THERE'S A
NEW WORLD
COMING

HAL LINDSEY

THERE'S A NEW WORLD COMING

HARVEST HOUSE PUBLISHERS
Eugene, Oregon 97402

OTHER BOOKS BY HAL LINDSEY:

The Late Great Planet Earth
Satan Is Alive and Well on Planet Earth
A Prophetical Walk Through the Holy Land
The Promise
The Rapture
The Liberation of Planet Earth
The Terminal Generation
1980's: Countdown to Armageddon

ACKNOWLEDGMENTS

Permission is gratefully acknowledged for reprinting from the following copyrighted material:

Expository Sermons on Revelation, by W. A. Criswell, Zondervan Publishing House, Grand Rapids, MI. Copyright 1969.

"I Wish We'd All Been Ready," by Larry Norman, Beechwood Music Corp./J. C. Love Publishing Company, Hollywood, CA. Copyright 1969.

Revelation Illustrated and Made Plain, by Tim LaHaye, Family Life Seminar, San Diego, CA. Copyright 1973.

The Revelation of Jesus Christ, by John Walvoord, Moody Press, Chicago, IL. Copyright 1966.

Except where otherwise indicated, all Scripture quotations in this book (including the text of Revelation) are taken from the King James Version of the Bible, with clarifying emendations from the original languages by Hal Lindsey.

Verses marked TLB are taken from The Living Bible, Copyright 1971 by Tyndale House Publishers, Wheaton, Illinois. Used by permission.

Contents

Introduction

The information in the book you're about to read is more up-to-date than tomorrow's newspaper. I can say this with confidence because the facts and predictions in these next few pages are all taken from the greatest sourcebook of current events in the world. We'll be centering our attention on one segment of this sourcebook—the Book of Revelation in the Bible. I think you'll be surprised to see what kind of predictions were made almost two thousand years ago!

For eighteen centuries the mysteries of the Book of Revelation remained largely unexplored. Churchmen of most faiths regarded it as a closed book. It was not until the nineteenth century that the renaissance of Revelation took place. Then people began to study the book with an intensity unparalleled in the history of Bible study. Scholars began to write lengthy volumes on the meaning of the mysteries.

On the shelves of my personal library I have at least twelve commentaries on the Book of Revelation. Most of these excellent works are carefully researched and are exhaustive in their contrasts and comparisons; I have often recommended them to my students and shall continue to do so. My book is not intended to replace these fine commentaries.

However, as I have quizzed many of my friends over the past few years, not more than a dozen of them have ever read the Book of Revelation or any commentary on it!

With statistics like that, something's got to be very wrong.

Revelation is the only book in the Bible that I know of which promises a special blessing to everyone who reads it and heeds the things that are written in it (Revelation 1:3). With a promise like that held out to every reader, you would think Revelation would be one of the most popular books in all world literature!

I'm sure the imagery and symbolism of the book are what scare most people away. However, I believe we need to see that the Book of Revelation is the "Grand Central Station" of the whole Bible. Nearly every symbol in it is used somewhere else in the Bible, but finds its ultimate fulfillment and explanation in this final prophetic book of the Bible.

There's no question that some great scholars have strong disagreements about the correct interpretation of certain passages in Revelation, and I'm sure I'm throwing my hat into the ring by presenting my own convictions. However, each man must do as he feels strongly led, and this principle of seeking after ultimate answers keeps men digging till the truth finally surfaces!

Some writers have chosen to interpret each symbol quite literally. For example, a locust with the face of a man, the teeth of a lion, a breastplate of iron, a tail that can sting, and wings that make the sound of many chariots would have to be specially created by God to look just like that description.

I personally tend to think that God might utilize in his judgments some modern devices of man which the Apostle John was at a loss for words to describe nineteen centuries ago! In the case just mentioned, the locusts might symbolize an advanced kind of helicopter.

This is just one example of the fast-moving, contemporary, and often deductive manner with which I have chosen to approach the Book of Revelation. I realize I'll be accused by some of making wild speculations; however, I have honestly sought to be as accurate and conservative as I know how to be, considering the awesome scope of this subject matter.

I genuinely believe the time has come for us to wake up and realize where we are on God's timetable. "Those" people on whom all these predicted calamities are going to come aren't just some people "out there" who are going to live at some other time in history. They may well be your closest friends or children or family.

In fact, it may be you, yourself!

Please be honest with yourself as you read this book, for at the end of the story there's a new world coming, and being ready for this is the only thing that really matters!

Hal Lindsey

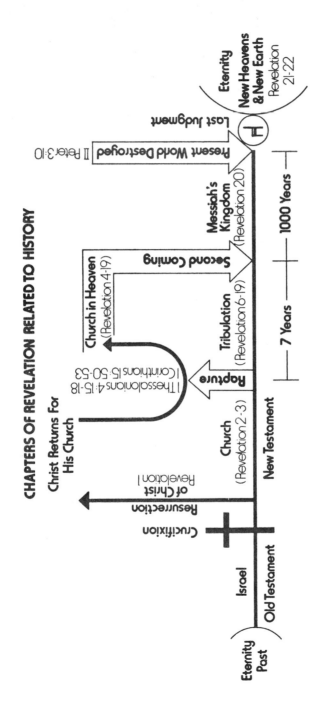

CHAPTERS OF REVELATION RELATED TO HISTORY

Eternity Past

Israel

Old Testament

Crucifixion

Resurrection
of Christ
Revelation 1

Church
(Revelation 2-3)

New Testament

Christ Returns For
His Church

Church in Heaven
(Revelation 4-19)

Rapture
1 Thessalonians 4:15-18
1 Corinthians 15:50-53

Tribulation
(Revelation 6-19)

Second Coming

Messiah's
Kingdom
(Revelation 20)

Present World Destroyed
II Peter 3:10

Last Judgment

Eternity
New Heavens
& New Earth
Revelation
21-22

7 Years

1000 Years

GOD'S OUTLINE OF HISTORY

ONE

The Real Jesus Unveiled

As the sun sank low over the Aegean Sea the old man stepped wearily into his grotto home. He longed for a night of renewing sleep. But as usual, it would not be his to enjoy. Sharing his cave were a band of criminals. All the men had been exiled to Patmos, that infamous desert island of the Aegean, for crimes they had committed on the mainland. But the old man's only crime had been sharing his new life in Jesus with everyone he met. For this offense Domitian, the Emperor of Rome, had banished him to Patmos to die of old age or starvation.

But God had other plans. Here in the seclusion of exile John the Apostle was to receive the most sweeping survey of future events ever to be granted to the mortal mind. God's revelations to John spanned twenty centuries, reaching past even our own sophisticated age of technology. Best of all, John saw Jesus Himself in such superlative grandeur that ordinary human words could never describe the sight.

TRUTH-IN-LABELING

> *(1) The Revelation of Jesus Christ, which God gave to Him to show to His servants the things which are going to happen soon; and He sent and signified it by His angel to His servant, John, (2) Who bore witness about the Word of God, and of the testimony about Jesus Christ, and about all things that he saw. (3) Blessed is he who reads, and those who hear the words of this prophecy, and keep those things which are written in it; for the time is at hand.* REVELATION 1:1–3

9

While many Bibles label the Book of Revelation as "The Revelation of John," it is more correctly called "The Revelation of Jesus Christ." This is the title which is given right in the first sentence of the book itself. It's more appropriate because *Jesus Christ* is the central figure of the book—not John the Apostle.

John didn't originate the ideas in this book even though he had had a long and intimate relationship with Jesus. Christ had called him to be an apostle when he was only a teenager, and now the fiery old man was writing somewhere between A.D. 85 and 90. Later John wrote a book which does bear his name—the Gospel of John. This book displays an especially intimate knowledge of the nature and work of Christ.

JOHN'S CHAIN OF ESP

In this Book of Revelation, however, John very frankly acknowledges both the divine source of his material and the unique procedure by which these words of revelation traveled from God Himself to John's pen and ink. The facts are stated in verse one:

> "The Revelation of *Jesus Christ*"—theme;
> "God gave . . . to show"—source and purpose;
> "Sent . . . by His angel"—intermediary;
> "To His servant John"—recipient and writer.

This is the chain of progression—from the Father, to the Son, to Christ's special messenger (the angel), to John, to us.

John emphasizes that he actually *saw and heard* everything he wrote in the book. Though he certainly could not fully understand everything he witnessed, John was careful to record the events exactly as they were given to him. None of his words were the product of a fertile imagination.

The Book of Revelation is unique among the books of the Bible in that it promises a special blessing to everyone who will study it with a receptive attitude. Curious tasters are not included in this promise, however, for the reader is told that he must also *heed* the words of the book in order to get the blessing.

THE KEY TO THE MYSTERY

In 1903 Dr. C.I. Scofield, the venerable old Bible scholar, described this promised blessing: "The book is so written that as the actual time of these events approach, the current events will unlock the meaning of the book." He pointed out that the Book of Revelation didn't have too much meaning to people a few centuries ago, and that for this reason very few people were willing to study its message. Revelation is written in such a way that its meaning becomes clear with the unfolding of current world events.

Interestingly, even the great church reformers of past centuries, such as Luther, Zwingli, and Calvin, knew little about prophecy. They were primarily interested in unlocking Biblical truths desperately needed for their own generation. They therefore didn't spend much time studying truths about the future. Possibly they sensed that their age would not witness the fulfillment of the Book of Revelation.

THE PROPHETIC ERA

Although I have read accurate interpretations of Bible prophecy written as early as 1611, more books have been written on this subject since the turn of the century than in all the previous centuries since Apostolic times!

This great revival of interest in prophecy is actually one of the important signs of the end times. The great Hebrew prophet Daniel wrote in the twelfth chapter of his book that he was very disturbed about some visions he had seen because he couldn't understand them. But the angel who had revealed these visions to him responded, "Thou, O Daniel, shut up the words, and seal the book, even to the time of the end: many shall run to and fro, and knowledge shall be increased." Daniel was told that his visions were prophetic in nature, and that their fulfillment wouldn't be understood by him or anyone else until the end of the age. The angel also informed him that as the end of this era approached, knowledge about prophecy would become widespread.

In speaking about these strange visions he had experienced, Daniel notes: "I heard, but I did not understand. Then I said, 'O my Lord, what will be the final outcome of these things?' And he said, 'Go your way, Daniel, for these words are closed up and sealed until the end. Many will be purified, made white, and tested, but the wicked will grow even more wicked, and none of the wicked will understand, but the wise will understand' " (Daniel 12:8–10).

Daniel observed that at the end of time the "wise" would understand. In Biblical terminology the "wise" are people who study what God has to say and become enlightened to its meaning by the Holy Spirit.

I believe that down through the centuries since John wrote these incredible revelations from God, men have received a blessing from reading them even if they understood very little of what they read. But today we live in a unique era. Now the promise of blessing carries an unprecedented comfort and practical fulfillment for every person who lets the Holy Spirit illuminate the words he reads.

A TIME WARP

One problem that even very sincere students sometimes encounter with the Book of Revelation is that its language seems so figurative. I think there are several key reasons for the heavy use of this symbolic style. For one thing, hostile critics of the book will find it pretty tough sledding and will thus be hampered in making sensible criticisms of it. But a more important reason for the symbolism is that the predictions of the book were so far removed from the language of John's day that ordinary Greek words (the *lingua franca* of New Testament times) couldn't adequately convey the message. After all, how could God transmit the thought of a nuclear catastrophe to someone living in the year A.D. 90!

THE TIME MACHINE

You might say that John was put into a "divine time machine" and transported nineteen centuries into the future. Try to put yourself in his place.

Suppose you were suddenly catapulted nineteen centuries into the future and confronted by the marvels of that time, then instructed to return to your own century and write what you had seen! How would you begin? You would have to describe things which have no existing terminology even in our own modern era. You would be forced to try to communicate in terms of things we know about now. If someone were to read your account nineteen centuries after it was written, they would be forced to search for clues to unlock the meaning of your symbols.

This is how John used his symbols. We can usually discover the meaning of the symbols by observing how they are used elsewhere in Scripture. The Book of Revelation is sometimes called the "Grand Central Station" of the Bible because so many Biblical symbols find their ultimate fulfillment here.

Sometimes John employed terminology which can be understood only when the prophecy's fulfillment is near. For example, John describes a horrible war in which fire and brimstone are rained down on people. In John's day the only thing capable of producing fire and brimstone was a volcano; it was one of the most dreaded forms of destruction. But this is really a classic description of the horrors of an atomic explosion; "fire and brimstone" says it pretty well! Before the development of the atomic bomb no destructive force known to man could equal the power of a volcanic eruption or even come close to fulfilling the description of "fire and brimstone."

In a number of cases in the Book of Revelation, John provides the interpretation of the symbology right in the same context. With the help of a good concordance (a book that lists Bible words and their Scripture references) we can pretty well determine the meanings of most of the other symbols.

A GREETING OF COMFORT

> *(4) John, to the seven churches which are in Asia: Grace be upon you, and peace, from Him who is, who was, and who is to come, and from the seven Spirits who are before His throne; (5)And from Jesus Christ, who is the faithful witness, the firstborn from among the dead, and the prince of the kings of the earth. To Him who loves us, and washed us from our sins in His own blood. (6) And has made us a kingdom of priests to God and His Father, to Him be glory and dominion forever and ever. Amen.*
> REVELATION 1:4–6

The original recipients of the Book of Revelation were seven churches in Asia Minor. But the book was obviously intended to reach much farther than to just those few hundred Christians of the first century A.D. John's greeting to them and us is "grace and peace from the triune God."

In many Bible narratives people greeted each other with the words "grace" and "peace." It would therefore be easy to assume that John's greeting was just a casual expression like "How do you do?" I am convinced, however, that this phrase is loaded with careful intent.

Remember, this book was penned only a few years after Nero's brutal persecution of Christians in Rome. These believers in Asia Minor had therefore experienced very little of this world's peace.

History also shows that after the death of Paul and John legalistic Judaizers began infiltrating many of the prospering little churches which the Apostles had founded or aided. The legalists tried to force the new believers back under the Mosaic Law as a way of life. John's greeting of "grace and peace" was thus rich with meaning for these struggling churches.

The Triune Source of the Prophecy

John reiterates emphatically the true source of the Revelation by graphically describing its three givers. He describes God the Father as "Him who is and who was and who is to come." This represents the present, imperfect, and future tenses of the verb "to be." There is simply no stronger way to describe continuous existence of being! The best definition of a life source that philosophy can give us is "an unmoved mover." John's God goes way back before that! He continuously existed before the beginning of all things (John 1:1).

An unusual description is given of one who I believe is the Holy Spirit. He is called "the seven Spirits who are before His throne." Seven is a number which always stands for completeness or perfection in Biblical symbolism. Since these "seven Spirits" are in a context which is speaking of God the Father and God the Son as being the source of the revelations, I believe these "seven Spirits" refer to the third member of the Godhead, the Holy Spirit.

The number seven speaks of the fullness of the Holy Spirit's powers and ministries to the believers. This "Spirit" is said to be "before God's throne." It's almost like One who is standing there waiting for instructions before going out, and we know that the Holy Spirit is that One who has been sent to fulfill the purposes of the One who sits on the throne.

John leaves no question as to the identity of the person who sends grace and peace to the brothers and sisters. It's Jesus

Christ Himself. Three marvelous titles are given to Him: *the faithful witness, the firstborn of the dead,* and *the prince of the kings of the earth.*

In what sense was Christ a faithful witness? As a true Prophet He revealed God to men. Christ did not merely reveal God by what He said (as other prophets had done), but He was, in His person, a perfect revelation and witness of all that God is.

Someone once said that Jesus was a perfect *portrait* of God. But He is really more than this. He is a perfect *photograph* of God. All that we can possibly conceive and understand of God, Jesus is (Hebrews 1:3; John 14:9).

FIRSTBORN OF THE DEAD

The reference to Christ as the "firstborn of the dead" clarifies a puzzling statement in Colossians 1:15, where He is referred to as "the firstborn of all creation." On the surface it almost sounds like Christ came into existence when He was born into this world—in other words, that He wasn't eternal. But this isn't the point of the statement. The point is that Jesus Christ was the first person ever to be permanently resurrected from the dead. (The resurrection of Lazarus was temporary—he died again.)

The term "firstborn" simply means that Christ is the first of a long line of people who will be resurrected with glorified, immortal bodies. I expect to be getting one of these bodies, and I've placed an order for a terrific one—one which won't ever get old or overweight!

THE RULER OF KINGS

When we see the mess the world is in, it's sometimes hard for us to believe that Christ is actually the "prince of the kings of the earth." This is because even though Christ has the *right* to rule the earth, He isn't exercising this authority over kings and kingdoms at this time.

Satan won a *temporary* legal right to rule the kingdoms of the world when Adam foolishly relinquished his God-given authority in the Garden of Eden. When Satan took Christ to a high mountain, showed Him the kingdoms of the world, and offered them to Jesus in return for worship, Christ didn't dispute Satan's temporary legal claim to these kingdoms.

The Lord knew that when His work on the Cross was finished, Satan would be too! (See John 12:31.) Now it's only a matter of time until Christ comes back to earth and claims His role as King of Kings and Lord of Lords over the rulers of this world! What a day that will be!

John assures his readers that they have not been left to themselves until that day, with only a *future* hope of redemption. In a flood of praise he proclaims that right now, just as we are in all our imperfections, we are loved with the continuous and pure love of Christ.

Sometimes we're tempted to think that the love of God had its highest culmination in the past, when God gave His Son to die for mankind. But the case is just the opposite. God's love then was for his *enemies*; now it's for His *friends*. *Then* God's love reached out to man in all his ugliness and sins; *now* it floods believers who have all been washed from their sins and clothed with Christ's robes of righteousness!

FREEDOM IS NOW

"He washed us from our sins in His own blood." Notice the past tense of that verb. If only we could get it through our heads that we *have been* cleansed from our sins and their eternal judgment! The fulness of God's great love is a *present* reality and His forgiveness of our sins is a *past* fact.

We don't have to wait and work to be forgiven. The work was fully accomplished when Christ shed His blood for us over nineteen hundred years ago. All that remains for us to do is to accept the pardon which God is so eager to give us and to delight in the realities of His ever-present love.

A KINGDOM OF PRIESTS

Whenever I think about the kingdom and the priesthood which Christ has given each of us as believers, I think of a line from a song I sang as a child:

> "This world is not my home.
> I'm just a-passin' through."

You know, the Kingdom of God on earth is a little like a secret society. No matter where I go in this world, whenever I meet a fellow believer-priest we have a special ability to communicate—a spontaneous love for each other—a mutual concern about the real issues of life and their solutions in Christ. We know that our kingdom is not of this world—that we're just travelers passing through. It's kind of like meeting an old friend in a foreign country.

Most of my Christian acquaintances don't wear backward collars, and perhaps you can't distinguish them from other people by their physical appearance. But *they* know, and *I* know, that we have been ordained as priests of God by Christ Himself. A priest's job is simply that of representing men before the throne of God. We have the joy of speaking to God on behalf of others and of speaking to men on God's behalf. Every believer has this tremendous privilege of priesthood (1 Peter 2:9; 1 Timothy 2:1–3).

THE GOD WHO HAS WOUNDS

(7) Behold, He is going to come with clouds, and every eye shall see Him, and they also who pierced Him; and all kindreds of the earth shall mourn because of Him. Even so, Amen.

(8) I am Alpha and Omega, the beginning and the ending, says the Lord, who is, who was, and who is to come, the Almighty.
                                                                REVELATION 1:7, 8

"Look! He's coming with clouds!" This exclamation is a prediction of the Second Coming of Christ—His glorious return to earth with His followers. It's an interesting fact that the Bible says at least seven times that Christ will return in or with clouds.

I used to wonder why it could possibly matter whether it was a cloudy day when Christ returned. Then I thought of Hebrews 12:1—"Wherefore, since we are surrounded with such a great cloud of witnesses, let us also lay aside everything that would slow us down and the sin which so easily trips us up, and let us keep on running with endurance the race that is set before us. . . ." In this verse the cloud refers to that great company of believers who have died in the past and are now observing our lives.

First Thessalonians 3:13 and Jude verse 14 state that Christ will return to earth with multitudes of saints. It's this throng of believers in Christ which I believe John is picturing as "clouds" in Revelation 1:7. To the people on earth God's multitude of saints, all dressed in spotless white robes, will appear as clouds descending from the sky.

TWO PORTRAITS OF A KING

In about 560 B.C. the Hebrew prophet Daniel described "one like the Son of man coming with the clouds of heaven." He predicted that this person would receive dominion and glory and an eternal kingdom in which all nations and peoples would serve Him (Daniel 7:13, 14).

For hundreds of years before Christ was born the Jews knew that this prophecy concerned their long-awaited King and Messiah. The kingdom He would establish would be a kingdom of peace and righteousness and prosperity, with all nations dwelling at peace with Israel. You can see why the Jews yearned and prayed for such a deliverer to come to them, since they had known so many cruel years under the yoke of oppression.

However, the Old Testament prophets also painted another portrait of their coming King—that of a suffering Messiah who would die because of the sins of the people. About a century before Christ was born a certain school of rabbis recognized this paradox. They reasoned that their coming Messiah could not be both a conquering King and a suffering Servant, so they began to teach that two Messiahs might come. One would be a son of David, and He of course would be the King. But the suffering Messiah, they reasoned, would probably be of the lineage of Joseph, since he had suffered so much at the hands of his brothers and the Egyptian Pharaoh before rising to prominence in the land of Egypt.

When Jesus Christ came to earth and presented His credentials—those of the suffering Messiah—the religious leaders rejected Him. What they wanted was a *conquering* king who would deliver them from Rome. They realized that a suffering Messiah could only be a spiritual deliverer—not a political one. By this time the religious leaders had degenerated in their thinking to the point where they taught that approval with God was based on the observance of certain religious regulations.

When Jesus began to preach about sin, stating in the Sermon on the Mount that even *wrong motives* were considered sin by God, this was more than the Pharisees could take, and they ultimately succeeded in having Him crucified. Tragically, they failed to see that no man or nation can have outer peace as long as there is inner turmoil of soul.

For anyone who cared to investigate, there was no lack of evidence to show that Jesus was indeed the long-awaited Messiah. Had the people received Him, He would have fulfilled the kingly prophecies in their day in addition to the ones regarding the suffering Messiah. But when the Jewish nation as a whole rejected Christ, the fulfillment of His kingship was postponed until the final culmination of world history. This is the subject of the Book of Revelation.

Unfortunately, many people today are making the same tragic mistake which the Jews did when they ignored the overwhelming evidence of Christ's claims at His first coming. Today we are standing at the threshold of Christ's return as King of Kings and Lord of Lords; yet men in general are totally ignorant of the event or have dismissed it as religious fantasy.

LOOK AND MOURN

When John says that all the tribes of the earth will mourn over Christ when they see Him coming, he is referring to the prediction in Zechariah 12:10, "And I will pour upon the house of David and upon the inhabitants of Jerusalem, the Spirit of grace and of supplications; and they will look upon Me whom they have pierced; and they shall mourn for Him, as one mourns for his only son, and will be in bitterness for Him, as one that is in bitterness for his first-born."

In this prophecy, the ancient prophet Zechariah declares that when Christ returns to the earth at the height of the coming war, called Armageddon, the Jewish people will for the first time recognize Him as their long-rejected Messiah. They will mourn as they gaze on the One they rejected nearly two thousand years ago.

GOD'S ULTIMATE STATEMENT: JESUS

"I am the Alpha and Omega." Alpha is the first letter of the Greek alphabet and Omega is the last. Christ is claiming, in other words, to be "everything from A to Z." He is everything that God has to say. If God wants to communicate with man, He'll do it through His "last word," Jesus Christ.

Two major attributes of Christ are emphasized in these opening comments of the Revelation: "Who is and who was and who is to come" conveys the idea of *eternity of existence;* that is, Christ existed *before* any specific point in time and will continue to exist *after* time gives way to eternity. Added to this attribute is the title *the Almighty.* This literally means "the omnipotent and all-powerful One." These attributes can only be true of someone who is God!

There is no limit to Christ's almighty power. Colossians 1:17 tell us that "in Him all things hold together." He is like the mysterious nucleus of an atom, holding tremendous explosive power from being unleashed. He Himself is that unfathomable source which keeps every atom from literally exploding!

Down from Heaven's Palaces

Can you imagine what the prospect of coming down to this world and becoming a human being must have meant to such an omnipotent One? He knew that His incarnation involved submission to the very people He had created, including death by crucifixion on the Cross at their hands. The poem expresses this contrast dramatically:

> "He came to die on a Cross of wood,
> Yet made the hill on which it stood."

At any moment that Christ had willed He could have stopped His crucifixion. He could have called ten thousand angels to deliver Him or simply used His own unlimited power. But He didn't. God's plan for man's salvation depended on Christ's willingness to endure the wrath of a holy God against man's sins.

Boldness That Couldn't Be Bound

(9) I, John, who also am your brother, and companion in tribulation, and in the kingdom and patience of Jesus Christ, was in the isle that is called Patmos, because of my stand for the word of God, and for the testimony about Jesus Christ. (10) I was under the control of the Spirit on the Lord's day, and heard behind me a great voice, that sounded like a trumpet. (11) Saying, "I am Alpha and Omega, the first and the last; what you see,

write in a book, and send it to the seven churches which are in Asia, Ephesus, Smyrna, Pergamos, Thyatira, Sardis, Philadelphia, and Laodicea."

REVELATION 1:9–11

John was an old man when he was exiled to Patmos. But he wasn't sent there because he was old—he was sent there because he was too much of a tiger at proclaiming the good news about Christ! The Roman Empire simply couldn't shut him up.

Evidently John had grown even bolder under the persecution he had received for being a believer, so that now the Romans were afraid to make a martyr of the Apostle by killing him! Exile therefore seemed like the best solution to this sticky problem. Little did the Romans realize that these letters from John to his fellow-Christians would unleash greater power than the combined might of all the empires in the history of the world!

WOE IS ME!

You know, John could have sat around on Patmos feeling sorry for himself and saying, "Lord, You've really let me down; after all these years that I've worked and suffered for You I can't count on You when I really need You." But John didn't say this. Instead, he was "in the Spirit on the Lord's day."

When you're filled with the Spirit you don't sit around feeling sorry for yourself and cursing your circumstances! The Spirit assures you that you're right where God wants you to be and that He has you there for some tremendous purpose. You may not be able to see the future, but you *know* the One who holds it. God wants every believer to be under the control of the Spirit all the time.

John was "in the Spirit" in a very unique sense here, however. The original Greek says, "I *became* in the Spirit." The idea here is that John became uniquely dominated by the Spirit of God at this time. He became infallible in what he saw and recorded. Every writer of Scripture experienced the same total domination by the Spirit; each one penned not only the *ideas* that God wanted man to know, but also the *very words* in which He wanted these concepts explained. "For no prophecy (of Scripture) ever originated in the mind of man, but men spoke from God as they were borne along by the Holy Spirit" (2 Peter 1:21).

While John was thus in the control of the Spirit, he heard

behind him a loud voice, like the sound of a trumpet. In general, trumpets in the Bible signify exceptionally important messages from God.

For example, a trumpet will sound when Christ comes in the air to call forth His own people. Seven trumpets will sound during some of the great judgments of the seven-year tribulation which will be unleashed upon this earth. Then, there's the great trumpet which will sound at Christ's final return to earth. A trumpet blast is a good way of getting attention. I guess that's why trumpets have always had such a prominent place on the battlefields of world history!

A BOOK FOR THE SEVEN CHURCHES

John was told to write what he saw in a book. This again emphasizes the fact that John actually *saw* the things he wrote down; he didn't dream them up. The fact that John really saw these events is mentioned seven times in the first chapter of Revelation.

There were several hundred churches in existence at this time, yet the angel specifies that John's book should be sent to only seven of them. Why do you suppose these were singled out for special instructions?

First, these congregations had problems which were typical of church problems everywhere, then and down through the ages.

Second, the order in which these seven church situations are presented in the Book of Revelation parallels the changing condition of the church as a whole down through the centuries from the time of Christ until the true Church is taken out of the world. Of course,the people who lived during the early centuries of church history would not have known of this parallel.

This kind of historical perspective of the church is invaluable because we can learn important lessons from the failures and successes of earlier Christians. Also, we can identify the period of time we are living in now by the condition of the church of our day.

AN OVERPOWERING VISION

(12) I turned to see the voice that was speaking with me. As I turned, I saw seven golden lampstands, (13) And in the midst of the seven lamp-

stands there was one like the Son of man, clothed with a garment down to the foot, and wearing about the chest a golden vest. (14) His head and His hair were white like wool, as white as snow; and His eyes were like a flame of fire; (15) And His feet like fine bronze, as if they were burning in a furnace; and His voice was like the sound of many waters. (16) And He had in His right hand seven stars; and out of His mouth went a sharp two-edged sword; and His countenance was like the sun as it shines in its strength.

(17) And when I saw Him, I fell at His feet as dead. And he laid His right hand upon me, saying to me, "Stop being afraid; I am the first and the last; (18) I am He who lives, and was dead; and, behold, I am alive forevermore, Amen; and have the keys of hell and of death."

REVELATION 1:12–18

The first and most important thing which John saw in his Patmos revelation was a vision of Christ Himself. Christ is so central to all of Biblical prophecy that without Him the whole program would collapse.

John saw Christ standing in the middle of seven golden lampstands. These lampstands symbolize the seven churches he is addressing. Now these are not just any kind of lampstands. They are likenesses of the lampstand that stood in the ancient Jewish Tabernacle. That single lamp provided all the light of the Tabernacle. Its purpose was to illumine all the articles of worship—to give them clarity.

This pictured the Messiah as the light of the world, illuminating mankind to the true meaning of the things of God. In the Gospel which bears his name, John says of Jesus, "In Him was life, and the life was the light of men." He adds that Jesus was "the true light which, coming into the world, shed light upon every man" (John 1:4, 9).

Why were these lampstands selected to symbolize the Church? The Apostle Paul gives us the answer to that question. In Ephesians 1:22, 23 he pictures the Church as the body of Christ on earth today. Its purpose is to spread the light of the gospel to this dark and needy world. Jesus told His followers, "You are the light of the world."

Christ is seen standing in the midst of these churches, hovering over them and guiding them to maturity. He is intimately interested in everything the Church does and everything that happens to it.

THE MAJESTY OF THE MESSIAH

The description John gives of Jesus is awe-inspiring. He wears the clothing of a priest and a judge—a long robe secured with a golden sash. He performs the role of a priest in behalf of all His children, but He is forced to manifest Himself as a *judge* to all who have rejected His offer of forgiveness. His white head and hair symbolize his pure, mature wisdom, while His flaming eyes seem to burn a hole through the man whose life is unrighteous. There's nothing quite so disconcerting as to have a pure person stare at you steadily, especially if you're harboring some secret impurity in your life.

We're told that Christ's feet were like burnished bronze glowing in a furnace. In the Bible bronze is always a symbol of judgment. The Old Testament altar of sacrifice and the implements used in the offerings were made of bronze. Christ is set forth here as the judge of the living and dead.

PAST, PRESENT AND FUTURE

> *(19) Write the things which you have seen, and the things which are, and the things which will happen after these things; (20) the mystery of the seven stars which you saw in My right hand, and the seven golden lampstands. The seven stars are the angels of the seven churches; and the seven lampstands which you saw are the seven churches.*   REVELATION 1:19, 20

In verse 19 God gave John a simple outline of the entire Book of Revelation. Far from being deeply mysterious, Revelation is actually one of the easiest of all Bible books to read and understand once we understand its symbols. Here is God's outline to John.

The things you have seen refers to the vision of Christ which John saw in Chapter 1.

The things which are alludes to the seven churches of Chapters 2 and 3 and looks at the entire church era up to Christ's return for His own.

The things which will happen after these things includes all the events after Christ takes His believers out of the world. This description starts in Chapter 4 and concludes in Chapter 22.

I am thoroughly convinced that *the things which are* are about to be terminated by the return of Christ for His Bride, the Church. He will *not* come to the earth itself at that event, but in the air above the earth. His followers, both dead and alive, will be caught up to meet Him there.

After this event, *the things which are to come* begin, starting with the horrors of the Tribulation which will break out on the earth for seven years. To save mankind from destroying itself, Christ will then return to the earth, subdue His enemies, and establish His kingdom on earth for 1,000 years.

In the last verse of this chapter God Himself explains what two of the symbols of Revelation mean. The "seven stars" represent seven angels or messengers to the churches, while the "seven golden lampstands" symbolize the churches themselves. God sets an encouraging pattern here by showing that *all of the symbols in the Book of Revelation have definite meanings.*

God intends not only to show John the most astonishing sights any human eyes will ever witness but also to carefully unravel their meaning for both him and us. As the mystery of this book is unfolded to you in the following chapters, I suggest that you be prepared for a journey that will not leave you the same as you began.

TWO

Panorama of Church History–I

In a very real sense, reading the Book of Revelation is like reading somebody else's mail. The whole revelation is addressed primarily to seven local groups of believers of John's day, although without question the intention of the revealing angel was that *all* people through all ages should benefit from it. But the primary recipients of this document were seven actual churches of the first century A.D.

It's significant that these letters of comfort and admonition to the seven churches found here in Chapters 2 and 3 are dictated to John by Jesus Himself. These letters represent the last recorded quotations of Jesus and are the only words He ever spoke directly to the Church on earth.

Notice that with all the terrible calamities of judgment that are about to fall on men, the first thing in Jesus' mind and His greatest concern is His Church. His "little flock." Before He shows them the horrors ahead, He first seeks to get them in shape spiritually, so that they'll see God's perspective of the coming judgments.

Why These Seven Churches?

At the time John wrote these messages, there were probably several hundred small congregations of Christians throughout Asia Minor. Many of these had experienced enough persecution to make them wary of meeting openly, so they met quietly and often in secret. Those who did gather openly were disdained by the populace at large.

The seven churches to whom these letters were sent were not the largest or best–known of their day. The churches at Rome and Antioch, for example, no doubt had bigger congregations and more prominent people as members.

Why were these *specific* churches chosen to receive these special messages of commendation, rebuke, exhortation, and challenge?

This question has intrigued Bible students for hundreds of years and has led to a variety of explanations. I personally agree with the four purposes described by the editorial committee of the *New Scofield Reference Bible.* This group of Biblical experts represents a long tradition of scholarly research on Bible prophecy.[1]

FOUR PURPOSES OF THE LETTERS

As you read through Revelation 2 and 3 you'll notice that each letter is a personal message from Jesus to a specific local church. He commends each church for any good deeds He finds and rebukes each one for any sin or worldly tendencies He sees. The Lord obviously chose these particular churches because they had the combinations of strengths, weaknesses, and differing characteristics that would convey many lessons to the Church throughout its history.

The second application of the truths of these letters is to the individual believers within each congregation. For instance, when Jesus says to the church of Laodicea that He's standing at its door and knocking for entrance, He isn't just requesting entrance into the door and life of the church itself; He also wants to come personally into the life of each *individual* in the church. From this truth we urge a person today to invite Jesus to come into his heart and life, since this is a valid application of this great statement of Jesus.

It's a shame that so few Christians through the centuries have availed themselves of the tremendous comfort and challenge Jesus gives in these letters. More than once when my

[1]*New Scofield Reference Bible,* Oxford Edition, pp. 1352, 1353.

money was running low and things weren't going as smoothly as I liked, I have read the letter to Smyrna and heard Jesus say, "You're not really poor; in My estimation you're rich, and the things you're suffering now are going to result in a crown of life for you if you have to endure to death itself."

On a few occasions I've also needed to hear Jesus' words to the church at Ephesus: "I have somewhat against you, Hal, because you've left your first love, Me! Remember what our relationship has been like in the past, and repent and come back into fellowship with Me."

WHAT EVERY PASTOR NEEDS TO KNOW

A third application of these epistles is for every church today to examine its spiritual status in the light of Jesus' exhortations to the first-century churches. I think every new pastor should become thoroughly familiar with the kinds of churches Jesus commended, the qualities that evoked His kind words, and the shortcomings that He rebuked. Many hours of pastoral heartache would be avoided if ministers patterned their churches as Jesus outlined in these letters!

The final message that we can learn from these unique letters is a prophetic one. We must keep in mind that everything in the Book of Revelation is presented from an *eternal* vantage point. In a book that's overwhelmingly prophetic in content, it's only reasonable to think that the messages to the churches in Chapters 2 and 3 would also have a prophetic application. I believe that this is the main reason Jesus chose these particular seven churches and placed them in this order.

A BIRD'S-EYE VIEW OF CHURCH HISTORY

Here in seven typical churches we see the predominant characteristics of seven successive eras of church history. The prophetic aspects were never understood clearly until much of the church history had unfolded, but now as we look back we can see striking similarities between the characteristics of each church in Revelation and the various periods of church history up to our present day. As one period of church history gave way to the next, the predominant church characteristic continued on in some of the succeeding churches although new traits characterized the churches in general.

That's why we can look at all the churches in the world today that call themselves "Christian" and find some that correspond with each of the seven church types described in John's Revelation. However, the dominant church characteristics of our day are those of the seventh church, the Laodicean church.

WHAT IS THE CHURCH, ANYWAY?

"Church" is a badly misunderstood word! It has come to mean something entirely different from what it meant to first-century Christians. In those days the term was used only by Christians. We're living at a time, however, when many people are reaching out for a new understanding and a new experience of what the church really is. They want to know whether the church is a building or the people in it or just some impersonal institution that's part of the "establishment."

The original Greek word for church, *ekklesia,* simply means a group of people that is called together for some special purpose. In the New Testament the word can mean several things. Sometimes it refers to all *true* believers in Jesus Christ. It doesn't make any difference what religious "brand" they're under as long as they're in a living union with Christ through a personal faith in Him as their Savior. When I use the word Church in this book to refer to the true believers in Christ, I've capitalized it.

There's a great word-picture of this union in the New Testament. It pictures Christ as the head of a body, and those who believe in Him as members or parts of His body. In fact, believers are said to be in an organic union with Jesus — "bone of His bone and flesh of His flesh" (1 Corinthians 12:12–14; Ephesians 1:22, 23; 5:30).

The word "church" is also used to refer to a group of people who meet in one specific location for worship and fellowship. In any one of these local congregations there are usually some true believers and some who are not.

THE CHURCH IS PEOPLE

The most common use of the word "church" today applies to any building in which people meet to consider spiritual matters, whether Christian or not. This use, however, is a rank perversion of the true meaning of the word, since "church" in the Bible *never* meant a building or anything inanimate. The church was *the people in the building.*

I'll never forget one church class I attended. A number of young people were chewing gum during class, and this got some of the old saints uptight. After awhile one of them had taken all she could and she said, "Pastor, some of the young people are chewing gum in the sanctuary!" Without batting an eye the minister shot back, "Madam, the sanctuaries are chewing the gum!"

No one in that class missed the lesson that the church is *not* the building but the saints in it.

WHEN IS A SAINT A SAINT?

Another word that has suffered badly at the hands of the church through the ages is the word "saints." This word is used all through the New Testament. Most people think it means either a very pious and good person or someone who's died and been declared a saint by the church because of his exemplary life.

But neither of these is the Biblical definition of a saint. The Bible teaches that *every* true believer in Christ, whether living or dead, is a saint in the sight of God, whether he acts like it or not (Romans 1:6, 7; 1 Corinthians 1:2).

AN OUTLINE OF THINGS TO COME

Before we look at each church letter in closer detail, let's pull together our facts so far.

In Revelation 1, Jesus gave John the simple, three-part outline he has to follow in writing down the Revelation. First he was to write about *the things he had seen* in the vision of the resurrected Christ, who had appeared and conversed with him. Then he was to write about *the things that are,* referring to the churches of his day and the letters which Christ was going to dictate to them.

The last division of the Revelation was to contain *the things which came after* the period of the churches. Everything from Revelation 4 to the end of the Book covers these events.

A Common Format in the Letters

Each of the seven letters was addressed to a literal church, and in each church a special messenger or representative would receive the letter and present its contents to the congregation. Each letter also follows a common, concise format, as follows:

1. *Destination* — this includes not only the city where the church is located but pertinent historical background of the city;
2. *Description of Christ* — in each letter Christ gives a description of Himself which is designed to meet some need existing in that church;
3. *Commendation* — Christ seeks to praise each church for something, but unfortunately no praiseworthy thing can be found about Thyatira, the counterfeit church, or Laodicea, the apostate church;
4. *Rebuke* — the only churches Christ doesn't have to rebuke for sinful activities are Smyrna, the suffering church, and Philadelphia the missionary church;
5. *Exhortation* — Christ counsels and encourages each of His churches to add what is needed to make them more godly and to remove anything that hinders their single-hearted devotion to Him;
6. *Promise* — Christ promises fabulous blessings to everyone who "has an ear" and heeds Christ's advice to the church and the individuals in it;
7. *Prophetic Application* — this is the historical role which each church was to play during the subsequent nineteen centuries.

Ephesus: Duty Without Love

(1) To the angel of the church of Ephesus write, "These things says the One who holds the seven stars in His right hand, who walks in the midst of the seven golden lampstands: (2) I know your works, and your labor and your patience, and how you cannot bear those who are evil; and you have tried those who say they are apostles, and are not, and have found them liars, (3) and have endured and have patience and for My name's sake have labored and have not fainted.

(4) "Nevertheless, I have something against you, because you have left your first love. (5) Remember, therefore, from where you have fallen and repent and do the first works, or else I will come suddenly to you, and will remove the lampstand out of its place, unless you repent. (6) But this you

have in your favor, that you hate the deeds of the Nicolaitans, which I also hate.

(7) "He who has an ear, let him hear what the Spirit says to the churches: 'To the one who overcomes I will give to eat of the Tree of Life, which is in the midst of the paradise of God.' "   REVELATION 2:1–7

DESTINATION

Ephesus was a large city with an excellent harbor, and it was known at this time as the marketplace of Asia. It was also a banking center because of its great vault in the Temple of Diana, which was considered the safest place in Asia Minor.

Ephesus was also an important religious city. The Temple of Diana (or Artemus, as the Greeks called her) was considered one of the seven wonders of the ancient world. The goddess Diana was the patron of all the prostitutes and, with her many-bosomed image, represented fertility and sexuality. Many writers in ancient times described the immorality of the city.

One pillar in the Ephesian economy was the production of silver images of Diana by the many silversmiths who plied their trade there. Devotees of this goddess brought much gain to the city (Acts 19:23–27). Black magic was also widely practiced in Ephesus. Paul met these occultists head on and led some of them to Christ as Savior (Acts 19:13–19).

The Christian church at Ephesus was extremely welltaught, having had Paul, Apollos, Timothy, and John as pastors. The Book of Ephesians in the New Testament was written by Paul to the Ephesian saints while he was in prison in Rome about A.D. 60.

DESCRIPTION OF CHRIST

Jesus describes Himself here as the One who "holds the seven stars (messengers) in His right hand." Each church "messenger" was both protected and held accountable for faithfully conveying God's message of grace and coming judgment.

As the Lord walks among the churches, He's intimately aware of their thoughts and attitudes. He sees what they've had to endure, where they've succeeded, and where they've failed. This intimate knowlege becomes extremely important in His evaluation of their affections and motives.

COMMENDATION

There was much in this church to commend and praise. The believers were zealous of good works and service for the Lord. Twice the letter speaks of how they labored for the name of Christ. These saints knew how to trust the Lord consistently under trial, which is the meaning of the word *patience*. They had held up under stress and been faithful.

Doctrinally speaking, these believers were not only competent but militant in their stand against false teaching. This was evidenced by their examination and expulsion of false apostles who had come to them. They also labeled immorality exactly for what it was and cast out the Nicolaitans—false teachers who claimed the actions of your body didn't affect your spirit, so go out and sin up a storm!

From all outward appearance, the church of Ephesus certainly looked like a model church, worthy of a high commendation.

REBUKE

Despite all these "pluses" the Lord discerned a deadly danger creeping into their attitudes: they had "left their first love" — Christ Himself! Though outwardly warm, they were inwardly cold! Day after day they went through the right routines, said the right words, dished out the right spiritual platitudes—and shriveled a little more inside!

No wonder Christ rebuked them, for He alone could see their inner motivation. No husband would be happy for very long with a wife who didn't really love him, no matter how well she cooked his meals and did the housework! And Christ wasn't happy with His bride in this church, either. She was His "cold fish"!

I've seen this pattern develop in both churches and individuals, and it seems to be the special weakness of those who are Biblically well-taught. I wouldn't for a moment suggest that the deep teaching of God's Word promotes spiritual coolness, but any prolonged study of the Bible which doesn't produce a greater love for Christ is unprofitable!

EXHORTATION

So these Ephesians are exhorted by Christ to *remember* and *repent*. These are two very significant words because many Christians suffer from short memories! Each time they get into a hassle they forget how Christ brought them through the last one. They forget how He met their needs for so many things in the past, and that since he was faithful then He will be the same in the present crisis!

Jesus tells the Ephesians to *remember* that love is the only acceptable motivation for Christian living. He urges them to *repent* of their loveless Christian duty and to get off their "works trip," returning instead to the love which they had when they first came to know Him, when they were flushed with the wonder and excitement of their new relationship with Him.

PROMISE

To the one who listens and overcomes, Jesus promises that he will eat of the Tree of Life in God's everlasting paradise. You'll see in Chapter 21 just what a fantastic promise this is! The Apostle John tells us in another writing that "the over-comer" is the one who believes in Jesus as the Son of God and has received Him as Savior and Lord (1 John 5:4, 5).

PROPHETIC APPLICATION: A.D. 33–100

The Ephesian church is a prophetic picture of the Apostolic church. Like the church of Ephesus, the dominant historical characteristics of this era were correct doctrine, circumspect conduct, and zealous labor for the Lord, but waywardness in heart attitudes.

As their love for Christ began to wane, they more and more served out of a sense of duty. In their own estimation, their acceptance by the Lord depended on their performance for Him. This opened the door to legalism.

One of the crucial issues for a vital faith is pure motives. As we remember how Christ has loved us, our natural response is to love Him in return (see 1 John 4:9, 10).

SMYRNA: POOR AND PERSECUTED, BUT RICH!

(8) And to the angel of the church in Smyrna write, "These things says the First and the Last, who was dead and is alive: (9) I know your works and tribulation and poverty (although you are really rich in the things that matter); and I know the blasphemy of those who say they are Jews, and are not, but are the synagogue of Satan.

(10) "Fear none of those things which you shall suffer. Behold, the Devil shall cast some of you into prison in order that you may be tried, and you shall have tribulation ten days. Be faithful to death and I will give you a Crown of Life.

(11) "He who has an ear, let him hear what the Spirit says to the churches; 'He who overcomes shall not be hurt in the second death.'"

REVELATION 2:8–11

DESTINATION

Smyrna was about forty miles north of Ephesus and was considered the safest seaport of its time. It had a thriving economy because it was on the main trade route from Rome to India and Persia. Alexander the Great personally planned the city, and it was called "the ornament of Asia" because of its beauty and splendor. Many Jews lived there, yet Smyrna was overwhelmingly pagan.

On one end of the main street, the "street of gold," stood the Temple of Zeus, and at the other end stood the Temple of Cybele, "the mother of the gods." Smyrna was also the center of emperor worship in the Roman Empire, boasting a temple to Tiberius Caesar.

DESCRIPTION OF CHRIST

Since the believers of Smyrna were experiencing severe suffering and even martyrdom, Jesus refers to Himself as the One who had suffered and died but is now alive. Because He conquered death, they will too; as the First and the Last He's already tasted death for each believer and removed its sting!

COMMENDATION

The Lord assures the Smyrnan believers that He knows about their faithful service despite great persecution and poverty. They are actuallly very rich in His sight, even though they have lost everything in this life for His sake, because they are earning eternal rewards.

The Smyrnan believers were victims of the "ten percenters." These people reported Christians to the Roman government and were rewarded with ten percent of the "heretics' " property. The believers were thus often wiped out financially, and many ended up martyred or in prison.

Eventually the Christians were given only the one choice—bow to Caesar as Lord or be put to a horrible death. Faithful believers answered with the vow that is forever written in God's hall of fame: "Jesus Christ is Lord, and none other."

In denying that Caesar was divine, the Jews were as persecuted as the Christians, since it was unthinkable for a devout Jew to worship anyone but Jehovah. In an attempt to take some of the heat off themselves, some Jews evidently turned in Christians to the officials and caused a great deal of persecution for them.

Jesus said that these were not true Jews, for they did not believe in Jehovah-God and His Messiah. If they had, they would not have allowed Satan to inspire hatred for the Christians. After all, the Jews had more in common with Christians than with the worshipers of Caesar.

REBUKE

There's not one word of rebuke to the Smyrnan church, which in itself suggests a great lesson. A church or individual suffering persecution for his faith is usually more devout and faithful than a comfortable, untested believer.

A European Christian leader once told me that during his frequent trips behind the Iron Curtain to visit the churches he found amazing examples of faith and devotion to Christ. One church that was undergoing considerable persecution said they were praying for God to send persecution upon their Western brothers so that they too might be purified!

Corrie Ten Boom, the Dutch survivor of Nazi gas chambers, told of another thrilling triumph in persecution. A group of believers was meeting in an Iron Curtain country when the church door burst open and two Russian soldiers with submachine guns strode in. They said they would give five minutes for anyone who wished to renounce Christ to leave, and that those who stayed would be shot immediately.

As each person searched his heart for the courage to face death, a few got up and left. The officers then walked to the door of the church, locked it, and turned to the congregation with the words, "Brothers and sisters in Christ, we are believers, too, but we did not want to worship where everyone was not completely committed to Christ and willing to die for Him. May we become part of your fellowship?"

EXHORTATION

The believers at Smyrna were encouraged by Jesus to face the coming trials and suffering for "ten days," Jesus said they would be given a "crown of life" as an eternal reward. We look further at believers' crowns in Chapter 4.

Many Bible interpreters believe that the "ten days of persecution" apply prophetically to the ten eras of persecution under ten diabolical Caesars: *Nero,* A.D. 64–68; *Domitian,* who exiled John to Patmos about 90–95; *Trajan,* 104–117; *Aurelius,* 161–180; *Severus,* 200–211; *Maximus,* 235–237; *Decius,* 250–253; *Valerian,* 257–260; *Aurelian,* 270–275; *Diocletian,* 303–312.

PROMISE

The one who heeds the message and overcomes by faith is promised that though he may die physically he will never face "the second death" — eternal torment in hell (Revelation 20:14, 15).

PROPHETIC APPLICATION: A.D. 100–312

The suffering of the church at Smyrna was prophetic of the great era of persecution under the ten Caesars named above. The motives of the church were purified during this long and difficult period. Millions of Christians met cruel martyrs' death rather than renounce Christ or swear allegiance to Caesar as Lord.

When I visited the ruins of the great coliseum in Rome, I found that the foundations are still stained with the blood of martyrs.

This was a period of tremendous witness and heroic faith. Even the wicked Roman Empire was finally shaken by the testimony of these Christians.

PERGAMOS: COMPROMISE WITH THE WORLD-SYSTEM

> *(12) And to the angel of the church in Pergamos write, "These things says the One who has the sharp sword with two edges: (13) I know your works, and where you are dwelling, even where Satan's throne is, and you hold fast My name and have not denied My faith, even in those days in which Antipas was My faithful martyr, who was slain among you, where Satan dwells.*
>
> *(14) "But I have a few things against you, because you have there with you those who hold the doctrine of Balaam, who taught Balak to cast a stumbling block before the childern of Israel, to eat things sacrificed to idols and to commit fornication. (15) So you also have those who hold the doctrine of the Nicolaitans, which is a thing I hate. (16) Repent, or else I will come to you quickly and will fight against them with the sword of my mouth.*
>
> *(17) "He who has an ear, let him hear what the Spirit says unto the churches: 'To him who overcomes I will give some of the hidden manna, and will give him a white stone, and on the stone a new name written, which no one knows except he who receives it.' "*   REVELATION 2:12–17

DESTINATION

The city of Pergamos was a blend of political power, pagan worship, and academic sophistication at its university. It was the capital city of Asia Minor, and royal officials filled it with beautiful palaces, temples, and idols.

There was an altar to Zeus that was a wonder of the ancient world. The patron god of the city was Aesculapius, the god of healing. In his temple a living serpent was the symbol of worship. All the pagan rites of antiquity were practiced here.

One of the great universities of the era was located here, with a library at one time of 200,000 books, second in size only to Alexandria's. Greek philosophy pervaded the city.

Pergamos also contained a temple to Octavius Caesar where Caesar-worship flourished. Each citizen was required to offer incense to the emperor once a year and declare that Caesar was Lord.

DESCRIPTION OF CHRIST

Jesus describes Himself as having a sharp sword with two edges; other verses of Scripture teach us this refers to the Word of God in its keen discernment of men's thoughts and motives. Jesus acknowledged that although their outward behavior was not all it could be, their motives toward Him were right, and that's what He was judging.

COMMENDATION

The Lord Jesus assures these believers that He knows they're dwelling where Satan's throne is — that is, in the heart of a city under Satan's control. He therefore understands the persecutions and temptations they're experiencing from the rampant Satanic religion.

Jesus praises these saints for continuing to boldly proclaim Him as the only Lord in the face of great danger and opposition. He also commends them for sticking steadfastly to the truth rather than watering it down or perverting it with the aberrations of the pagan religions.

No doubt many Christians in the church of Pergamos died for their faith, but Jesus singles out one man especially and calls him "My faithful martyr."

Church tradition tells us that this first martyr, called Antipas, was brought before a statue of Caesar and told to swear that Caesar was God. But Antipas boldly proclaimed that Jesus alone was the Lord, and that there was no other God but He. The Roman official exclaimed. "Antipas, don't you know that the whole world is against you?" to which he replied, "Then Antipas is against the whole world!" Antipas was put inside a brass bull which was heated with fire until he was roasted to death.

Antipas was just an obscure man of history who was totally committed to Christ. But he's the one we remember when we think of ancient Pergamos.

REBUKE

The Lord deals with our sins according to our maturity and the circumstances of our failure. This church was tolerating serious evil in the teachings and practices of Balaam and the Nicolaitans, yet the Lord's rebuke shows understanding of the pressures Satan can bring.

The teachings of Balaam drew God's people away by using voluptuous women as enticement to sexual sins. The teachings of the Nicolaitans may have originated with Nicholas, one of the seven original deacons (Acts 6:5). Nicholas drifted into Greek philosophy and began to accept its tenet that the spiritual part of man is inherently good and the material part inherently evil. He reasoned that a man's indulgence of his body didn't defile his spirit. That gave religious sanction to the playboys of his day!

Nicholas also taught his followers to go to the pagan temples as well as to the church. In fact, he sought to merge Christianity with paganism. Cozy compromise with the world was the heart of his teaching.

EXHORTATION

Jesus hated these teachings because they lured believers away from fellowship with Him and compelled Him to discipline them. No sin can be committed, whether in body or in mind, that doesn't affect the believer's communion with Christ until it's judged and forsaken. Jesus warns the church to expel all who teach and practice such error unless they repent. Otherwise He Himself will fight them with the sword of His Word.

PROMISE

The people of that day were enamored with the "mysteries" of the pagan religious rites. But Jesus promised *greater* mysteries for His followers to enjoy *forever* — "hidden manna" and a "stone with a new name which only the receiver knows." Just as Israel received manna from heaven as its food while in the wilderness, so the believer will be fed and sustained by the Bread of Life, Jesus Christ.

Some law courts of John's day gave a white stone to a defendant when he was acquitted and a black stone when found guilty. Being given a white stone with a new name on it suggests the believer's complete acceptance and favor with God.

PROPHETIC APPLICATION: A.D. 312–590

During the historical era that the church of Pergamos symbolized, the church merged with the state. Emperor Constantine made Christianity the official religion of the empire and massive persecution ceased. But this apparent blessing to the church became a curse.

The church compromised its position more and more in order to gain favor and power. A church hierarchy began to develop, with the Bishop of Rome claiming increasing prominence because of his proximity to the ruler of the empire. He sought to strengthen his claim with the declaration of apostolic succession — alleging that this office in Rome was linked directly to Peter and that the Big Fisherman was the foundation of the church.

As the church at Pergamos therefore compromised with the world's paganism and immorality, its symbolic counterpart in the fourth and fifth centuries committed spiritual adultery in an impure alliance with the Roman Empire.

THYATIRA: THE GREAT COUNTERFEIT

(18) And to the angel of the church in Thyatira write, "These things says the Son of God, who has eyes like a flame of fire and His feet are like fine bronze: (19) I know your works and love and service and faith and patience and more works: and your latest works are greater that your first.

(20) "Nonetheless, I have a few things against you, because you allowed that woman Jezebel, who calls herself a prophetess, to teach and to seduce My servants to commit fornication and to eat things sacrificed to idols. (21) And I gave her an opportunity to repent of her fornication, and she did not repent.

(22) "Behold, I will cast her into a bed, and those who commit adultery with her into great tribulation, unless they repent of their deeds. (23) And I will kill her children with death, and all the churches shall know that I am He who searches the minds and hearts. And I will give to every one of you according to your works.

(24) "But to you I say, and to the rest in Thyatira, as many as have not accepted this doctrine and who have not known the deep things of Satan (as they call them), I will put no other burden upon you. (25) But what you have already hold fast until I come.

(26) "And to him who overcomes and keeps My works to the end I will give power over the nations, (27) and he shall rule them with a rod of iron: as the vessels of a potter shall they be broken to pieces, even as I received this authority from My Father. (28) And I will give him the morning star."

(29) He who has an ear, let him hear what the Spirit says to the churches.   REVELATION 2:18–29

DESTINATION

As a city, Thyatira was the least important of the seven addressed. Its main industry was dyeing cloth a beautiful red or purple. For this it was famous throughout the empire.

The first believer in Christ in Europe that we know about was a seller of purple cloth named Lydia, and she was from the city of Thyatira. There were many trade guilds in the city, and it was almost impossible to do well in business without belonging to one of these guilds. That became a problem for believers because paganism and immorality were rife in guild life.

There was also a temple for fortune-tellers in Thyatira, with a powerful female oracle presiding over it at this time.

DESCRIPTION OF CHRIST

Jesus describes Himself as having eyes like a flame of fire. This depicts His piercing appraisal of their hearts, a search which exposed impure motivations in their worship of Him. Jesus' feet of bronze symbolized the judgment that was going to fall on this church if it didn't shape up.

COMMENDATION

The Lord praised the Thyatirans for their love, faith, service, patience, and works. In fact, He mentions works twice, because as a growing church their service for Christ in recent years had been greater than at the beginning. In some ways, members of the church were very commendable. They had love and faith, which Paul the apostle affirmed as "the real goals that the commandments of God should produce in believers" (1 Timothy 1:5).

REBUKE

Leaders and certain other believers, however, had allowed an occultic prophetess to ensnare some of the immature believers in the church. This woman was probably the chief oracle of the large shrine for occultic mediums and fortune-tellers in the city of Thyatira when this letter was written. Her actual name was Sambathe, but here she is given a very descriptive nickname, "Jezebel."

Just as Jezebel had led Old Testament Israelites into idolatrous religious rites and debased sexuality, this heathen prophetess induced the people at Thyatira to mix idolatry and sexual impurity with their Christianity.

Today some leaders of churches and "Christian" colleges who *ought* to know better are doing the same sort of thing. They invite noted fortune-tellers to speak in churches and classrooms to satisfy curiosity. These occultic mediums are trojan horses in the midst of God's camp: only evil can come from listening to their poisonous doctrines.

EXHORTATION

The most severe and unusual warning given to any of the churches is given to Thyatira. Interestingly, instead of destroying or removing the prophetess. Christ casts her "into a bed" so that those who lack genuine love for God will confirm their infidelity by consorting with this spiritual harlot.

Those who commit adultery with the harlot will be brought into "great tribulation" unless they repent and evidence true faith in the Lord. He also warns that her "offspring" will be *killed*—those who mix occultism *in any way* with the teachings of the Bible and Christianity will perish. This includes all users of mediumistic paraphernalia, such as crystal balls, cards, and astrological charts.

The Lord declares that all the churches will realize through His treatment of the harlot and her followers that He examines the motives behind religious practices.

Many "religious" people don't desire a *personal* relationship with the true God; that would place too many demands on their selfish plans. They merely want religion to boost their ego from time to time as they perform their "good" deeds.

PROMISE

But now Jesus turns to the sincere seekers in the midst of this idolatry and immorality with some marvelous promises.

First He assures them that no other burdens will be added

to them: what He'd told them to do and to stop doing was all He intended to "lay on them," since they were already laboring with heavy responsibilities. He reminded them to hold zealously to their faith until He returned. This indicates prophetically that a remnant of this particular kind of church will continue on earth until the Rapture.

The believing remnant of this church is also promised that it will be a co-ruler with Christ over the Kingdom that will be established for a thousand years on earth. (This is explained in detail in Chapter 20).

PROPHETIC APPLICATION: A.D. 590–1517

Prophetically speaking, the major characteristics of Thyatira fit the church era that spanned the Middle Ages. During this time the dominant church fabricated a system that, like Jezebel, bound the people to image-worship, superstition, and priestcraft. These Scripture verses indicate this church will still have some adherents and some power *into* the "great tribulation" (verse 22). But the *believing* remnant from this prostituted form of Christianity is promised it will be present at the Rapture and will be delivered from the clutches of the "mother" church by Christ's return (verse 25).

THREE

Panorama of Church History–II

(1) And to the angel of the church in Sardis write, "These things says He who has the seven spirits of God and the seven stars: I know your works, that you have a reputation that you are alive, but you are dead. (2) Wake up and put some strength into what remains to be done before it dies, for I have not found any of your works completed in the eyes of God. (3) Remember, therefore, what you have received and been taught. Hold to those things and repent. If you will not wake up, I will come to you as a thief, and you will not know what hour I will come upon you.

(4) "You have a few people even in Sardis that have not soiled their garments, and they will walk with Me in white, for they are worthy to do so. (5) He who overcomes will thus be clothed in white robes, and I will not blot his name out of the Book of Life, but I will confess his name before My Father and His angels."

(6) He who has an ear, let him hear what the Spirit says to the churches. REVELATION 3:1–6

DESTINATION

Five hundred years before John wrote this letter, Sardis was one of the richest and most powerful cities in the world. It became ethically complacent and morally degenerate, and was conquered by Cyrus of Persia, then by Alexander the Great, and then it was leveled by an earthquake in A.D. 17. Later it was rebuilt by Tiberius Caesar.

Sardis was still a comparatively important city, but nothing like it had been in its heyday. The people tended to live in the glories of the past, and the church in Sardis was guilty of the same backward look.

Sardis was noted far and wide for its idolatrous worship of the goddess Cybele.

DESCRIPTION OF CHRIST

Christ describes Himself as the One who has "the seven spirits of God." As noted in Chapter 1, this refers to the omnipresent and omniscient nature of God the Holy Spirit. It's significant that Christ says that *He* has the Spirit. Unfortunately He didn't see any evidence that *they* had the Spirit! The ministry of the Holy Spirit is to empower, teach, guide, and equip believers for Christian living—this was tragically missing in the church at Sardis.

The Holy Spirit wasn't totally absent from the church (since He's always present wherever the real Church is), but the "dead church" label was a sure giveaway of its need for the *filling* ministry of the Holy Spirit.

The Lord also speaks of holding the "messengers" of the churches in His right hand. The messengers were the men responsible to deliver Christ's message to each of the churches. Christ's words are intended to remind all messengers (ministers) of their responsibility to Him to proclaim the true message. When the people of a church are "dead," spiritually speaking, God holds the minister accountable to Him. That minister needs to preach and demonstrate the absolute necessity of walking in the Spirit.

COMMENDATION

There's very little commended in this church of Sardis. Jesus said, "You have a *few* people, even in Sardis, who have not soiled their garments." This refers to walking in the ways of the ungodly world and being squeezed into its mold. That happens to us when we fail to fully appreciate the great salvation Christ gained for us on the Cross or fail to realize the richness of life Christ is eager to give us if we'll just take it! It's substituting the world's rags for God's riches—what I call a real "bummer"!

REBUKE

The church in Sardis was living on a moth-eaten reputation. The people had once been spiritually vibrant, but now they were apparently existing "in the flesh," which is the meaning of the word "dead" in verse 1.

There are few more pitiful sights than a stately, old church building that was built by and filled with enthusiastic Christians but now draws only a handful of parishioners on Sunday morning. It always reminds me of what Jesus said about the Pharisees: "Outside they looked like lovely, newly whitewashed tombs, but on the inside they were full of dead men's bones."

EXHORTATION

No believer can live on past spiritual victories. Complacency and lack of spiritual vision lead from stagnancy to actual retrogression in spiritual life. In fact, if we're not moving steadily forward we're losing ground in the Christian life because things are changing so rapidly in our world. A believer or church that has lost its vision and dynamic soon falls far behind and is neutralized as far as effectiveness for God is concerned.

Christ exhorts the church at Sardis and other churches like it to "wake up" and revitalize the good things they do have going for them. If they don't, what they have will "die"—they'll lose what progress they have made.

If believers fail to apply the truth they've learned in the past, it will eventually be taken away—they'll *forget* the principles of Christian living, and when they need to draw upon them they won't be there. This is what Jesus meant when He said, "Be sure to put into practice what you hear. The more you do this, the more you will understand what I tell you. To him who has shall be given; from him who has not shall be taken away even what he (thinks he) has" (Mark 4:24, 25, *TLB*).

I know several guys who were terrific Bible teachers in the past, but because they failed to consistently apply to their own lives all the truths they were teaching others, they began to slip noticeably. It grieves me to see this, but even sadder is the fact that these men haven't yet realized that their real power is gone.

PROMISE

The overcomer—one who truly believes that Jesus is the Son of God and his personal Savior—is promised wonderful blessings in this life and the next. Here Jesus names three up ahead:

First, the overcomer will walk with Christ in white, symbolizing the spotless and perfectly righteous character given to those who believe (Romans 4:4–8).

Second, his name will remain in the Book of Life. This Book contains the names of all the individuals ever born. If a person does not receive Jesus Christ as Savior by the time he dies, his name is blotted out of the Book of Life.

Third, Jesus will declare the overcomer's victory before the Father and His angels. Earlier Jesus had promised: "Whoever will confess His relationship with Me in front of men, the Son of Man will confess His relationship with Him in front of the angels of God. But whoever denies a relationship with Me before men shall have his relationship with Me denied before the angels of God" (Luke 12:8, 9).

PROPHETIC APPLICATION: A.D.1517–1750

The church of Sardis symbolized the Reformation Era. During this period of history the church was reformed, but not revived! Some essential doctrines were reclaimed, such as the truth that people can be justified with God only by faith, but the changes did not shake loose the elaborate rituals and human traditions of the medieval church. Complacency and a new legalism set in, and only a few tasted the power of the Holy Spirit for Christian living.

PHILADELPHIA: REVIVAL AND EVANGELISM

(7) And to the angel of the church in Philadelphia write, "These things says He who is holy, He who is true, He who has the key of David, He who opens and no man shuts, and shuts and no man opens: (8) I know your

works; behold, I have set before you an open door, and no man can shut it, for you have a little strength and have kept My word and have not denied My name.

(9) "Behold, I will make those of the synagogue of Satan (who say they are Jews, but are actually lying) come and worship before your feet and know that I have loved you. (10) Because you have obeyed my admonition for patient endurance, I also will keep you out of the hour of trial which will come upon all the world, to test those who dwell upon the earth.

(11) "Behold, I am going to come suddenly. Hold fast to what you have, so that no one takes your crown. (12) I will make the one who overcomes a pillar in the Temple of My God, and he shall never leave it. I will write upon him the name of My God and the name of the city of My God, the New Jerusalem, which comes down out of heaven from My God. And I will write upon him My new name."

(13) He who has an ear, let him hear what the Spirit says to the churches. REVELATION 3:7–13

DESTINATION

Philadelphia was about thirty miles southeast of Sardis. It was destroyed in A.D. 17 by the same earthquake that toppled Sardis. Tiberius Caesar, the great builder of cities, reestablished it.

Philadelphia was at the center of a great vineyard district and had a thriving business in wine. Because of this, Bacchus, the god of wine, had many devotees there. Quite naturally, drunkenness was a chronic social problem in the district.

The very large Jewish population in Philadelphia was apparently responsible for some of the persecution of Christians. The Jews were no strangers to persecution; Roman laws were hard on them as well as on the Christians.

DESCRIPTION OF CHRIST

To this missionary-minded church, Jesus presents Himself as the One who opens doors of evangelistic opportunity where and when *He* chooses. No mere man can *open* a door of witness or *shut* one except by the will of the Father. This is a stirring illustration of the sovereignty of God. If every missionary really believed this truth about Jesus, there would be fewer heartsick and frustrated missionaries!

When Jesus says that He possesses the "key of David," it's a reminder to the Jews in Philadelphia that the Davidic Covenant—which promised eternal blessing through David's greater Son, the Messiah—will be fulfilled in Jesus Himself. The startling statement that the Jews will come and worship at the feet of Christians means that the foes of Jesus will one day acknowledge the Christians' Lord as the true God.

COMMENDATION

Jesus praises the Philadelphians for their "work," which was obviously evangelism. He sets before them an open door for witness which no one can shut. Paul used this same symbol for evangelistic outreach when he said, "For there is a wide-open door for me to preach and teach here" (1 Corinthians 16:9, *TLB*).

Christ had promised to open doors as these believers sought to reach the lost world with His message of salvation. They were smart enough to realize that they had only "a little strength," and so they relied on Christ to open the way. He faithfully does just that for those who trust Him. But when there's *human* maneuvering to do *God's* work, things never work out right!

REBUKE

There's not a hint of rebuke to this church! It's important for us to see the characteristics that made this church so highly approved by the Lord.

EXHORTATION

Jesus' admonition is a simple encouragement to hold fast what the believers have learned and experienced in their walk with Him. He tells them they're doing great and to keep up the good work!

PROMISE

Most of this letter is composed of promises. Someone has counted over seven thousand promises in the Bible which God has made concerning His children and their welfare. Several very important ones are in this letter.

The first one is the "open door of opportunity" for believers to reach out to the unbelieving world. You'll notice that it doesn't say only *certain* people are supposed to go through that door and witness. The door is open for *every* child of God who will simply walk through it.

Often when we think about witnessing to someone we know, we think he couldn't possibly be open to the gospel. But the next time an opportunity comes along to speak to someone about Christ, we need to remind ourselves of the door which Christ says *He* has opened to their minds! They must open the door of their hearts, but He will open the door to their minds.

The greatest promise given to any of the seven churches is in this letter. Jesus promises that these Philadelphian believers will not go through the time of testing which is coming upon the whole world (verse 10).

The scope of this promise goes far beyond the little church in the ancient city of Philadelphia. There are several reasons for this. First, this promise speaks of a specific time or hour when the whole world will be in turmoil. A crisis of this kind has never faced the whole world at one time since this promise was given.

Second, this promise is unique because the believers who constitute the "Philadelphia-type" church are promised they will be "kept out of the hour of trial." Note they are not told they will be safeguarded *in* the trial but they will be kept *out of it altogether.*

A third reason for wider application of this promise is that the global judgment is to test "those who dwell upon the earth." This is a very specialized designation in the Book of Revelation. Listen to the Apostle John's description of these people in Chapter 13, verse 8.

"And all who *dwell upon the earth* will worship him (the Antichrist), that is, those whose names are not written in the Book of Life of the Lamb who was slain from the foundation of the world." See Revelation 6:10; 8:13; 11:10; 17:8 for further information. These people are unquestionably men and women who have rejected Jesus Christ as Lord of their lives.

I believe this is a clear and tremendously comforting promise to true believers in Christ that He will snatch them out of the world before unleashing the global judgments which are discussed in depth in Chapters 6 through 19.

PROPHETIC APPLICATION: A.D. 1750–1925

This was the great missionary era of the Church. Believers awakened to the millions who had never heard the name of Jesus, and many missionary movements began during this period. The China Inland Mission, the Student Volunteer Movement, and the Salvation Army were typical of the sacrificial enterprises reaching a vast cross-section of unevangelized peoples.

During this period the Church sensed its need for spiritual revival when God sent men like Wesley, Whitefield, Edwards, Finney, Spurgeon, and Moody (to name a few) across England and America. Revivals swept across the English-speaking countries and out of this great spiritual awakening rose many universities and churches dedicated to Christ.

Unfortunately, missionary zeal began to wane after World War I, and though some evangelistic movements continued to flourish, many of the schools and churches that arose during this era have long since abandoned their Christian heritage.

The Philadelphia type of church is still present in the world and it will be here until the Rapture, but it is not the dominant force in the professing Christian church today.

I wish that it were!

LAODICEA: COMPROMISE AND APOSTASY

(14) And to the angel of the church of the Laodiceans write, "These things says the Amen, the Faithful and True Witness, the Beginning of the Creation of God: (15) I know your works, that you are neither cold nor hot, I wish you were either cold or hot.

(16) "So then because you are lukewarm, and neither cold nor hot, I will spit you out of my mouth. (17) Because you say, 'I am rich and increased with goods and have need of nothing, and do not realize that you are wretched, miserable, poor, blind, and naked, (18) I counsel you to buy gold from Me that has been tried in the fire that you may be rich, and white raiment that you may be clothed and that the shame of your nakedness does not appear. And anoint your eyes with salve that you may see.

(19) "As many as I love I rebuke and discipline. Be zealous therefore and repent. (20) Behold, I stand at the door and knock. If any man hears

My voice and opens the door, I will come in to him and will fellowship with him and he with Me. (21) To him who overcomes I will grant to sit with Me on My throne, even as I also overcame and sat down with My Father on His throne."

(22) He who has an ear, let him hear what the Spirit says to the churches. REVELATION 3:14–22

DESTINATION

Laodicea was an extremely wealthy banking center about forty miles east of Ephesus. It had a medical school which was noted for a healing eye ointment.

The city was very pleasure-conscious, with a huge race track and three lavish theaters, one of which was half again as large as a football field.

DESCRIPTION OF CHRIST

Jesus first reveals Himself to this church as the "Amen," which means "I believe" and is usually spoken in response to some truth or promise of God. This affirmation was sadly lacking in this church, and Jesus emphasizes His own belief in the Father. This was meant to convict and rebuke the people into sounding their "Amens" to God.

As the "Faithful and True Witness" of God's truth, Jesus wanted these indifferent church members to also look at Him in a different light. Evidently they held Christ in low esteem and gave only casual consideration to His words.

Jesus uses a name for Himself here that appears nowhere else in Scripture: "The Beginning of the Creation of God." This church had become so satiated and smug with all its worldly possessions that it had forgotten its reason for existence was to proclaim the message that "God so loved the world that He gave His only-begotten Son. . . ."

COMMENDATION

There's not one word of commendation for this compromising, ingrown, unbelieving church. You'd think Jesus could come up with something to commend, but He hates compromise and spiritual indifference so intensely that He will not encourage them in any way. I feel sure this church was grinding away at doing their thing, oblivious to the fact that Christ had no part in their pitiful performance.

REBUKE

Most of this letter is divine denunciation. The Lord first rebukes the Laodiceans for being neither apathetic nor fervent. As witnesses for God, they were absolutely neutralized by their adoption of the world's views. (How painfully this reminds me of the double-talk of neo-orthodoxy today, which takes the Biblical terms of our historic faith and subtly redefines them to cloak unbelief!)

Jesus says that this kind of church nauseates Him and He will vomit this sham of a church out of His mouth.

Next Christ rebukes the church for its focus on material wealth as the criterion for success. They had accumulated properties, buildings, and opulent appointments, thinking they were doing God a favor to call themselves His children!

However, Jesus' estimation of their true condition was much different than theirs: "You are wretched, miserable, poor, blind, and naked." What a contrast to Jesus' appraisal of the church at Smyrna, the church that was materially poverty-stricken but spiritually rich!

I'm sure it's not too hard to see the lesson for churches today!

EXHORTATION

Christ's exhortation is aimed more to individuals than to the church as a whole. Apparently the church was almost past reforming. Every now and then I talk to believers who are members of large, spiritually dying churches. Though they know the church isn't giving them spiritual nourishment, they sometimes feel they should stay on and try to change the church. But I think Jesus is saying here that there is little hope for a church when the leadership lacks spiritual life or concern for God's primary business of winning souls and building them in the faith.

Jesus exhorts these Laodicean church members to "buy from Him gold that's been tried in the fire" of testing. Peter explains what this testing is designed to do: "These trials are not only to test your faith, but to see whether it is strong and pure. It is being tested as fire tests gold and purifies it and your faith is far more precious to God than mere gold" (1 Peter 1:7, *TLB*).

It appears that Jesus is urging these lukewarm, professing believers to pray for a little persecution in order to help them get their spiritual priorities in order. When fire is put to gold to refine it, the impurities rise to the top and can be skimmed off. This is what Jesus has in mind for this church!

The Lord urges them to "buy white raiment to cover their spiritual nakedness." This always reminds me of the fable of the emperor's new clothes. You remember how he was hoodwinked into buying some beautiful and costly clothes that were reputedly invisible to fools and incompetents. He paraded down the streets of his city for everyone to see how regal he looked in his new wardrobe—but he was naked!

This was really the case with the Laodicean church. They needed the covering of Christ's white robes of righteousness which He freely gives to each person who receives Him as Savior from sin.

Jesus further counseled these misguided religionists to "anoint their eyes with salve so they could see." These people were familiar with the healing aspects of eye-salve since it was produced in their own city. Jesus used this as a symbol of healing their spiritually blind hearts. This can only occur by being born again through the Holy Spirit's power. Jesus said, "Unless a man is born again, he can't even *see* the kingdom of God" (John 3:3).

This letter to Laodicea also contains an exhortation to the real believers. They're challenged to respond to God's love as He expresses it in His discipline. They should have been grateful to receive God's discipline because God chastens only His own children, as revealed in Hebrews 12:5–8.

This is what the writer of Hebrews meant when he said, "My son, do not despise the discipline of the Lord, nor faint when you are corrected by Him, for whom the Lord loves He disciplines, and chastens every son whom He receives. But if you are without discipline, of which all God's children are partakers, then you are bastards and not God's sons" (Hebrews 12:5, 6, 8).

One of the greatest symbolisms of Christianity is found in Christ's exhortation to these dead, apostate church members.

He addresses the church at large and the individual members specifically when He says, "Behold, I stand at the door and knock. If any man hears My voice and opens the door, I will come in to him and fellowship with him and he with Me."

The application usually made from this statement of Christ is that He's waiting at the door of each human heart, seeking to be admitted to the life of each person who senses his spiritual emptiness and invites Jesus to enter and fill the void. This is a perfectly valid application, as the essence of being a Christian is having "Christ in you, the hope of glory" (Colossians 1:27).

PROMISE

Jesus speaks again about the glory in store for the overcomers in this church. They had to overcome a lot to be true believers in the midst of that carnal, sterile indifference to God. Yet they overcame by inviting Jesus into their lives.

He says these overcomers will one day sit on His throne with Him and rule with Him through eternity. No higher privilege will ever be granted to humans—and we'll read more about its wonders in Chapter 21.

PROPHETIC APPLICATION: A.D. 1900—Tribulation

Near the turn of this century the scholars at many theological seminaries, particularly in Europe, began to introduce what they called "higher criticism" of the Scriptures. They were eager to examine the historicity and accuracy of the Biblical documents by using research methods developed in secular education.

Many of the leading critics possessed, at best, a lukewarm relationship with Christ, and this was reflected in their hazy views of Scripture. The more open skeptics began to deny outright the supernatural aspects of the Biblical faith—all in the name of scholarship—and before long they had "demythologized" Jesus into a mere man.

This Satanic infection spread like wildfire through the seminaries in Europe and the U.S., and by the 1920's it was echoing from the pulpits of American churches. The Western world was caught up in scientific and philosophical rationalism and the church got sucked into the vortex because so many of its leaders had never experienced a deep faith in Jesus.

The sad truth is that thousands of churches around the world today call themselves Christian but Christ is nowhere to be found in them. Tragically, most of the unbelieving world look at them—and want no part of their sham. And I don't either!

Although this Laodicean lukewarmness is the predominant characteristic of the church age today, there are signs that the Philadelphian evangelistic fervor is reviving in these closing days of human history. That's consistent with God's pattern of always showering down grace before hurling blasts of judgment.

The unbelievers of this era will find themselves enmeshed in the judgments of God during the Great Tribulation which is soon coming upon the earth. But everyone within this church age who is a true believer in Jesus will be taken out of the world before the judgment, and will be rewarded for his faith by spending eternity with Jesus.

THE CONCLUSION OF THIS MATTER

To sum up the great lessons for us today which are found in these seven letters to seven churches, I want to quote John Walvoord, President of Dallas Theological Seminary.

> Taken as a whole, the messages to the seven churches of Asia constitute a tremendous warning from Christ Himself, as expressed in the exhortations to each of these churches. He warns the churches today to "hear what the Spirit says to the churches."
> The church at Ephesus represents *the danger of losing our first love*, that fresh ardor and devotion to Christ which characterized the early church.
> The church at Smyrna represents *the danger of fear of suffering*. They were exhorted by Christ to "fear none of the things that they would suffer." In this day when the persecution of the saints has been revived in many places, the church may well need this admonition.
> The church at Pergamos illustrates *the constant danger of doctrinal compromise*, which is often the first step toward complete defection from the faith. Would that the modern church, which has forsaken so many fundamentals of Biblical faith, would heed that warning!
> The church at Thyatira is a monument to *the danger of moral compromise*. The church today has not only tolerated but in many cases *encouraged* compromise of Biblical moral standards.
> The church at Sardis is a warning against *the danger of spiritual deadness*, of orthodoxy without life, of mere outward appearance but no inward reality.
> The church of Philadelphia is exhorted to *keep enduring with patience*

and maintain the "little strength" that they had while they wait patiently for the Lord's return.

The final message to the church at Laodicea is the crowning indictment, a warning against *the danger of lukewarmness,* of self-sufficiency, of being unconscious of desperate spiritual need.

The invitation given long ago to the seven churches of Asia to hear what the Spirit says is extended to all men and churches today. A loving God would have men hear and believe, turn from their idols of sin and self, and look in faith to the Son of God, who loved them and gave Himself for them.[1]

[1]John Walvoord. *The Revelation of Jesus Christ,* Moody Press, 1966.

FOUR

The Church Goes Extraterrestrial

After considering the inconsistent showing of Christ's church over the past centuries, we might be inclined to think that Christ would give up on it! But I'm happy to say that is far from the case. In fact, just the opposite is true. As the centuries have rolled by, Christ has been preparing the place in heaven for all who continue to join God's family, and each passing year has brought nearer God's appointed day for our happy reunion with Him.

The Old Testament saints looked forward to spending eternity with the Lord, but they knew they would have to face death before they could face their Lord. They didn't know—because it wasn't revealed until the New Testament—that someday Jesus would return to the sky and take a whole generation of believers to heaven without dying physically. There would be no "valley of the shadow of death" for them!

In each of the seven phases of church history that we looked at in Chapters 2 and 3, earnest believers longed to be in that select group who would witness the coming of Christ. But God has a perfect time schedule for His program, and the long interlude between Jesus' first coming and His second has given opportunity for countless millions more to receive His love and forgiveness of sin.

We're eternally indebted to the New Testament writers for the picture they've given us of Christ on earth and of His new creation called the Church. But to the Apostle John alone was granted the privilege of actually *leaving* this earth and *recording* for us the scenes of the Church's final destination in heaven with Christ.

You'll remember that John was an old man exiled to the Island of Patmos when Christ appeared to him in His resurrected and glorified body. The sight so overwhelmed John that he lost consciousness. When he revived, Jesus told him the reason for His visit. John was to see God's future for mankind and creation, and he was to record it so that everyone could read it and be aware of what was coming.

Jesus told John to write about three things: first, the things he'd seen in the glorified Person of Jesus; second, the things that were spiritually significant in the churches of John's day—churches whose experiences would typify conditions throughout church history until Jesus returned for His people; third, things that would take place "*after* all these things" (Revelation 1:19)—in other words, events at the end of the world.

Although John didn't comprehend many of the things he saw, he faithfully recorded it all. In Chapter 1 we saw his description of Christ in His glory. Chapters 2 and 3 witness the spiritual condition of the church through the ages. These visions were given to John while he was still on Patmos.

But now in Revelation 4 begins the story of John's space travel to heaven where he saw the things that will take place both there and on earth following the close of church history.

AN OPEN DOOR IN HEAVEN

(1) After these things I looked, and, behold, a door was opened in heaven; and the first voice that I heard, like that of a trumpet talking with me, said, "Come up here, and I will show you what must happen after these things."
REVELATION 4:1

It's important to note that the Church has been the main theme of the Revelation until Chapter 4. Starting with this chapter, the Church isn't seen on earth again until Chapter 19, where we suddenly find it returning to earth with Christ as He comes to reign as King of Kings and Lord of Lords.

The big question is: "Where is the Church during the earthly devastation described in Chapters 6 through 19, and how did it get wherever it is?"

I Love a Mystery!

The Apostle Paul gives us the prophetic answer to the question, calling it a "mystery." When the word "mystery" is used in the Bible, it usually refers to a secret that no one can know until God chooses to reveal it.

Since the Church itself was a mystery to the believers of Old Testament days, its final destiny was also unknown. Not until after Jesus' resurrection and the birth of the Church did God choose to reveal His plans for this new body of followers, and Paul was given the responsibility of unveiling the secret.

In First Corinthians 15:51, 52 Paul writes, "Behold, I show you a mystery: we shall not all die, but we shall be changed from mortal to immortal, in a moment, in the twinkling of an eye, at the last trumpet. . . ."

The mystery revealed here is the promise that a certain group of people wouldn't have to die before going to be with the Lord, but could be changed from mortals to immortals without going through physical death.

Paul further amplifies this in First Thessalonians 4:15–17: "For this we say to you by the authority of the Lord, that we who are alive and remain until the Lord returns will not be raised up before those who have died. For the Lord Himself will descend from heaven with a shout, with the voice of the archangel, and with the trumpet of God; and the dead in Christ will rise first; then we who are alive and remain will be caught up together with them in the clouds, to meet the Lord in the air, and so will we ever be with the Lord."

The Great Snatch!

It's obvious from these verses and from others that Paul predicts a time when Jesus will raise the bodies of dead believers and simultaneously change living believers to immortals. The word for "caught up" actually means to "snatch up," and that's why I like to call this marvelous coming event "The Great Snatch"! It's usually referred to as the "Rapture," from the Latin word *rapare*, which means to "take away" or "snatch out."

Why would Jesus promise that a special group of His people would be taken from earth to heaven without first dying as millions of other believers have done?

The simple, wonderful answer is that they will be alive when God's striving with rebellious men turns into an avalanche of judgment upon the Christ-rejecting world and Satan himself—a judgment so terrible that God isn't going to let His Church go through it. This Tribulation isn't for God's people, but for those who have rejected His salvation.

WILL THE CHURCH GO THROUGH THE TRIBULATION?

This question has caused a great deal of controversy among true believers in Christ. Many Bible students who believe that a time of great testing and judgment will culminate in the return of Jesus as King of Kings are disagreed on whether the Church will have to endure this suffering along with the unbelieving world.

I personally believe that the Bible teaches the Church will escape these calamities. Although believers may well experience severe persecution as the day of Christ's return draws near, I believe Scripture teaches clearly that believers will be kept *from* the "time of trial" which God will send upon the world to try unbelievers (Revelation 3:10).

Part of the confusion on this issue rises from a failure to distinguish *two stages* in Jesus' second coming. One passage of Scripture speaks of Christ's coming *in the air* and in *secret*, like a thief coming in the night. Another part of the Scripture describes Christ's coming in power and majesty *to the earth*, with *every eye* seeing Him.

Both of these can be true only if there are two separate appearances of Christ in the future. Although Revelation 4:1 does not specifically refer to Christ's reappearance at the Rapture, I believe that the Apostle John's departure for heaven *after* the church era closes in Chapter 3 and *before* the Tribulation chronicle begins in Chapter 6 strongly suggests a similar catching away for the Church.

CONSPICUOUS BY ITS ABSENCE

As I said earlier, the Church is mentioned *nineteen times* in the first three chapters of the Book of Revelation and isn't mentioned *once* as being on earth from Chapters 4 through 19! And it's in these chapters that the great outpouring of God's wrath is described in detail!

It's also very interesting that in Chapters 2 and 3 we read "He who has an ear, let him hear what the Spirit says *to the churches*" repeated seven times, while in Chapter 13 we see: "If anyone has an ear, let him hear." This is the same warning except that the *church* is left out! It seems unthinkable that God would omit mention of the Church if it were still on earth during these devastating judgments.

THE SIGNS OF HIS COMING

The best authority on Jesus' return is, of course, Jesus Himself. As He was answering three great questions by His apostles (When would the Temple be destroyed? What would be the *sign of His coming?* What would be the sign of the end of the age?), He gave His reply in a parable and an historical allegory (Matthew 24:32–44). From these we can deduce when He will return to catch up the Church.

The parable involved a fig tree sprouting its first leaves. Jesus said that as new fig leaves indicate the nearness of summer in Israel, the accumulation of certain signs on the earth and in the skies would signal the arrival of God's judgments upon the generation which saw *all* the signs begin to appear. He said no one would know the exact *day* or *hour* of His coming, but we could know which *generation* would see Him.

THE SIGN OF NOAH

To illustrate this, Jesus gave an historical allegory about the great Flood of Noah's day. He said the people were going about their business as usual—eating, drinking, and marrying—but paying no attention to Noah's warnings about God's impending judgment. They had no idea God's prophetic time of judgment had come until the Flood destroyed them all.

Jesus said His coming would be *exactly like that*. But—which coming? His secret coming for the Church, or His coming in power and glory at the end of the Tribulation?

The answer comes into focus when we understand what the *Flood* symbolizes.

The Flood was a judgment on everyone who rejected God's

prophetic warning and offer of forgiveness. In Jesus' allegory, the Flood symbolizes a judgment which is coming upon the unbelieving world, and it must therefore refer to the period known as the Great Tribulation. Jesus pointed out that first there was a prophetic warning, then God removed His people to safety, and *then* judgment fell.

THE SIGN OF SODOM

We're also told that Jesus' coming will have similarities to the destruction of Sodom. Two angels told Lot that God was going to punish the wicked residents of the city, and then they escorted Lot and his family to safety. As the people of Sodom went about their daily routines, God rained down fire and brimstone and destroyed the entire city (Luke 17:20–36).

There's the pattern! First a prophetic warning, then God removes His people, and judgment falls on unbelievers.

If Jesus' historical illustrations refer to His coming for His people at the *end* of the Tribulation, as some teach, then believers as well as unbelievers would pass through its incredible horrors while doing their business as usual—eating, drinking, marrying, building, buying, planting, and selling.

But no one can live a *normal* life in the chaos of the Tribulation, as we'll see in the following chapters of Revelation.

RAPTURE BEFORE JUDGMENT

I think you can see why these two illustrations of Jesus teach His return for His own *before* the Tribulation judgment begins. We are now living in a period of prophetic warning about God's impending judgment. Books, preaching, mass media, and word-of-mouth messages about Jesus' return are having a wider dissemination than at any time in history. Following this prophetic warning, Christ will remove His people in the Rapture, and then judgment such as man has never known will sear the world for seven years. After that, Christ will lead His rescued followers into God's kingdom of peace and righteousness on a beautiful new earth.*

*For a thorough presentation of the pre-Tribulation Rapture view, see *The Rapture Question,* by John F. Walvoord, Zondervan, 1970.

IS THE RAPTURE NEAR?

Since the Bible teaches the Rapture is going to occur *before* the Tribulation period begins, and since there are increasing signs that this time of God's judgment is nearing, it would be good to briefly summarize the major signs that Jesus and the prophets said would herald the Tribulation and the return of Jesus to this earth.† Even though many of these signs are appalling in themselves, their tremendous significance should gladden the heart of every true believer in Christ.

Many of these predicted signs are amplified in various chapters of the Book of Revelation. Here I'm simply going to list them to get them focused in our minds as a group.

1. The return of the dispersed Jews to Israel to become a nation again in 1948.
2. The Jews' recapture of the Old City of Jerusalem in the 1967 Arab-Israeli War.
3. The rise of Russia as a powerful nation and enemy of Israel.
4. The Arab confederation against the new State of Israel.
5. The rise of a military power in the Orient that can field an army of 200 million soldiers. (Red China alone boasts that she has this number of troops!)
6. The revival of the old Roman Empire in the form of a ten-nation confederacy. (I believe the European Common Market is ultimately going to be this power.)
7. The revival of the dark occultic practices of ancient Babylon.
8. The unprecedented turn to drugs.
9. The increase of international revolution.
10. The increase of wars.
11. The increase of earthquakes.
12. The increase of famines through the population explosion.
13. The coming of plagues.
14. The increase of pollution.
15. The departure of many Christian churches from the historic truths of Christianity.
16. The move toward a one-world religion.
17. The move toward a one-world government.

†For amplification and documentation of each of these signs, read the author's book, *The Late Great Planet Earth,* Zondervan, 1971.

18. The decline of the United States as a major world power.
19. The increase in lawlessness.
20. The decline of the family unit.
21. Global weather changes.

THE GREAT HOPE

Several times in the New Testament the coming of Christ at the Rapture is called a great "hope." It can only be a hope, however, for people who are ready by having personally received Jesus as their Savior.

Jesus described the sudden parting of believers from unbelievers when He comes secretly for His own. He said two men will be working in a field, and one will be taken and the other left. Two women will be employed side-by-side, and one will suddenly disappear and the other one will be left (Matthew 24:40–44).

Larry Norman, a popular American folk singer and a friend of mine, summed it up beautifully in his song, "I Wish We'd All Been Ready."[1]

> Life was filled with guns and war,
>   and everyone got trampled on the floor—
> I wish we'd all been ready!
>
> Children died, the days grew cold,
>   a piece of bread could buy a bag of gold—
> I wish we'd all been ready!
>
> There's no time to change your mind,
>   the Son has come and you've been left behind!
>
> Man and wife asleep in bed,
>   she hears a noise and turns her head, he's gone—
> I wish we'd all been ready!
>
> Two men walking up a hill,
>   one disappears and one's left standing still—
> I wish we'd all been ready!
>
> There's no time to change your mind,
>   the Son has come and you've been left behind!

[1]Copyright 1969 Beechwood Music Corporation/J.C. Love Publishing Co., Hollywood, Cal. Used by permission.

There's no time to change your mind,
How could you have been so blind?
The Father spoke, the demons dined,
    the Son has come, and you've been left behind!

JOHN'S FIRST GLIMPSE OF HEAVEN

(2) And instantly I was caught up in the Spirit and saw a throne that was set in heaven, and the One sitting on it. (3) And He who was sitting there looked like a jasper and a sardius stone; and there was a rainbow encircling the throne that looked like an emerald. REVELATION 4:2, 3

In verse 2 John tells us of his first glimpse of the One whose voice had thundered out, "Come up here and I will show you what must happen after *these things.*"

These things refers to the events of the church age. John has been called up into heaven to be shown the things which must happen *after* the Rapture, both in heaven and on earth. The first sight that greeted his eyes was a magnificent throne and an indescribable Person sitting on it.

Throughout the rest of The Revelation, the throne of God is the central object of focus. Around it everything else revolves, from it pour forth the judgments of God, and toward it all the inhabitants of heaven bow in worship.

Of course, the throne is only as important as the One who occupies it. We know that it's the throne of God the Father, but the description given of the One sitting on it appears to be that of God the Son. He's not described in the form of a man, however, and since we know that Jesus is in heaven in His human body, it's most likely that John's vision was that of God the Father.

THE SPLENDOR OF GOD

The impact on John was overwhelming! The glory and splendor was breathtaking. At a loss for words, John attempts to describe God in majestic terms. He saw the Occupant of the throne as jasper and sardius stones in appearance. A rainbow around the throne was emerald in color.

A jasper is a precious stone, but many scholars believe this to have been a diamond. As John looked at the throne, he was impressed with something that radiated like a many-faceted gem. He also saw what appeared to be a beautifully cut ruby.

The sardius stone has this appearance and emits a deep, rich, red glow.

The significance of this is tremendous. The jasper pictures the glowing radiance of God's holiness and flawless perfection, while the deep red sardius symbolizes the immense value of the shed blood of Jesus Christ. Just as the jasper and sardius stones have many facets which reflect their radiance and beauty, so the countless ages of eternity will show the unlimited facets of God's love and riches for us.

MERCY IN JUDGMENT

The purpose of a rainbow is given in Genesis 9:11–17, where God reveals that He set His bow in the sky as a symbol of His promise that He would never again completely devastate the world with water. He also proclaimed that as long as the present earth existed the four seasons would continue, and that there would be light and darkness as well as the sun for heat. The rainbow around God's throne is therefore a gracious reminder that God will remember His post-flood promise of mercy even during the awful days of the Tribulation.

In the Bible the color green symbolizes life, and circles symbolize eternity. The circular, emerald-colored rainbow therefore also pictures God's gift of eternal life which He will offer to those on earth even in the midst of the horrors of Tribulation judgment.

THE TWENTY-FOUR ELDERS

(4) And round about the throne were twenty-four thrones, and I saw twenty-four Elders sitting on the thrones, clothed in white robes; and they had crowns of gold on their heads.   REVELATION 4:4

The identity of these twenty-four enthroned Elders is not certain. Many Bible scholars feel that they are a special group of angels who minister to God and assist in the administration of the universe. That's a possibility, but I personally believe that they are representative of the Church. Twenty-four is the number associated with priestly service and is symbolic of the Church operating in its role as priest.

You'll notice that these twenty-four enthroned Elders are clothed in white and are wearing gold crowns. Both of these are true of born-again humans, but not of angels. White robes symbolize the righteous garments given to believers the moment they trust in Christ, and the golden crowns here are victors' laurels. They're the type presented to winners in the original Olympic games; believers have been victorious over death and hell, but angels have not faced those perils.

THE BELIEVER'S CROWNS

In passing, I think it's important to note that there are also other crowns promised to believers as rewards for various kinds of faithfulness in this life.

One of these eternal rewards is going to be a *crown of life.* It's a martyr's crown. Revelation 2:10 describes it. This crown is granted as a reward for dying as Christ's martyr. James 1:12 also mentions this crown, and this would be a particularly blessed crown to win.

Another trophy is called the *crown of glory.* According to First Peter 5:4, this is given to shepherds who pastor their congregational flocks well. Ministers who are faithful in their God-given task will receive a crown of glory at the Judgment seat of Christ.

Then there's the *crown of righteousness,* described in Second Timothy 4:8. I don't know whether I'm going to get any other kind of crown, but I know I'm going to get this one! You may think, "You're awfully conceited to be saying that!" But this crown is given to those eagerly expecting Christ's appearing— and I'm sure doing that! Aren't you?

A special crown is promised to the *soul-winner*—the believer who leads people to faith in Christ. This crown is mentioned twice by the Apostle Paul when he speaks of his converts as being his rejoicing and his crown (Philippians 4:1; 1 Thessalonians 2:19).

THE THRONE AND THOSE AROUND IT

(5) And out of the throne proceeded lightnings and thunderclaps and voices; and there were seven lamps of fire burning before the throne, which are the seven spirits of God. (6) And before the throne there was something like a sea of glass, like crystal.

And near the throne on both sides were four Living Beings full of eyes in front and in back. (7) And the first Living Being was like a lion, and the second Living Being like a calf. The third Living Being had a face like a man, and the fourth Living Being was like a flying eagle.

(8) And the four Living Beings each had six wings, and these creatures were full of eyes all over; and they do not rest day and night from saying, "Holy, holy, holy, Lord God Almighty, who was and is and is to come."
REVELATION 4:5–8

The throne of God in heaven, like the North Star, is the sure reference point that humans and angelic beings can fix their course of life upon. Around this unchangeable throne is a cast of heavenly characters and objects that will play critical roles in God's future dealings with men.

WHO MOVED THE LAMPS?

The first of these objects is the group of seven lamps. In Chapter 1 we saw these same seven lamps *on earth*, with Christ walking among them. Now these seven lamps (which, as we saw, portray the Church), are *in heaven*. This is further evidence that God will remove the Church from earth before His outpouring of judgment.

In Chapter 1 we were also introduced to the seven Spirits of God, and we saw that this symbolized the sevenfold characteristics of the Holy Spirit. In Isaiah 11:2 the prophet made a prediction about the coming Messiah, saying that the Spirit of the Lord would rest upon Him. Then he delineated the seven attributes of the Holy Spirit. He called Him (1) the Spirit of the Lord, (2) the Spirit of Wisdom, (3) the Spirit of Understanding, (4) the Spirit of Counsel, (5) the Spirit of Might, (6) the Spirit of Knowledge, and (7) the Spirit of the Fear of the Lord.

THE SEA OF CRYSTAL

The word "sea" in Biblical symbolism often pictures the restless masses of mankind. The word is used this way in Revelation 13 and several times in the Book of Isaiah. In Isaiah the prophet compares the nations with a *troubled* sea in a storm. Yet the sea before the throne of God is motionless like a sea of glass. This pictures the believers at rest in the presence of God. There's no more storm upon *this* sea; it's calm, quiet, and peaceful before the throne of God.

THE FOUR LIVING BEINGS

Surrounding the throne are four strange-looking creatures full of eyes. Although the King James Version of the Bible calls them creatures, they really aren't that. While we can't be dogmatic about it, these Living Beings seem to be angels who represent the four portraits of Christ that we find in the four Gospels—Matthew, Mark, Luke, and John.

The "lion," king of the beasts, pictures Christ as the King of the Jews. This is especially emphasized in the Gospel of Matthew. The hard-working ox pictures Christ as the fully obedient servant of His Father. This quality is highlighted in the Gospel of Mark.

The Living Being with the face of a man represents Christ as the ideal and perfect man, as vividly portrayed in the Gospel of Luke.

The flying eagle suggests Christ's heavenly origin—in other words, His complete oneness with the God of heaven. This is the special message of the Gospel of John.

The four Living Beings, with their continual song of praise, "Holy, holy, holy. . ." will remind us night and day forever of the sublime nature and work of the Lord Jesus Christ while He was on earth.

THE AWE OF THE UNDESERVING

(9) And when the Living Beings give glory and honor and thanks to Him who is seated on the throne, who lives forever and ever, (10) the twenty-four Elders fall down before Him who is seated on the throne and worship Him who lives forever and ever, and cast their crowns before the throne, saying, (11) "You are worthy, O Lord, to receive glory and honor and power, for You have created all things, and for Your pleasure they are and were created." REVELATION 4:9–11

Evidently whenever the four Living Beings begin to praise the Lord, it's the cue for the twenty-four Elders to fall down before the throne and worship God also. As a part of their worship of Him, the Elders throw their crowns at His feet.

I said earlier that the crown which each Elder wore was a victor's crown. Actually there are many crowns promised as rewards to faithful believers, and the victor's crown seems to symbolize them all. It may be that a believer who has earned more than one crown will be given stars to attach to his victor's crown to designate how many crowns he has won.

Or it may be that the faithful Elders, who are symbolic of all believers, will somehow be able to wear more than one crown at a time. In any case, though the crowns of the Elders have been honorably won, they will realize how unworthy they are to claim *any* rewards for faithful service, and out of hearts of love and gratitude they will cast their crowns in praise at the Father's feet! Just as you and I may someday do!

FIVE

The Lamb Becomes a Lion

One of the unique things about the Bible is that it speaks with the same matter-of-fact tone about things which man has never seen as it does about the common, everyday things of life. The Book of Revelation talks with unwavering assurance about the magnificent residence for believers in heaven. It also describes with authority the events that will scourge the earth for seven years after believers are taken to heaven.

These seven years will be the most fateful in all human history. They are "the countdown," because at the termination of this period Jesus will return to earth in a cataclysmic personal appearance to establish the Kingdom of God on earth.

During this seven-year period known as "the Tribulation," the human race will witness the most terrible judgments ever to fall on God's creation. Chapters 6 through 19 of Revelation describe in detail the unprecedented horrors of this time.

Before any judgment lashes the earth, however, a portentious scene must unfold in heaven. This event is described for us in Revelation 5.

THE SCROLL OF JUDGMENT

(1) And I saw in the right hand of Him who sat on the throne a scroll written within and on the back, sealed with seven seals. (2) And I saw a strong angel proclaiming with a loud voice, "Who is worthy to open the scroll

*and to loose its seals?" (3) And no one in heaven or on earth or under the
earth was able to open the scroll or to look on it. (4) And I began to weep
uncontrollably because no man was found worthy to open and to read the
book or to look on it.* REVELATION 5:1–4

About 2,600 years ago, God revealed to the Prophet Daniel
many predictions about future world events, including the return of Christ to this earth to set up God's earthly Kingdom.
As Daniel puzzled over these fantastic predictions, God told him
to seal up all of his prophecies until the end of the age (Daniel
12:4).

During all the centuries since God spoke to Daniel, men
have had comparatively little interest or knowledge concerning
the events of that final period of man's history often called the
"end times." Prophecy has indeed been a closed subject.

But John tells us in this chapter about one of the first events
that will take place after the Rapture of the Church. It will be
the unsealing of a scroll that reveals all the judgments which
will descend on the world during its coming seven years of tra-
vail. John also describes the dramatic search for someone worthy to open the scroll and set in motion its dreadful forces.

THE SIGNIFICANCE OF SCROLLS

Sealing a scroll was a common and important practice in
Biblical times. The wills of both Emperor Vespasian and Caesar
Augustus, for example, were secured with seven seals.

For such a document, a scribe would procure a long roll of
parchment and begin writing. After a period of writing he would
stop, roll the parchment enough to cover his words, and seal
the scroll at that point with wax. Then he would resume writing, stop again, roll the scroll, and add another seal. By the
time he was finished, he would have sealed the scroll seven
times. The scroll would be read a section at a time, after each
seal was opened.

Why was this process used? Evidently it was to prevent un-
authorized persons from tampering with the scroll or reading
and revealing its contents. Only a "worthy" person—that is,
someone with proper authority—could have legal access to the
scroll's message.

W. A. Criswell presents one of the best explanations of the
use of a sealed scroll in his *Expository Sermons on Revelation.*

He points out that when a Jewish family was required to forfeit its land and possessions through some distress, the property could not be permanently taken from them. Their losses were listed in a scroll and sealed seven times, then the conditions necessary to purchase back the land and possessions were written on the outside of the scroll. When a qualified redeemer could be found to meet the requirements of reclamation, the one to whom the property had been forfeited was obligated to return the possessions to the original owner.

MAN'S FORFEITED INHERITANCE

Since the major part of the Book of Revelation deals with a seven-sealed scroll and its mysterious contents, it's very important for us to understand the significance of these contents.

I believe the scroll represents the forfeiture to Satan of man's original inheritance from God. You see, when God created Adam and Eve, he gave them dominion over the earth and everything in it. Man was the delegated sovereign of Planet Earth.

However, when Adam obeyed Satan and simultaneously turned his back on God, he became the Benedict Arnold of eternity and the universe. He officially forfeited to Satan his authority to rule the world. At that point the arch-enemy of God legally took over dominion of this earth.

Earth rightly belongs to Adam's race, but as a result of our forefather's capitulation to Satan, none of his descendants can qualify to pay the redemption price of the forfeited world. Someone must be found—if humanity is to escape eternal loss—who is "worthy" to make restitution for man's deficiency.

As John looked at this great scroll and sensed its importance, he wept uncontrollably because no man could be found who was untainted with Adam's sin. No man or angel in the universe would claim the right to open this scroll. Could anyone be found to redeem man's lost heritage? Dr. Criswell eloquently describes John's quandary.

THE TEARS OF ALL MANKIND

John's tears represent the tears of all God's people through all the centuries. They're the tears of Adam and Eve as they view the still form of their dead son, Abel, and sense the awful consequence of their disobedience. They are the tears of the children of Isreal in bondage as they cried to God for deliverance from their affliction and slavery. They're the sobs and tears wrung from the heart and soul of God's people as they have stood beside the graves of loved ones and experienced the indescribable heartaches and disappointments of life.

Such is the curse that sin has laid upon God's beautiful creation. No wonder John wept so fervently. If no redeemer could be found to remove the curse, it meant that God's creation was forever consigned to remain in the hands of Satan.[1]

In this chapter John is going to reveal the *one Person* who qualifies to pay the redemption price of man's lost inheritance. It is the God-man, Jesus Christ, who would pay the debt by forfeiting His own life. In the pages that follow we'll see that a day is coming when the resurrected and glorified Christ will cast out the usurper who's been ravaging the world, punish those who refuse His salvation, and redeem our bodies, the earth, and all creation!

The Lion Who Was a Lamb

(5) And one of the Elders said to me, "Stop weeping, behold, the Lion of the tribe of Judah, the Root of David, has conquered so as to be worthy to open the scroll and to loose its seven seals." (6) And I looked, and standing there in the midst of the throne and of the four Living Beings and in the midst of the Elders was a Lamb as though it had been slain, having seven horns and seven eyes, which are the seven spirits of God sent forth into all the earth. (7) And He came and took the scroll out of the right hand of Him who sat upon the throne. (8) When He had taken the scroll, the four Living Beings and twenty-four Elders fell down before the Lamb, and every one of them had harps and golden bowls full of incense, which are the prayers of saints. Revelation 5:5–8

As John stood weeping, one of the Elders assured him that a personage worthy to open the scroll had been found. He was none other than the Lion of the tribe of Judah and the Root of David, the promised Deliverer of Israel and the Redeemer of mankind.

Judah was one of the twelve sons of Jacob, the patriarch from whom the twelve "tribes" of Israel originated. In Genesis 49:10 Jacob prophesies of his son Judah's leadership: "The scepter (rulership) shall not depart from Judah . . . until Shiloh (the Messiah, to whom it belongs) comes. . . ."

Judah was the tribe from which King David came. Through

---

[1]W. A. Criswell, *Expository Sermons on Revelation*, Zondervan, 1969.

several prophets in the Old Testament, God promised David a royal Kingdom that would last forever. He told David that one of his descendants would be called the "Prince of Peace," and that this Prince would reign over an eternal Kingdom of righteousness and justice (1 Chronicles 17:11–14; Isaiah 9:6, 7). In Revelation 5:5, 6 we're introduced to the One who is the fulfillment of these predictions: Jesus of Nazareth, from the tribe of Judah and the family of David. Curiously, he's described here by two terms that seem to be contradictory: He's called both a "lion" and a "lamb."

But rather than being contradictory, these terms are actually perfect descriptions of Jesus in His two primary roles.

When Jesus came to earth the first time He came in humility to offer Himself as the Lamb of God to die for the sins of men. But when He comes again He'll return in the strength and supremacy of a lion. His previous lamblike meekness and gentleness will give way to regal power. The first time Christ came as a Savior, offering pardon and cleansing from sin and its consequences; when He comes the second time, He will wield a rod of iron as the Judge of all men.

A DESCRIPTION OF THE LAMB

The Lamb which John saw was no ordinary specimen. It was a composite of all the marvelous attributes of Jesus. Even the word John uses to refer to the Lamb is full of tender meaning. It's the Greek word *arnios*, which means "a little, pet lamb." It's used only one other place in the New Testament, when Jesus told Peter to take care of Jesus' *lambs* while He was gone (John 21:15).

This isn't the first time we're introduced to Jesus as a lamb. John the Baptist called Jesus "the Lamb of God who would take away the sins of the world." He meant that Jesus was destined to take the place of the ceremonial "Passover lamb," and that by bearing men's sins Jesus would reconcile God and man.

Remember, in the directions for the Passover, the people were not to go out and slay just *any* lamb. The lamb was to be carefully chosen from the firstlings of the flock for its beauty and perfection, and it was to be placed in the bosom of the family for four days, that is, until the children loved it and it was looked upon as a member of the family; a pet lamb, held next to the hearts of those who lived in that household. That little *arnios* was identified with the family, loved, cuddled, petted, and caressed.[2]

Such is the Lamb that John sees standing next to the throne of God and in full view of all the redeemed in heaven. This was God's "pet," if you please, the darling of His heart, and yet it had to be slain to purchase redemption for all of God's creation.

THE EVERLASTING WOUNDS

This slain Lamb is *standing* here in the heavenly vision, indicating that it's no longer dead. However, the fact that John could tell that it *had been* dead means that there must have been mortal wounds visible. That's consistent with what John tells us of Jesus later in the Revelation, for on several occasions Christ shows His wounds to those who've rejected Him.

It's very interesting to stop and think about the fact that even though Jesus has a perfect, immortal body, it still has scars in it. When God raised Jesus from the dead, He could very easily have erased the nailprints and the spear wound in His side. Yet for some reason He left them there.

I'm not sure of all the reasons why Jesus still has His wounds, but personally, I'm very glad He does. I want to look at those scars and touch them often, just to be reminded of what it cost Jesus to make it possible for me to be in heaven.

John further describes this Lamb as having seven horns and seven eyes. This symbolizes a composite image of what Christ is like. The number seven in Biblical usage denotes completeness and perfection. Throughout the Old Testament horns represent power, and a multiplicity of eyes implies knowledge and intelligence.

This unusual picture of Jesus speaks of the fact that as the all-powerful, resurrected Savior of men, He exercises constant vigilance and care over all His children. It also implies that those who've rejected IIim will one day experience the searching scrutiny of their deeds by the omnipotent Judge whom they've rejected.

THE LAMB TAKES THE SCROLL

Finally Christ, the Lamb, takes the seven-sealed scroll from the right hand of the One who sits on the throne. Instantly the

[2]Ibid.

four Living Beings and twenty-four Elders fall down before the Lamb in worship, for they realize that the events resulting in the redemption of creation are about to begin.

In their hands the Elders hold harps and golden bowls filled with incense, which represents the earnest prayers of believers of all past ages begging God to judge Satan and his followers and to liberate mankind and creation from its curse.

This marvelous picture of intercession shows just a part of what believers in heaven will be doing while judgment is raging on the earth for seven years. They will be functioning as priests, interceding with God on behalf of their Tribulation brothers and sisters who are still on earth.

That's exciting to me! Right now Christ is our High Priest, representing us in person before the Father's throne. The day is soon coming when we will have the privilege of representing our fellow believers in person before the Lamb in heaven.

THE CHOIR THAT COULDN'T BE NUMBERED

> *(9) And they sang a new song, saying, "Worthy are You to take the book and to break its seals, for You were slain, and purchased for God with Your blood men from every tribe and tongue and people and nation. (10) And You have made them to be a kingdom and priests to our God, and they will reign upon the earth." (11) And I looked, and I heard the voice of many angels around the throne and the Living Beings and the Elders; and the number of them was myriads of myriads, and thousands of thousands, (12) saying with a loud voice, "Worthy is the Lamb that was slain to receive power, riches, wisdom, might, honor, glory, and blessing." (13) And I heard every created thing which is in heaven and on earth and under the earth and on the sea, and all things in them saying, "To Him who sits on the throne and to the Lamb be blessing and honor and glory and dominion forever and ever." (14) And the four Living Beings kept saying, "Amen." And the Elders fell down and worshipped.* REVELATION 5:9–14

Have you ever stopped to think how important singing is in our lives? We sing at weddings, funerals, political rallies, football games, graduations, and church services, not to mention the singing we do in private moments.

What is it about song that soothes us when we're sad, cheers us when we're lonely, and exhilarates us when we're happy?

If you notice the songs of our day, you'll realize that most of them have words that express deep feelings of the composer or singer. Love songs extol the virtues of the lover—or the beloved, and this theme has always marked one of the most popular types of songs.

Another popular kind of music is the ballad. This song tells of someone's exploits or deep hopes and longings, like many of the psalms in the Old Testament. These were originally put to music and sung. A current revival of the ballad-type is known as "country music." This is my favorite.

I like this kind of music because it runs the gamut of emotions from gloom to glee. After a Johnny Cash concert I'm worn out! That music comes right up out of his soul and grabs me!

I wouldn't be at all surprised or disappointed if the *new* song which the hosts of heaven sing to extol the incomparable Son of God has a "country music" style! I know one thing—no one will be able to sing this new song without being overwhelmed with emotion toward the One whose praises they're singing.

I can hardly read these matchless words without tears coming to my eyes: *"Worthy is the Lamb that was slain!"* Never have human words sounded so inadequate to me! Never has there been a greater understatement about anyone!

"And the four Living Beings kept saying, 'Amen!' And the Elders fell down and worshipped!"

SIX

The Beginning of Sorrows

In Chapters 6 through 19 of the Book of Revelation we're given an unfolding chronological picture of a future seven-year period of the greatest tribulation this earth will ever experience. This period is God's final countdown for mankind, culminating in the personal, visible return of Jesus Christ to this earth to reclaim it as His own possession.

The "Tribulation," as this period is called, is well named, for there will be sorrow and suffering on this earth such as man has never known before and will never know again. These are the days Jesus spoke of when He said that if He didn't return to end the Tribulation there wouldn't be anyone left alive.

Men who have studied Bible prophecy all their lives are startled by the fact that right before their eyes the entire setting for the events of the Tribulation is coming into focus. Long ago the prophets of Israel made specific predictions about this period of God's judgment, but this century is the first to witness the beginning of the fulfillment of so many of these prophecies.

For those of us who know what the prophets have taught, picking up our morning newspaper is practically a traumatic experience. Headline after headline screams out a confirmation of these remarkable predictions.

A LOOK AT THE TRIBULATION

A question that many have asked is, "Why is there going to be a time of Tribulation and judgment on the earth, and how can we know it will last only seven years?"

In Chapter 5 we've seen several reasons for the outpouring of God's judgment upon the earth. One is for Christ to finally annul the authority of Satan who usurped control of the earth from Adam. The second reason is to judge all who oppose God, in preparation for the final redemption of mankind and the whole universe.

But, one of the most important reasons for an allotment of seven years for God's final dealing with mankind has to do with an incredible prophecy of Daniel made in the sixth century B.C. (Daniel 9:24–27).

In this amazing prediction, Daniel set forth a divinely ordained time period of "seventy weeks" of years (490 years) in which God would primarily reach out to the unbelieving world through His chosen people, the Jews. The time period was like a great, divine "time-clock" with 490 years of time marked off on it.

A specific event was to mark the *beginning* of this 490 years of Jewish evangelistic outreach. When the Persian King, Artaxerxes Longimanus, gave the Jews permission to leave their Babylonian captivity and restore and rebuild the city of Jerusalem, God's finger pushed down on the stop watch and the 490-year alloted countdown began clicking off. That was April, 445 B.C.

Daniel predicted that after sixty-nine weeks of years (483 years) had clicked off on this allotment of time, the Messiah of Israel would be revealed to the Jews and then killed, and the city of Jerusalem and their Temple would be destroyed.

We know the exact time of the fulfillment of this prophecy, because 483 years had transpired on the *very day* that Jesus presented Himself to the nation of Israel as their Messiah and was rejected by them and put to death. Within forty years of this event, Titus and the Roman legions destroyed the city of Jerusalem and tore down their beautiful Temple.

ISRAEL IS MISSING "ONE WEEK"

With these events, God's finger once again pushed in on the divine time-clock and the alloted time of Israel's special outreach to the unbelieving world was stopped, *seven years short of the promised 490 years.*

When the nation of Israel rejected the One who called Himself "the Way, the Truth, and the Life," God took the spotlight *off* of Israel and set the nation aside as the special messengers of His truth for men coming to know Him. The spotlight of God turned to a group who would be made up of both Jews and Gentiles, a group who would accept His Messiah as Savior and proclaim that message to the world. This group is known as the *Church.*

Because we know that God would never go back on His Word, we're positive that He intends to give the Jews the seven years left on their alloted time to finish the purposes for which God called them as a chosen race, namely that of being His witnesses to the whole world.

In Chapter 7 we'll see how God lays His hand on 144,000 Jews who will more than make up for Israel's failure to preach the message of Messiah. In the seven years left to them they'll evangelize the whole world. No one has done that yet!

But before God can shift His emphasis back to Israel, the Church must be taken out of the world since His hand is now on it. In Chapter 4 we saw how that happened at the Rapture.

The Threefold Judgments of God

In this chapter of the Revelation, John begins to unfold the sobering judgments of God that will begin the seven-year countdown until Jesus returns to the earth. The Book of Revelation presents these Tribulation judgments in *three* distinct series. They're presented in chronological order in Chapters 6 through 19 of The Revelation and each contains an unleashing of seven specific horrors, each getting progressively worse.

The first of these judgments is depicted here in Chapter 6 as the breaking and unrolling of the seven-sealed scroll of God. Out of it come the unforgettable Four Horsemen of the Apocalypse with their reign of terror.

The second series of God's outpoured wrath is signaled by the successive sounding of seven trumpets. The earth itself is devastated by these judgments.

The third series of punishments is unleashed by the pouring

out of seven bowls full of the wrath of God. These are the most severe of all.

Until this point, John has been overwhelmed and awed by the revelations of Jesus as the Creator and Savior of mankind. But as the seven seals are opened and the wrath of God is poured out, the vision of Jesus changes from Savior to *Judge*, from Lamb to *Lion*.

The sight of these calamities about to be experienced by man must have brought grief and terror to John. I'm sure the hand that penned the following words was trembling!

"BEHOLD, A WHITE HORSE!"

> *(1) I saw when the Lamb opened one of the seals, and I heard as it were the noise of thunder, one of the four Living Beings saying, "Come." (2) And I looked, and behold, a white horse; and the one who sat on it had a bow; and a crown was given to him, and he went forth conquering and to conquer.*   REVELATION 6:1, 2

SEAL NUMBER ONE: THE FUEHRER!

The command "come" in verse 1 of the King James Version should actually be translated "go." The translation of this word is determined by its context, and in this context one of Christ's servants (the Living Being) is giving the command for the action to start. He instructs the rider of the white horse to begin his campaign of conquest on the earth.

Who is the white horse rider? It's the Antichrist himself! In the symbology of the ancient world a white steed stood for conquest. When a victor triumphantly entered a newly-conquered kingdom he would invariably ride a white horse. The conquering Antichrist carries with him a warrior's bow, symbolizing his control over the weapons of war. On his head rests a crown, for he has succeeded in conquering more and more of the peoples of the earth. Eventually the whole world will claim him as its sovereign.

It becomes obvious that the only person who could accomplish all of these feats at this particular stage of the seven-year Tribulation is the person called the Antichrist. He is the scintillating personality who will be personally indwelt by Satan and will have such spiritual magnetism that the whole world will actually worship him.

The Bible indicates that there will actually be *two* Antichrists. One will be a European who will rule the political and religious world from Rome. The other Antichrist will be a Jew posing as a religious prophet. He will rule from Israel as a pseudo-messiah and will help establish the worship of the Antichrist of Rome.

The white apocalyptic horseman of Revelation 6 is the *European* Antichrist. I personally believe that this man is alive somewhere in the world at this very moment!

At this point the important thing to note about this charismatic character is that he is presented as the *first* of the great judgments of God upon the Christ-rejecting world. This person whom the world will view as its savior will turn out instead to be its Trojan Horse—its greatest possible curse!

Much more will be said about this incredible conqueror and his conquests in Chapters 13, 17, and 18.

SEAL NUMBER TWO: WAR!

(3) And when He had opened the second seal, I heard the second Living Being say, "Go!" (4) And there went out another horse that was red, and power was given to him who sat on it to take peace from the earth, and that men should kill one another; and there was given to him a great sword.

REVELATION 6:3, 4

During the first three and one-half years of the Tribulation the Antichrist will bring a pseudo-peace to the world. Everyone will be singing his praises as the greatest leader in all human history.

But at the midpoint of the Tribulation the second seal is opened and, according to Ezekiel 38 and Daniel 11, Russia, the rider of the red horse, snatches peace from the earth. With her Arab allies she invades the Middle East and attacks Israel. The war escalates until it involves all the major powers on the earth and becomes the greatest battle in the history of mankind—the Battle of Armageddon. This is developed fully in Chapter 16.

SEAL NUMBER THREE: ECONOMIC CATASTROPHE

(5) And when He had opened the third seal, I heard the third Living Being say, "Go!" And I looked, and behold, a black horse; and he who sat on it had a pair of balances in his hand. (6) And I heard a voice in the midst

*of the four Living Beings say, "A measure of wheat for a denarius, and three
measures of barley for a denarius, and see that you do not hurt the oil and
the wine."*   REVELATION 6:5, 6

The judgment symbolized by the rider of the black horse
seems to be a worldwide financial catastrophe. With war
spreading across the world from the Middle East, food, fuel, and
other life-supporting commodities will become more and more
scarce. The hungrier people become, the itchier become their
trigger fingers!

The "pair of scales" indicates scarcity of food, for the food is
weighed out as carefully as gold. Numerous passages in the Old
Testament associate the weighing of food with its scarcity.

The frightening thing is that a day's ration of wheat will
cost a denarius, the Biblical equivalent of an average worker's
entire daily wage. Or one day's pay could instead buy three
quarts of barley (a lesser grain). In other words, during the
Tribulation the average man will have to pay out his entire
day's salary just to purchase food for his family. There's not
much chance that the Antichrist will be issuing food stamps,
either!

Olive oil and wine were the luxury foods of John's day. The
horesman was told not to tamper with these items. Evidently
all the luxury foods will still be around to tempt people, but the
common man will have no means to purchase such items. Only
the rich will be able to function in a normal way economically.
The saying that "the rich get richer while the poor get poorer"
will really be true during the Tribulation. I have an idea that
those who retain their wealth will do so as a result of a moral
sell-out to the Antichrist.

Today we see the beginnings of this economic catastrophe
foretold in Revelation as the nations of the world become tied
up in a tightening noose of financial knots. Many headlines
reflect the growing concern over the indebtedness of Third World
countries to the West's international financial system.

A. W. Clausen, president of the World Bank, stated that the
total debt of 103 developing nations stood at 810 billion dollars
in 1983. Since 1982, when Mexico found itself in trouble, over
30 of these countries have found the enormity of their share of
this burden so hard to pay that they have had to renegotiate
their loans with creditor nations or face bankruptcy. Even political considerations are sidestepped on this issue as the Rea-

gan administration's bailout of the Polish goverment at the height of the Solidarity crisis demonstrated. More ironic, these poor nations saw a drop of 11 billion dollars in their living standards as they paid out more in loan repayments than they received in new loans.

And that has led to the fear of a "debtors' revolt." This reared its head recently in April 1984, when Argentina said that it would not meet the deadline to pay 500 million dollars in overdue interest to U.S. banks. At the last minute, the crisis was averted—temporarily—by new foreign financing giving Argentina the needed cash infusion to pay the interest, thus avoiding financial calamity to at least 25 U.S. institutions.

However, the debt in Latin America alone stands at 330 billion dollars now, and the U.N. Economic Commission for Latin America issued a report predicting that the red ink will grow to 451 billion dollars by 1990 unless something is done to cut the 35 billon dollars a year that this depressed region of the world is paying in interest payments alone!

There seems to be no relief to this problem in sight. In fact, economist William Cline of the Washington, D.C.-based Institute for International Economics warns, "There will be some countries in difficulty at some time over the next ten years." And what's frightening about this prediction is that the United States could be among those nations facing bankruptcy! While Brazil, Mexico, Poland, and Argentina lead the "international club of debtors" (as one reporter so aptly put it), C. Fred Bergsten, director of the IIE, says the U.S. could find itself owing 100 billion dollars to foreign nations by 1985. How is this possible? "We've been lulled into complacency by the recent improvement in the U.S. economy," he says. "But as we move ahead, there are a lot of bombs ticking along the way in the international mine field—and any one of them could go off down the road."

It doesn't take much adding—even in this era of billions—to see that one time bomb (financial debt of developing nations) plus another (overextension of U.S. and world banks) equals a worldwide explosion, just as the Apostle John prophesied almost 2000 years ago!

This worldwide condition can lead to a global economic collapse. The resulting panic, fear, and suffering could bring the exact conditions for the acceptance of the world dictator known in Bible prophecy as the Antichrist.

What is interesting here is that even though the Antichrist apparently temporarily solves the global financial collapse, it comes back again in the middle of the Tribulation after war breaks out.

SEAL NUMBER FOUR: MASS DEATH

> *(7) And when He had opened the fourth seal, I heard the voice of the fourth Living Being say, "Go!" (8) And I looked and, behold, a pale horse, and the name of him who sat on it was Death, and Hades followed along with him. And authority was given to them over the fourth part of the earth, to kill with sword, and with hunger, and with death, and with the beasts of the earth.*   REVELATION 6:7, 8

Following close on the heels of the second and third horsemen is the pale horse. With his grim companion Hades he brings the inevitable aftermath of war and calamity—*death on a massive scale.*

It staggers the imagination to realize that one-fourth of the world's population will be destroyed within a matter of days. Dr. Carl Sagan, the noted astronomer, summarized a report by the World Health Organization on the dangers of a nuclear holocaust for *Parade* magazine in 1983. In part he wrote, ". . . in a recent detailed study chaired by Sune K. Bergstrom (the 1982 Nobel laureate in physiology and medicine), (WHO) concludes that 1.1 billion people would be killed outright in such a nuclear war, mainly in the United States, the Soviet Union, Europe, China and Japan. An additional 1.1 billion would suffer serious injuries and radiation sickness, for which medical help would be unavailable. It thus seems possible that more than 2 billion people—almost half of all the humans on Earth—would be destroyed in the aftermath of a global thermonuclear war. This would represent by far the greatest disaster in the history of the human species and, with no other adverse effects, would probably be enough to reduce at least the Northern Hemisphere to a state of prolonged agony and barbarism. Unfortunately, the real situation would be much worse."

When I think about this awful judgment that awaits the Christ-rejecting world, it gives no satisfaction to my heart; it fires me up to get out the message that God has provided an alternative in Jesus.

MODERN-DAY PROPHETS OF DOOM

Today it isn't just the religious world that's warning us the world is headed for chaos. "Prophets" in the academic, scientific, and political world are telling us the same thing.

In the shocking study done at Massachusetts Institute of Technology for the Club of Rome and presented in the book *Limits To Growth,* the computers time after time told the same story: "Without a complete change of basic values and goals at individual, national, and world levels there is no chance to avoid international catastrophe."[1]

Six thousand years of recorded human events makes it fairly obvious that man's trend is toward self-seeking—*not* toward the noble goal of the world's best interests.

George Borgstrom in his book *Hungry Planet* cautioned in the 1960's, "It is sobering to realize that no part of the world, in the event of serious crop failure, is more than one year away from critical starvation, and even the rich United States with all its surpluses is not more than two years away."[2]

William and Paul Paddock warned in their sobering book, *Famines—1975!* that "the crisis of population explosion versus static agriculture is indeed formed. The nations of the undeveloped world are no longer grain exporters; they are grain importers. There is no more unused land to bring into cultivation; even the deficient marginal land is by now in use. Hunger is rampant throughout country after country, continent after continent around the undeveloped belt of the tropics and subtropics. Today's crisis can move in only one direction—toward catastrophe. Today hungry nations; tomorrow starving nations."[3]

Time has not changed the value of these grim predictions— to the contrary. Coupled with major weather changes, 1984 has seen a quickening of the factors that the Paddocks wrote about over a decade ago. The population explosion has not abated but is mushrooming, especially in Third World nations, where the extra burden of more hungry mouths and no increase in agriculture production is a continuous cycle. According to the U.N.'s

---

[1]Dennis L. Meadows, *The Limits to Growth,* Universe Books, 1972
[2]George Borgstrom, *Hungry Planet,* Macmillan, 1967.
[3]William and Paul Paddock, *Famine—1975,* Little, Brown, 1968.

Population Reference Bureau, today's global community of 4.4 billion will double in 50 years to 9 billion! In Brazil alone, the nation's population of 131 million will triple to 333 million.

If the future of this vast South American nation is to be anything like its present, it will spell trouble. Recently, a five-year drought that lasted from 1979 to 1984 claimed the lives of 250,000 Brazilians and caused the uprooting of 25 million people who live in an area twice the size of Texas. The Associated Press reported that "famished peasants were eating rats and lizards to stay alive."

Although it doesn't get much play in the media, famines today are not unique to one continent or people. For the last six years, the Soviet Union has been experiencing a prolonged drought—hence the constant need for grain supplies from the U.S. and elsewhere. The *Los Angeles Times* in its May 4, 1984, edition reported briefly that "the official Soviet media have indicated growing alarm in the Kremlin over the drought."

In 1983, while it was already reeling from a two-year drought, Southern Africa was affected by that now-famous weather system El Nino (Spanish for the Christ Child) which prevented the return of rain. The result, according to the National Geographic, ". . . was devastating. Livestock by thousands died of thirst and hunger. Those losses along with crop failures sharply aggravated malnutrition in [Botswana], where nearly one child in four already was undernourished." According to Carol Heald, secretary of the Interministerial Drought Committee, the number of children suffering from malnutrition "in spite of outside help has climbed toward one in three." More about El Nino later.

North of this devastation, in the sub-Saharan regions of Africa, the population has doubled since 1960 to almost 400 million, and the growth rate increases 2.9 percent annually—the fastest in the world! At the same time, the area has been plagued by drought for the last decade and now accounts for half the world's 10 million refugees. While both animals and humans search for water and food, the "desertification" of Africa continues to increase, with experts predicting that the current 20 percent of land now considered desert will leap to 45 percent in 50 years if these trends continue. Accompanying these modern-day, famine-burdened nomads is an upswing in pestilence as livestock and humans contract disease after disease feeding on their malnutritioned bodies.

While some might see modern technology as a way out for our bleeding African brothers and sisters, *Time* magazine reported, "In rural Senegal a $250,000 U.S.-made, solar-powered irrigation system lies idle, mainly because of maintenance problems." Caught in the grip of economic debt, wars, revolutions, famines, and plagues, Africa may well be beyond the saving of modern man and a portend of things to come.

At the same time, while "believers" in science see a renaissance for modern man, the greenhouse effect—a by-product of modern technology's pollutants—continues to produce major changes in the earth's balance. The Environmental Protection Agency warned in 1983 that the earth is experiencing the greatest rise in temperature in recorded history and that the results could be "catastrophic," with a prediction that farmland in the Southwest of the U.S. may become so arid that it will be useless.

THE SPECTER OF PLAGUES

Pestilence is another word for epidemics. Whenever you have a combination of poverty and famine, disease is close kin, as the situation in Africa so vividly portrays. But how can disease of epidemic proportions happen in today's world of miracle drugs?

A decade ago I was in a doctor's office browsing through some of his professional journals when I came upon an article that really intrigued me. It described new "super-bacteria," so-called because of their remarkable resistance to all known miracle drugs. The article went on to say that doctors around the world were becoming alarmed at the possibility that certain of these bacteria would give rise to the greatest outbreak of dread diseases that the world has ever seen.

In the time since then, a virus-caused disease has become a doctor's nightmare. I don't think there's anyone reading this book who has not become familiar with the term AIDS. Unknown ten years ago, the frightening rise of Acquired Immune Deficiency Syndrome has come out of nowhere and spread to 4000 people in the U.S. alone since the first reported case in 1981. More than 1700 people have died from this often-fatal disease. Notably, most of the victims of AIDS have been homosexual men. The cities of New York, San Francisco, and Los Angeles—urban centers with a large gay population—are reporting major outbreaks.

But AIDS knows no boundaries, whether geographical or sociological. In Orange County, California—a suburb of Los Angeles— "AIDS is as epidemic here as it is in Los Angeles and San Francisco," Dr. Thomas Prendergast, head of the county's AIDS program, told the *Los Angeles Times*. The epidemiologist said the county could expect a "doubling every six months" of AIDS cases—the fastest rate in the nation!

While scientists in both France and the U.S. believe they may have isolated the virus which causes AIDS, they don't expect a vaccine for at least two years—if their findings prove correct. Meanwhile, the National Center for Disease Control in Atlanta reports a nationwide increase of 53 percent in known AIDS cases and a 61 percent increase in the death rate just between the months of October 1983 and March 1984.

As the time of the Great Tribulation draws even closer, one cannot rule out another way for the specter of plagues to wipe out large segments of population: in the form of biological warfare. For a fraction of the cost of a single hydrogen bomb, scientists can produce a bacteriological bomb that would wipe out the entire population of California! And if you believe that governments would balk at using this type of weapon because of its immorality, just look at the behavior of the Soviets in Afghanistan and the Iraqis in their war with Iran—both have thought nothing of using chemical warfare against their enemies despite so-called treaties banning their use, and the Soviets are well-trained in such tactics.

Nineteen hundred years ago as Jesus was telling His disciples what the world would be like just before He returned to set up His kingdom on earth, He said: "Nation will rise against nation, and kingdom against kingdom, and in various places there will be great earthquakes, famines and *plagues;* and there will be fearful sights and great signs from outer space" (Luke 21:10,11).

As world conditions increasingly fall into the pattern that Jesus spoke of, it may sadden the believer but it should give us a sense of intense anticipation that we are indeed the generation that is standing on the brink of seeing the return of Jesus Christ to this earth!

SEAL NUMBER FIVE: MASS MURDER OF BELIEVERS

(9) And when He had opened the fifth seal, I saw under the altar the souls of those who had been slain because of the word of God, and because of their testimony which they had held. (10) And they cried with a loud voice, saying, "How long, O Lord, holy and true, do You not judge and avenge our blood on those who dwell on the earth?" (11) And white robes were given to every one of them; and they were told to rest for just a little while longer, until their fellow servants also and their brothers, that should be killed as they were, should be fulfilled. REVELATION 6:9–11

The opening of the fifth seal reveals something which Christians have shrunk back from with compassion for nineteen centuries—the knowledge that countless brothers and sisters in Christ must seal their newfound testimony with persecution and martyrdom during the Great Tribulation. It's a sobering fact that if people will not give their hearts to Christ *now*, while it is still easy and small cost is involved, when the Tribulation judgment sets in, although they can still be saved, it will be "so as by fire."

Those who become believers after the Tribulation has started will be easy to identify. The Antichrist will require that all men on earth worship him as God. All who refuse to profess this allegiance by receiving the Antichrist's identifying mark on their forehead or hand will be prohibited from buying or selling.

The worldwide computer banking system that will allow the Antichrist to accomplish this is already in its fledgling stages as we see more in-home computers and automated tellers with secret access codes springing up all over. Bank of America, the world's largest bank, has already begun penalizing customers monetarily who are not using their automated system in order to quicken the pace of change to a virtual cash-free society. The banks want to be freed from all the paperwork and expense generated from check and credit card expenditures. Individuals in the future may not handle money, but instead see their paychecks go right into the bank, much like many senior citizens now have their Social Security checks processed for security reasons.

In order for this worldwide system to work, everyone must have a personal identification number—much like Social Security—and Western society is certainly not adverse to this numbering as more and more people are given their own secret access codes for automated teller machines and in their work-place in order to sign on to a computer. Eventually, one secret number will give a person access to all his individual needs, both at work and at home. Of course, all information about your personal and credit habits which could affect your credit rating would be on file under your number and would be instantly available by computers to anyone needing the information, both friend and foe.

All of this is happening because of the expense and inconvenience of paperwork. Imagine what will happen when the Antichrist sinks his fangs into this system! By the time of the Great Tribulation, it will be set up and waiting for him to take over.

Since Revelation 14:9–11 warns that all who *do* receive the mark of the Beast (the number 666) will suffer eternal judgment at the hand of God, true believers will obviously refuse the mark and suffer the wrath of Antichrist instead.

SEAL NUMBER SIX: A MASSIVE NUCLEAR EXCHANGE

(12) And I looked when He opened the sixth seal, and there was a great earthquake, and the sun became black as sackcloth of hair, and the moon became like blood; (13) And the stars of heaven fell to the earth, even as a fig tree drops its untimely figs, when it is shaken by a mighty wind. (14) And the atmosphere was pushed apart like a scroll when it is rolled together; and every mountain and island were moved out of their places. (15) And the kings of the earth, along with the great men, the rich men, the chief captains, the mighty men, every slave, and every free man, hid themselves in the dens and in the rocks of the mountains, (16) then said to the mountains and rocks, "Fall on us, and hide us from the face of Him who sits on the throne, and from the wrath of the Lamb; (17) for the great day of His wrath has come, and who is able to stand?"   REVELATION 6:12–17

The opening of the sixth seal introduces a tremendous earthquake. Earthquakes have always been a particularly terrifying experience for people to go through.

It has been estimated that in the past 4000 years earthquakes have caused a loss of 14 million lives! Experts agree that the frequency of earthquakes is increasing significantly and that "killer quakes" are happening more often than ever before. The U.S. Geological Survey's National Earthquake Information Center in Golden, Colorado, estimates that it receives reports of approximately 8000 quakes worldwide every year!

Here are just some of the most intense and unusual quakes we've witnessed in the last decade:

—December 1983: 2800 people killed by powerful earthquake in Yemen.

—October 30, 1983: two days after two schoolchildren are killed in an Idaho quake, 1200 people lose their lives in a quake located in Turkey. The next day, 30 people are killed by a jolt in northeast China. Earlier in the month, people who have always lived in the area from Boston to Toronto feel an earthquake for the first time in their lives. Scientists again examine the theory that quakes striking close together in time are interrelated no matter how far apart they are in miles.

—May 1983: 104 people die when Japanese coastal lands are hit by earthquake-generated waves. Previously in the month, the town of Coalinga, California, is virtually wiped off the map by an intense quake.

—March 1983: 250 die in Colombian quake.

—In 1976, the city of Tangshan, China, was hit by a massive earthquake. The death toll (though never officially revealed by the authorities) was put as high as 750,000! Also, 4000 people lose their lives in Mount Ararat quake in Turkey.

These are just a few of the thousands of quakes rattling our planet. Most, like one felt in the unlikely state of Delaware, go unreported by the media.

So many authorities have warned Californians to expect a giant quake along the San Andreas Fault that the people who live anywhere near it tend to keep their fingers crossed. Dr. C. Barry Raleigh, director of the Lamont-Doherty Geological Observatory in Palisades, New York, told *U.S. News and World Report* in 1983, "A great earthquake, with severe destruction of property and high loss of life, is inevitable in California. . . . Since about 1978, California has had a significantly higher frequency of moderate-to-large earthquakes. . . ."

However, in 1984 the Federal Emergency Management Agency gave the Midwest a shock that most Americans thought was reserved only for Californians. Said agency Director Louis Giuffrida, "While California is normally thought of . . . as the worst for earthquakes, the most severe area is really the New Madrid Fault." This fault touches the states of Tennessee, Arkansas, Indiana, Missouri, Kentucky, Illinois, and Mississippi. The agency said that a quake registering a magnitude of 8 or better on the Richter scale would affect a 200,000-square-mile area, injure thousands of the millions of people living near the fault, and cause damage estimated at 60 billion dollars. "Near-total destruction would occur close to the epicenter, producing a natural disaster unequaled in the nation's history in terms of human life and economic losses," Giuffrida said.

The last time the New Madrid Fault struck was in 1811, and scientists estimate that it was 8.6 on the Richter scale. The ground shook from the Rockies to the Atlantic and as far north as Quebec, Canada! Within two months' time, two more quakes struck registering 8.4 and 8.7. Thousands of aftershocks rocked the nation.

Annually, these earth tremors kill 10,000 to 15,000 people and rack up 7 billion dollars in damages, according to *U.S. News and World Report*. John Filson, chief of the USGS, told the magazine, "Without doubt there are going to continue to be earthquakes in most parts of the United States. Sites in California have the highest likelihood of very destructive earthquakes, but major population centers on the East Coast and parts of the Midwest should also be considered vulnerable."

Professor R. A. Daly said in the book *Our Mobile Earth* that "by far the most awful earth shock is yet to come." Seismologist Otto Nuttli of St. Louis University, and the man who pointed out the dangers of the New Madrid Fault, said a jolt like the one in 1811 "would cause a disaster whose magnitude would only be eclipsed by an all-out nuclear war."

The earthquake described in this sixth judgment will be of a magnitude never before known by mankind. It will be "the granddaddy of them all"! The particular Greek word used here actually means "a violent, catastrophic shaking." This meaning, coupled with the darkening of the sun and the moon, leads me to believe that the Apostle John is describing an earthquake set off by many nuclear explosions. As you can see, with all the earthquake faults previously undiscovered by man, a world-wide nuclear war could set them all off together in an inter-related shaking of our planet. Remember, John had to describe phenomena of a very advanced technical age in terms of his first-century understanding.

Recently as I was studying about nuclear weapons I discovered that science has perfected a cobalt bomb—one of the most lethal weapons known to man. A cobalt bomb is made by placing a shield of cobalt 59 metal around a hydrogen bomb. By this comparatively simple operation the destructive capacity of the hydrogen bomb is doubled. More significantly, however, the radioactive contamination of the cobalt bomb is tremendous. Scientists have dubbed it "the dirty bomb" because of its fallout. This is what I believe may be pictured in Revelation 6:12.

Verse 13 states that "the stars of heaven fell to the earth." This word for star can refer to either a star or a meteor. In this verse it seems more likely that meteors are intended. When meteors first strike the atmosphere of the earth they glow with a fiery red color. Man-made satellites glow the same way when they return to earth.

However, verse 13 may be referring to more than ordinary meteors. Russia now has a weapon called a "fractional orbital bomb." It consists of a dozen or so nuclear-tipped missiles which can be fired simultaneously from an orbiting space platform. Because the missiles come straight down from the sky, they can strike several cities simultaneously and with virtually no warning. When these missiles streak through the air they'll look like meteors showering the atmosphere!

Another marvel of horror in our nuclear age which I believe John saw in prophetic preview is the MIRV intercontinental ballistic missile. These weapons of unbelievable accuracy and destructive capabilities normally carry ten independently targeted warheads per missile. Each one of these warheads is capable of vaporizing a city the size of London.

According to Senator Jake Garn of Utah in the July 16, 1979, issue of *U.S. News and World Report*, the Soviet "SS-18 has more destructive power all by itself than all of our nuclear warheads put together from every source."

To give some idea of the kind of power to which Senator Garn is referring, it is reported that the Soviet Union has 308 launchers for the monster SS-18 ICBM. Each launcher is capable of refiring—which means the Soviets can attack with 616 of these SS-18 ICBMs. One SS-18 can deliver such a heavy throw weight that it can hurl either one 100-megaton warhead, or two 50-megaton warheads, or 10 five-megaton warheads, or 30 one-megaton warheads.

All the bombs used by all forces in World War II equal less than 25 megatons of explosive power. Some of the SS-18s are believed to carry warheads equal to four times this power. This is enough to destroy a state the size of Ohio. A one-megaton warhead is enough to destroy Los Angeles.

The Apostle John's description of the sun becoming black as sackcloth and the moon becoming like blood perfectly describes the phenomena that would result from massive amounts of dust and debris blown into the sky by multiple nuclear bursts. The "Nuclear Winter" scenario described by Dr. Carl Sagan and other prominent scientists would also result from this same condition. (More on this later.)

"And the atmosphere was pushed apart like a scroll when it is rolled together" (Revelation 6:14). Do you know what happens in a nuclear explosion? The atmosphere rolls back on itself! It's this tremendous rush of air back into the vacuum that causes much of the destruction of a nuclear explosion. John's words in this verse are a perfect picture of an all-out nuclear exchange. When this happens, John continues, every mountain and island will be jarred from its present position. The whole world will be literally shaken apart!

THE BLINDNESS OF UNBELIEF

What will be the human reaction to this event? You know the saying, "There are no atheists in foxholes." The whole world will know that this is the doing of the Lamb, Jesus Christ. But will they fall on their knees and turn to him for mercy? Let's see!

> (15) And the kings of the earth, along with the great men, the rich men, the chief captains, the mighty men, every slave, and every free man, hid themselves in the dens and in the rocks of the mountains, (16) then said to the mountains and rocks, "Fall on us, and hide us from the face of Him who sits on the throne, and from the wrath of the Lamb; (17) for the great day of His wrath has come, and who is able to stand?"   REVELATION 6:15-17

Notice to whom they prayed—not to God, even though they had just acknowledged His existence, but to the inanimate rocks and mountains!

There are lots of people like this in the world today. Instead of trusting in the God of heaven, they put their faith in superstition or the horoscope. Some of these people even profess to believe that there is a God who rules the universe, but when the chips are down this unknown God has no personal relevance to their lives. They have what is called a "head knowledge" of God, but it's eighteen inches away from reality; that's the distance from their heads to their hearts!

SEVEN

144,000 Jews for Jesus

The awful judgments described in the last chapter give rise to the desperate question of man, "Who is able to stand?" (Revelation 6:17). Revelation 7 answers that question. It also shows once more that "even in judgment God remembers mercy." God will provide an opportunity for the whole world to hear the gospel of Christ during this awful time of tribulation (Matthew 24:14).

So far six seals of judgment upon the earth have been opened. But before the seventh seal is opened, Revelation 7 gives us a parenthetical panorama of the evangelistic activity of the Tribulation period. The chapter begins by flashing back to the very *beginning* of the seven-year period, where God sends 144,000 evangelists out with the gospel message *before* any judgments at all are permitted to fall upon the earth.

These evangelists are Jews who may have been witnessed to by some Christians prior to the Rapture; when they discover that all the believers are gone, they turn in faith to Christ to become their Messiah. On many occasions I have spoken to Jewish acquaintances about accepting Jesus as their Savior; when they don't wish to, I tell them about the Rapture, urging them to reconsider their decision when this event happens.

Most of us know that when a Jewish person determines to do something, it usually gets done. The latter part of Chapter 7 shows the great success of the Jewish evangelistic efforts.

Their converts are shown at rest before the throne of God. There is such a great multitude of them from all nations, tongues, and tribes that they cannot be numbered.

WHY JEWS ONLY?

But the greater question of this chapter is, "Why are the 144,000 chosen evangelists only of the Jewish race?"

In order to answer this question, we must understand why God called the nation of Israel into being in the first place, and why they are called "the chosen race."

God's purposes for the Jewish people are woven throughout the entire Bible, starting with Genesis 11 and continuing uninterrupted through the Gospel of Luke. (Other New Testament books, such as Hebrews and James, also have a strong Jewish emphasis.) The sheer fact that over three-fourths of the Bible is about the Hebrew race indicates the importance which they hold in the eternal purposes of God.

Four thousand years ago God called Abraham out of Assyria and presented him with several fantastic promises and sobering responsibilities. He promised Abraham a son from whose loins would be born a unique race of people—a nation chosen and blessed in a special way by God Himself.

GOD'S PURPOSES FOR ISRAEL

What were God's purposes for creating this race? Although there were numerous reasons for the choice, I've narrowed them down to the four I consider most important.

First, the Jewish people were to receive and write down God's revelation to man. Though the Jewish people have failed in performing some of the things God wanted them to do, they did fulfill this main purpose for them—to write the Bible. Virtually every book of both the Old and New Testaments was penned by a Jewish writer. There are a handful of possible exceptions, but none of these has ever enjoyed proof of Gentile authorship.

The *second* reason the Jews were chosen was to protect and preserve the textual purity of the Scriptures they had penned. The degree of success which the Jewish scribes had in doing this is one of the wonders of the ancient world. When you consider the turbulent history the Jews endured and the unbelievable job they did in preserving their Scriptures, every Jew and Christian today should give them humble thanks.

A startling example of the accuracy of the Jewish scribes in copying and caring for their beloved Scriptures is the scroll of Isaiah, discovered among the Dead Sea Scrolls in the late 1940's. The date of this Scroll of Isaiah has been fixed at 200 B.C., while the earliest Isaiah manuscript we had known about before this discovery is dated A.D. 900! Though 1,100 years separated the two manuscripts, they were virtually identical when compared with each other!

In 1983 another important discovery was made which further confirmed the accuracy of the Scriptures. An Israeli archaeologist, Adam Zartal, found what he believes to be a 30-centuries-old altar built by Moses' successor, Joshua. In an interview with the Associated Press, Zartal said his group found the altar on Mount Ebal and that the 27-foot-by-21-foot altar fit the one described in the Book of Joshua 8:30–35 exactly. Covered with sheep bones, ashes, and a dark substance believed to be blood, Professor Benjamin Mazar said there was no doubt about the holiness and antiquity of the excavation. The professor, one of Israel's most respected archaeologists, went on to say that carbon 14 tests on ceramic potteries found at the site were dated to be from the 12th century B.C.—the very era during which Joshua conquered Canaan! The report concluded that if further tests prove the authenticity of the altar, "it will lend support to those who argue the literal nature of the Scriptures rather than their allegorical nature."

MESSIAH JESUS PREDICTED

The *third* reason for Israel's existence was to serve as the human family through whom Messiah, the Savior of mankind, would be born. There are over three hundred specific prophecies in the Old Testament which refer in some way to the Messiah's coming. The great paradox is that when Messiah did come with His credentials of fulfilled prophecy, the very people who had predicted His coming rejected Him! Nevertheless, the New Testament begins, "These are the ancestors of Jesus Christ, a descendant of *King David* and of *Abraham* (Matthew 1:1, *TLB*).

The *fourth* reason the Jewish race was selected was to witness to the pagan world that there is only one true God and to show men how to come to know Him. Throughout their four thousand years of existence, the Jews have not always been willing witnesses of this fact to the world. However, even the rebellion and unbelief of the Jews against their God has been a continuing witness of God's reality, because this history of rebellion and its consequences were foretold by God. History is strewn with the evidence of fulfilled prophecy concerning the Jewish people and their ancient homeland, Israel.

SPIRITUAL BLINDNESS

Because the Jewish people through their long history so persistently rejected their promised and long-awaited Messiah, God allowed to come upon them a national spiritual blindness— an inability to comprehend the simple truth of the Messiah's message. This blindness was true of the Jews even before Jesus came into the world (Acts 7:51–53).

Of course, there have always been individual exceptions to this overall national blindness. Some Jews have accepted Jesus as Messiah in every generation since the first century. In Biblical terminology these are called "the believing remnant."

There has been much infidelity in Jewish history, and their present worldwide dispersion and persecution have been their divine discipline. However, God made unconditional promises of eternal blessings to the Jewish patriarchs and will someday restore the Jews to a position of special favor with Himself.

Right now the Church (all true believers in Jesus Christ) is enjoying God's special blessing. The drama of this shifting emphasis is told in Romans 9, 10, and 11. God has promised never to abandon His chosen people, no matter how despicably they treat Him (Romans 11:1, 2). The divine hand of protection of the Jews during their Six-Day War was just a token of that protective care.

A simple way I have of remembering God's dealing with the nation of Israel is as follows: Romans 9, *election;* Romans 10, *rejection;* Romans 11, *restoration.*

BLIND—BUT NOT FOREVER!

According to Romans 11:25 this national blindness will not last forever: "For I don't want you, brothers, to be ignorant concerning this mystery, lest you should become wise in your own eyes, that a partial blinding has come upon Israel *until* the fullness of the Gentiles has been brought in."

"The fullness of the Gentiles" is that point in time when the Church is removed from the earth by the Rapture. Then God's special focus and blessing will shift back again to the Jew. This fact is guaranteed to Israel by hundreds of unconditional promises in the Bible. The Jews will once again be responsible, as God's representatives, to take His message to the world. But this time these 144,000 Jews will do in only seven years what their nation has failed to do in all its history—evangelize the whole world!

GOD STOPS THE WIND

> *(1) After these things I saw four angels standing on the four corners of the earth, holding the four winds of the earth, so that the wind could not blow on the earth or on the sea or on any tree. (2) Then I saw another angel ascending from the east, having the seal of the living God; and he cried with a loud voice to the four angels, to whom it was given to hurt the earth and the sea, (3) saying, "Do not hurt the earth or the sea or the trees, until we have sealed the servants of our God in their foreheads.* REVELATION 7:1–3

Although the subject of *angels* is usually associated with fairy tales or myths, these creatures are spoken of very matter-of-factly in the Bible and they play a very important part in the predicted judgments of God on the earth. The Bible speaks of three categories of angels. *First,* there are the angels of God who remained faithful to Him when Lucifer (who later became known as Satan or "the Devil") rejected God and led a rebellion against Him.

The *second* category are the angels who followed Lucifer in the rebellion but are still free to work against God's purposes. These are fallen, unbound angels and are usually called *demons.*

The *third* group are fallen angels who are bound and imprisoned. Apparently these are a particularly vicious group who so overstepped their authority that God cast them into a place called "the abyss" to wait the final execution of their sentence— to be cast with Satan and the other demons into the Lake of Fire (see 2 Peter 2:4).

GLOBAL WEATHER CHANGES

Because angels have superior power and intelligence, the four mentioned in verse one have apparently been given authority over the weather conditions of the earth. I say weather conditions because if the world's wind patterns are changed, radical effects will occur in all the rest of nature because of its delicate ecological balance.

You'll note that verse 2 says "...the four angels, to whom it was given *to hurt* the earth." This harm will be upon the earth, the sea, and the trees.

Have you ever thought about how much destruction has been caused by wind? If you've ever experienced the terror of a great hurricane, typhoon, dust storm, or tornado you know what I'm talking about. I've been at sea during a hurricane, and I can tell you it tested my agnosticism of those days right to its very core!

Many of the prophecies relating to the Tribulation indicate freak weather conditions and storms of unprecedented intensity. In fact, Jesus Himself predicted that strange phenomena would occur regarding the relationship of the earth to the sun, moon, and stars. "Then there will be strange events in the skies—warnings, evil omens and portents in the sun, moon, and stars; and down here on earth the nations will be in turmoil, perplexed by the roaring seas and strange tides. The courage of many people will falter because of the fearful fate they see coming upon the earth, for the stability of the very heavens will be broken up" (Luke 21:25, 26, *TLB*).

Many scientists have soberly warned that the earth's weather patterns are already beginning to change radically.

FREAK WEATHER PATTERNS

While scientists have been issuing all sorts of dire warnings during the last 20 years on the changing scope of the earth's weather systems, no one was quite prepared for the devastation caused in 1983 when El Nino wreaked havoc throughout the globe. Five continents felt the impact of the world's largest weather system when, for reasons still unkown to man, the ocean currents of El Nino warmed up to as much as 4 degrees in some places. This caused a collapse in El Nino's jet streams, and the dislocation of this usually stable weather machine brought disastrous effects around the world:

—Australia hit by worst drought of the century, coupled with dust storms and brushfires. Seventy-five people killed and 2.5 billion dollars in damage.

—Indonesian crops fail, 340 people starve to death. Damage: 750 million dollars.

—Western Europe flooded, in grip of unseasonable heat wave; 25 die, 200 million dollars in damage.

—Northern Africa hit by drought, also notes loss of 200 million dollars.

—Southern Africa continues drought, crop production down by 70 percent, a billion-dollar loss.

—Middle East cold and snow claims 65 victims and posts 50 million dollars in damage.

—Indian drought costs 150 million dollars, epidemics break out.

—China struggles with a million people working around clock against flooding that claims 600 lives and costs 600 million.

—Philippines and Micronesia also drought victims; 450 million in damage.

—Hawaii hit by unusual hurricane that leaves one dead and 230 million in damage.

—Christmas Island nestings abandoned by 17 million birds.

—Mexico and Central America also hit by drought; 600 million in damage.

—South America caught in grip of flooding and drought; almost 800 dead, over 4 billion in damage.

—Cuba and Gulf Coast states get five months of rain resulting in flooding; 65 die and 1.2 billion in damage assessed.

—East Coast plus Mountain and Southern states flooded by bad storms. Over 100 die and damage is estimated at 1.1 billion.

—California and Western states wracked by high tides plus torrential winds and rains, including tornadoes. Fishermen find marine life not native to California coast and can't find those that do belong. Los Angeles, known for its sunshine, has triple the amount of normal rainfall. Forty-five die; 1.1 billion in damage.

Officials of the National Atmospheric and Oceanic Administration claimed there was nothing like it in memory. When

El Nino's toll was added up, *National Geographic* magazine noted that over a thousand people died and almost 9 billion dollars in damage was estimated, but the "human suffering [was] beyond calculation."

And 1984 shows no letup in freak weather patterns. Already this year is being called the worst tornado season to hit the U.S. in a decade—and it's not even half over yet! The first two weeks of May alone recorded 303 tornadoes throughout the nation.

These stories point out the close relation of shifts in wind currents with freak weather and violent storms. I believe that the pollution of the upper atmosphere is already beginning to cause a shift in weather patterns which will be greatly accelerated during the Tribulation.

GRACE BEFORE JUDGMENT

Before the four angels are allowed to execute their judgment of shifting the wind patterns, another angel appears, coming up from the rising sun. This angel has the "seal of the living God" with which he seals the special servants of God who will be His witnesses during the Tribulation period.

God has never allowed Himself to be without witnesses on earth to proclaim His way to receive forgiveness and acceptance. The spiritual vacuum that will be left by the removal of all true Christians at the Rapture will be quickly filled with these 144,000 Jewish "bond-servants of God."

Several very interesting things should be noted about the "seal of the living God."

The verb "to seal" means to make an imprint in wax with a signet ring. This was done in ancient business transactions of all kinds, and signified that whatever was thus sealed belonged to the one whose mark was on it. The idea of a *visible* mark of ownership and guarantee of protection is inherent in the word.

In the New Testament, the seal of God is the Holy Spirit Himself. In fact, in Ephesians 1:13, 14 the same word used here for "seal" is used to describe the Holy Spirit. This is also borne out in Ephesians 4:30 and Second Corinthians 1:22 and 5:5. Jesus had this same seal of God, the Holy Spirit, upon Him (John 6:27).

The seal of God—the Spirit—gives a special empowering to

these servants to perform their awesome mission.

Revelation 7:3 also speaks of a visible *mark* on the forehead of the servants. You can be sure this mark will be in vivid contrast to the mark which the followers of Antichrist will receive when they swear allegiance to him. A person might be a "secret service" believer today, but in those days God's men will really be "marked men." No one will be able to mistake them!

GOD LOOKS OUT FOR HIS OWN

A seal also guarantees the protection of the person bearing it. Since these are marked men, they will be under constant attack by the followers of Antichrist as well as demonic forces. But God will supernaturally protect them against all attacks. They will apparently suffer from hunger, exposure, ridicule, torture, and imprisonment at times, but all of these special servants will be preserved to continue their witness through the whole Tribulation period. This is evidenced by the fact that when the scene shifts to the *end* of the Tribulation in Revelation 14:1–5, the 144,000 witnesses are seen standing on Mount Zion with Jesus.

I personally believe that the ones whom Jesus describes as "these brothers of mine" in Matthew 25:31–46 are the 144,000 described here. The way a person treats these evangelists during the Tribulation will reflect whether he is a believer in their message or not, because it will be extremely perilous to help these men who will no doubt be on the Antichrist's most-wanted list.

The great lesson I learn from this forecast is that God's man or woman is indestructible until God is finished with him here on earth!

THE EVANGELISTS SELECTED

(4) And I heard the number of those who were sealed; and there were sealed a hundred and forty-four thousand of all the tribes of the children of Israel. (5) Of the tribe of Judah were sealed twelve thousand. Of the tribe of Reuben were sealed twelve thousand. Of the tribe of Gad were sealed twelve thousand. (6) Of the tribe of Asher were sealed twelve thousand. Of the tribe of Naphtali were sealed twelve thousand. Of the tribe of Manasseh were sealed twelve thousand. (7) Of the tribe of Simeon were sealed twelve thousand. Of the tribe of Levi were sealed twelve thousand. Of the tribe of Issachar were sealed twelve thousand. (8) Of the tribe of Zebulun were sealed

twelve thousand. Of the tribe of Joseph were sealed twelve thousand. Of the tribe of Benjamin were sealed twelve thousand. REVELATION 7:4–8

WHO SAYS THE TRIBES ARE LOST?

I never cease to be amazed at how far afield many interpreters go when they approach the Book of Revelation. This particular passage seems to drive some to new heights of imagination. Some say that these couldn't possibly be literal Jews. Others add that the numbers certainly are merely symbols, not to be taken literally.

To all of this sort of speculation I say, "Why not?"

The fact that God redeems 144,000 literal Jews and ordains them His evangelists not only makes good sense but fits in with the counsel of God's purposes as previously noted in the introduction to this chapter.

So may I say loud and clear: the 144,000 described here are *not* Jehovah's Witnesses, or Mormon leaders, or some symbol of the Church; they are Jews, Jews, Jews!

It's amazing to realize that even though most Jews today don't know which tribe they stem from, God does, and He selects twelve thousand from each of the twelve tribes of Israel. There's a religious group called the British Israelites who believe that the ten tribes of Israel (who lived in the north of Israel and were taken captive in the eighth century B.C. by the Assyrians) were subsequently intermingled through repeated inter-marriage and turned into the modern Anglo-Saxons! With such spokesmen as Herbert W. Armstrong and his son, Garner Ted, this view has gained credence with a growing number of people. The physical differences between an Anglo-Saxon and a Jew ought to be sufficient to dispel such a myth, but if not, surely this passage should. The tribes certainly aren't lost to God!

LAST-INNING SUBSTITUTES

As you read through the list of the twelve tribes in verses 5 through 8 perhaps you noticed that two of the original tribes, Dan and Ephraim, are missing, and that two others are substituted in their places.

Many scholars believe that the tribe of Dan is missing because the Jewish Antichrist (the False Prophet), will come from it. This certainly seems to be the meaning of an ancient prophecy that Jacob gave about the tribes of Israel in the last days: "Dan will be a serpent in the way, a venomous viper by the path, that bites the horse's heels so that his rider falls backward" (Genesis 49:17).

Ephraim is left out because it led the way in causing the civil war which divided the ten tribes of the North from the two in the South. The tribes of Dan and Ephraim were the first to lead Israel into idolatry.

Individual members of these tribes can certainly be brought into God's kingdom by faith, but no representatives of these tribes are given the honor of being the great evangelists of God in the Tribulation. The priestly tribe of Levi is substituted for Dan, and Joseph (Ephraim's father) is substituted for Ephraim.

HOW ARE THE 144,000 CONVERTED?

Many have asked the question, "If all the Christians are snatched out of the world in the Rapture, how are these evangelists going to be saved?"

There are several ways.

Some Jews will have been witnessed to by Christian friends and will surely have heard something about prophecy related to the disappearance of Christ's followers. Though it may sound wild to them now, when "cloudfulls" of Christians all around the world are suddenly missing, the Holy Spirit will convince His selected witnesses that the gospel message is indeed true, and they will believe.

Others will surely be perplexed by this strange phenomenon of missing people and will not accept the reasons given by various Satanically-inspired groups. They will seek out an answer, find Christian literature of years past which explains the prophetic gospel, and then believe.

To some, Jesus may even appear in person in much the same way that He did to Saul of Tarsus, who became the Apostle Paul.

It's important to remember that the Holy Spirit will still function in His role of drawing people to Jesus. However, He will relate to believers as He did during Old Testament times. He will regenerate the human spirits of those who accept the Messiah, but he will indwell and empower only those whom

God has chosen for special service. This will surely include more than the 144,000, for never will believers be more in need of the Spirit's sustaining power!

By whatever means, however, God will see that these Jews are quickly brought to true faith in Jesus as their Messiah and will send them on their ways with His message of forgiveness and deliverance.

They will be like 144,000 Jewish Billy Grahams turned loose at once!

WHAT A REVIVAL!

(9) After this I looked, and behold, a great multitude, which no man could number, of all nations, and kindreds, and peoples, and tongues stood before the throne, and before the Lamb, clothed with white robes, and palms in their hands, (10) and cried with a loud voice, saying, "Salvation is of our God who sits upon the throne, and of the Lamb." REVELATION 7:9, 10

The effectiveness of the evangelism during the Tribulation is overwhelming. What a revival! It's enough to make a Southern Baptist evangelist's mouth water!

It's almost impossible for us to really appreciate what these converts of the 144,000 will have to endure because of their faith. The fact that they are standing here before the throne of God in white robes during the Tribulation confirms that they were martyred because of their belief in Christ.

PRAISE THE LORD!

(11) And all the angels stood around the throne, and about the Elders and the four Living Beings, and fell before the throne on their faces, and worshipped God, (12) saying, "Amen! Blessing, and glory, and wisdom, and thanksgiving, and honor, and power, and might is of our God forever and ever. Amen." REVELATION 7:11, 12

What a scene for John to have witnessed! At the center of everything was the throne of God. Closest to it were the four Living Beings, and surrounding them and the throne were the twenty-four enthroned Elders. An unspecified number of angels encircled this whole scene, and when they saw the great multitude of martyred Tribulation saints waving their palm branches and praising God they fell on their faces before the throne and worshipped God.

I really like that! Every opportunity these angels and Elders get, they drop on their faces and praise the Lord. Perhaps you've heard it said that the angels in heaven rejoice when one sinner is saved. I'm sure they're happy for the sinner that has been redeemed, but I have a suspicion that the real reason for their joy is that it gives them another opportunity to fall down on their faces and praise the One who made the sinner's salvation possible.

IDENTITY OF THE MULTITUDE

(13) And one of the Elders answered, saying to me, "Who are these who are clothed in white robes? And from where did they come?" (14) And I said unto him, "Sir, you know." And he said to me, "These are they who came out of the Great Tribulation, and have washed their robes, and made them white in the blood of the Lamb. (15) Therefore they are before the throne of God, and serve Him day and night in His temple: and He who sits on the throne shall dwell among them. (16) They shall hunger no more, neither thirst any more; neither shall the sun beat down on them, nor any heat. (17) For the Lamb who is in the midst of the throne shall feed them, and shall lead them unto living fountains of waters; and God shall wipe away all tears from their eyes."   REVELATION 7:13–17

Isaiah, the prophet of Israel, said that any "robes of righteousness" which men weave from their own good deeds are nothing more than dirty, soiled rags (Isaiah 64:6). But a beautiful thing is pictured here of these martyred saints—they took their *soiled* robes and washed them in the *crimson* blood of Jesus and they came out *white!*

God graciously rewards these persecuted children of His with the new, immortal bodies which all believers will eventually receive. Notice what an improvement they are over the old ones. Night and day they serve, but they don't get tired. No more hunger, no more thirst, no more discomfort in the heat or cold; and God Himself shall wipe away every tear. One of the tenderest memories an adult has is that of his mother kissing his sore finger and wiping away the tears from his eyes. Oh, what we have to look forward to in heaven!

SUMMING IT UP

Revelation 7 tells three incredible stories. One is about the ancient people of God, the Jews. Though they failed repeatedly to fulfill God's purposes in choosing them, God provides one final opportunity for obedience. This time a "remnant" of 144,000 Israelites hand-picked by God Himself and empowered by the Holy Spirit enjoys astounding success in evangelizing the world. The second amazing story of Revelation 7 concerns the new converts of these 144,000 evangelists. Despite unprecedented persecution and eventual martydom, these believers from every ethnic group on earth remain unwaveringly loyal to Christ, and they ultimately inherit God's rich blessings in eternity.

The third and perhaps most remarkable story of Revelation 7 is the record of God's graciousness in judgment. Even while He is justly punishing the world for its persistent rejection of Christ, God offers both Jews and Gentiles still another opportunity to change their minds and receive the Savior.

Eight

The Death of World Ecology

Let's take a minute to review what we've covered so far.

We've seen that Revelation 6 and 7 describe the Tribulation period, the seven-year reign of terror on earth which precedes Christ's final return to earth. We've examined the successive breaking of six of the seven seals of the rolled-up scroll, and we've seen that each broken seal ushers in a specific judgment of a holy God on a Christ-rejecting world.

The *first* seal releases a dictator, the Antichrist, who ultimately succeeds in subduing the entire world. The *second* seal takes peace from the earth. Russia and her Arab confederates attack the young State of Israel, resulting in an intense, wide-ranging war that lasts three-and-a-half years. The *third* seal results in a worldwide economic collapse. The *fourth* seal precipitates a tremendous outbreak of death through famines, epidemics, and civil violence. The *fifth* seal marks the beginning of the greatest persecution of all time—a period when believers will be slaughtered in the streets.

The horrors of the first five seals seem to be the inevitable results of what will happen when men's evil natures are totally unrestrained. The *sixth seal* unleashes a worldwide nuclear holocaust and is God's judgment on the world for its persecution of His saints.

Revelation 7 flashes back to the beginning of the Tribulation period, shortly *after* the Rapture but just *before* the judgments begin. Though all true believers will have been caught up to heaven at the Rapture, God will provide a continuing witness for Christ by calling forth 144,000 Jewish evangelists, 12,000 from each tribe. For seven years they will perform a remarkably effective job of bringing people to faith in Messiah Jesus.

THE GOLDEN SILENCE

> *(1) And when He had opened the seventh seal, there was silence in heaven for about a half-hour. (2) Then I saw the seven angels who stood before God, and they were given seven trumpets. (3) Then another angel came and stood at the altar, having a golden censer: and there was given to him much incense, so that he might offer it with the prayers of all the saints upon the golden altar which was before the throne. (4) And the smoke of the incense, which came with the prayers of the saints, ascended up before God out of the angel's hand. (5) And the angel took the censer, and filled it with fire from the altar, and cast it upon the earth: and there were voices, and thunderclaps, and lightnings, and an earthquake. (6) And the seven angels who had the seven trumpets prepared themselves to sound.*
>
> REVELATION 8:1–6

Verse one of this chapter speaks of a half-hour interlude of eerie silence in heaven just after the seventh seal is opened and *before* its judgment is released. This silence is awesome in its significance and stands in stark contrast to the joyous sounds of Elders and angels crying their praises in Chapters 4 and 5. This half-hour pause might be called "the lull before the storm" because the seventh seal, which has just been opened, will bring the greatest judgments yet. I'm sure the enormity of what is about to take place causes even God to pause and soberly assess what must be done to His errant creature, man.

The seven angels who stand in the presence of God are real personalities—not just figments of someone's imagination. The Bible indicates that angels are grouped in clearly defined ranks, much as in a military command structure. The highest of all angelic beings are these seven "archangels" who stand in the presence of God. These are the ones who will announce with trumpet blasts God's next seven judgments on the earth. These seven trumpet judgments are all a part of the *seventh seal*.

A BOWL OF PRAYERS

But before they can blow their trumpets to begin the judgments, "another angel" appears on the scene. He stands at the altar holding a golden censer filled with a special kind of incense—the prayers of saints. These He offers to God.

Although many good Bible scholars believe that the "other angel" here at the altar is simply another high-ranking angel, I believe that this "angel" is none other than Christ Himself functioning in His ministry of High Priest. The golden censer was only used in the Holy of Holies by the high priest in the ritual of prayer. It was this prayer-offering function of the coming Christ which was pictured by the Old Testament altar of incense.

After the believers are taken up to heaven at the Rapture they will apparently share in Christ's priestly ministry of interceding for the Tribulation saints. Revelation 8:3 specifies that *all* the saints in heaven, those believers who have been raptured, as well as believers still on earth at that time, will offer up prayers to God for the suffering brothers going through the Tribulation. They won't just be watching the agony on earth—they'll be vitally involved! That's thrilling to me, because as a believer I'm not especially interested in sitting on a cloud and plucking a harp night and day! I want to have a meaningful responsibility as a king and a priest.

After Christ finishes offering the prayers of the saints to the Father, He fills the golden censer with fire from the altar and throws it to the earth. The earth erupts with thunder, lightning, and an earthquake. None of these things is intended to destroy anyone, but rather to warn the people on earth of the approach of additional judgments.

It's extremely important to see that God seeks to extend the interlude of quietude as long as He can. He will give men more than adequate opportunity to think over the sixfold judgments which the world has just experienced. He'll wait eagerly for them to turn in repentance to Christ.

God always proceeds reluctantly toward judgment. However, the remaining judgments of the trumpets and bowls are the direct answer to the prayers of the martyred saints for justice. These judgments will occur near the *end* of the Tribulation period.

THE KEY TO THE TRUMPETS

It's once again very important for us to realize that the Book of Revelation is John's firsthand account of what he saw and experienced when he was taken up into heaven. How difficult it must have been for him with his first-century orientation to find adequate descriptive words to verbalize the incredible things he viewed! Even fifty years ago the things described in the Book of Revelation were so far beyond our comprehension that no one dreamed they could happen apart from some supernatural assistance.

Now such things as John described are not only possible, but could happen within thirty minutes! There are already enough nuclear-tipped missiles on station and ready for launching to do everything predicted in this chapter. Dr. W. H. Pickering of Cal Tech confirmed this when he warned, "In half an hour the East and the West could destroy civilization."

Although it is possible for God to supernaturally pull off every miracle in the Book of Revelation and use totally unheard-of means to do it, I personally believe that all the enormous ecological catastrophes described in this chapter are the direct result of nuclear weapons. In actuality, man inflicts these judgments on himself. God simply steps back and removes His restraining influence from man, allowing him to do what comes naturally out of his sinful nature. In fact, if the Book of Revelation had never been written, we might well predict these very catastrophes within fifty years or less!

JUDGMENT ON VEGETATION

(7) The first angel sounded, and there followed hail and fire mixed with blood, and they were cast upon the earth: and the third part of trees was burnt up, and all green grass burnt up. REVELATION 8:7

To John's eyes, unsophisticated as to ICBM's, the holocaust he witnessed looked like "hail and fire, mixed with blood" raining down from the atmosphere.

This devastation seems to be a massive nuclear attack much larger than the first one described in the sixth seal of Chapter 6. The nations involved in this particular nuclear exchange will be identified in Chapter 16. The scope of the damage done to the earth is unbelievable.

Sometimes the trumpet judgments are referred to as "the judgment of thirds," since one-third of several kinds of things is destroyed by them. If you've ever been in a forest fire you can imagine the terror of watching one-third of all the trees on

118 *There's A New World Coming*

earth go up in smoke! Think of the famine that will occur when *all* of the green grass is wiped out by fire! The word "grass" also includes the idea of grain, such as wheat, rice, and oats.

With this massive loss of vegetation will come soil erosion, floods, and mudslides. Air pollution will be immense; the smoke of the fire will fill the atmosphere, and the remaining vegetation will be unable to adequately absorb the hydrocarbons from automobiles and industry. Ecology will be thrown chaotically out of balance.

Notice that God continues to be gracious even in this awful judgment: He leaves two-thirds of the greenery untouched! But even this mercy-tempered judgment fails to induce the populace to change its mind about God.

JUDGMENT OF THE OCEAN

(8) And the second angel sounded, and something like a great mountain burning with fire was cast into the sea; and the third part of the sea became blood; (9) And the third part of the creatures which were in the sea, and had life, died; and the third part of the ships were destroyed.
REVELATION 8:8, 9

Notice that this verse specifies "something *like* a great mountain burning with fire." Again John describes this phenomenon in terms of how it looked to him. This is probably either an enormous meteor or, more likely, a colossal H-bomb. A hydrogen bomb exploded in the ocean would look like a huge, flaming mountain smashing into the sea. In addition to destroying one-third of all marine vessels, the "mountain" will wipe out one-third of all marine life, turning the sea crimson with the blood of the dead.

It's hard to imagine the enormity of what's being predicted here. Yet such a thing is technically possible right now. If enough super-thermonuclear weapons were to be set off in the ocean, a large percentage of marine life would be destroyed.

I recently spoke to a member of the Senate Arms Race Committee. He said that there is a growing paranoia among the military and government leaders of the world about the other nuclear powers. Everyone is worried about the other guy pushing the button. His own opinion was that a future full-fledged thermonuclear war is inevitable unless all nuclear weapons are scrapped. There doesn't seem to be much possibility of this in spite of all the "summit talks" between nations!

Some of you might be reading all these judgments that can be inflicted upon mankind through an atomic holocaust and thinking that they all comprise an important reason why there should be an end to the nuclear arms race. But as much as the United States and Soviet Union talk about resuming arms negotiations, make no mistake about it—the Soviets are too paranoid to ever really disarm. Besides, it's not in their game plan of world conquest and Communist domination.

The behavior of the Soviets both publicly and clandestinely as their military might grows leaves U.S. leaders no choice but to maintain a strong deterrent—the so-called Mutual Assured Destruction. With this "MAD" technique, the weaponry systems of both nations are growing more sophisticated in their abilities to wipe out life as we know it.

Of course, I would love to be optimistic about a "build-down" in the arms race, but my understanding of current events and Bible prophecy forces me to believe that just the opposite is true and that the world is indeed headed for grave times.

THE MASS "POSEIDON ADVENTURE"

One of the reasons why such devastation occurs on the ocean may be that thermonuclear missiles are targeted toward large armadas of naval vessels. Revelation 8:9 says in effect, "One-third of all ships of the world are destroyed." Obviously one of the repercussions of hitting these naval warships is that merchant ships are hit too.

When you couple the destruction of at least one-third of all vegetation with the annihilation of one-third of all marine life, it amounts to a massive reduction of the world's food supply. Add to this the loss of a great majority of the merchant fleet so that food cannot be distributed to the suffering nations, and it equals famine on an unbelievable scale. Just think of how many nations today depend upon merchant vessels for most of their food supply, and you will get some idea of the magnitude of this judgment!

FRESHWATER POLLUTION

(10) And the third angel sounded, and a great star fell from heaven, flaming like a torch, and it fell upon the third part of the rivers, and upon

the fountains of waters. (11) And the name of the star is called Wormwood; and the third part of the waters became wormwood; and many men died of the waters, because they were made bitter.   REVELATION 8:10, 11

I believe that this "star" is another thermonuclear weapon which is a part of a series of exchanges between the nuclear powers. This particular "star," which is given the name "Wormwood," contaminates a third of all freshwater sources on earth.

While I was living in Dallas in the late '50's, a tremendous drought hit the city. It intensified to the point that the supply of drinkable water actually ran out. The officials cleaned up the polluted water of the Red River enough so that it was safe to drink, but it still tasted salty. Finally, in desperation, some of the residents of the city drove out to the rural areas and bought farm well-water just to get a taste of fresh water again!

The "bitter" water of this third trumpet judgment will be so poisonous that numbers of people will die from drinking it.

LIGHT DIMINISHED

(12) And the fourth angel sounded, and the third part of the sun was smitten, and the third part of the moon, and the third part of the stars, so that the third part of them was darkened, and the day did not shine for a third part of it, and the night likewise.   REVELATION 8:12

Here we have all natural light diminished by one-third: sunlight will be reduced by one-third and the night will be one-third darker than usual. I believe that this light reduction will result from the tremendous pollution in the air left from nuclear explosions. This would be an inevitable consequence of a big nuclear exchange.

In 1983 the third annual conference on the worldwide effects of a nuclear holocaust was held in Italy. Describing the findings of scientists at the Lawrence Livermore National Laboratory, the *San Francisco Examiner* gave these details on what researchers call the "Nuclear Winter": "Within a few weeks of an all-out nuclear war, a devastating freeze would settle on the Northern Hemisphere. Massive amounts of soot from burning cities and forests would diffuse through the atmosphere, blotting out the sun. High noon would look like the dead of night. The average temperature would drop as much as 72 degrees at the centers of the continents in the Northern Hemisphere. Although slightly warmer temperatures would be found on the coast, the average North American temperature might be 15 degrees. The freeze would last from several weeks to several months."

It is important to note that even in the violence of these judgments, not all life would perish, as most poeople believe. According to the article, Michael MacCracken, an atmospheric scientist at Livermore, stated that "although the effects would be severe, they do not substantiate claims that nuclear war would end life on Earth."

Let's stop and look back over these judgments for a moment. Think of the threat to human life posed by the destruction of a third of all green vegetation! The blow to agriculture will be staggering.

Think of the consequences of losing one-third of all marine life. Do you know how many nations depend on fish as their basic diet? To destroy all this marine life would critically extend the famine that will already be sweeping the earth. To wipe out a third of all ships would result in a virtual standstill of world commerce and distribution of foodstuffs.

Then add to this the poisoning of the freshwater sources and the curtailment of natural light by a third, and you can see that the rapid succession of all these judgments is designed by God to shock man into changing his mind about Christ—to repent and receive God's gift of forgiveness while there's still time.

The Blindness of Unbelief

(13) And I beheld, and heard an angel flying through the midst of the atmosphere, saying with a loud voice, "Woe, woe, woe, to the inhabiters of the earth because of the other voices of the trumpet of the three angels, who are yet to sound!" REVELATION 8:13

At this point God interrupts the quick succession of trumpet judgments with a pause and a warning. His flying messenger informs men that the worst is yet to come. Hopefully this announcement will motivate men to turn to Christ for forgiveness. Most men, however, will ignore this warning too. Thus they must face the full fury of the last three trumpet judgments. These judgments are called "woes" because of the intensified suffering which they unleash.

A WORD FOR GOD

We should note carefully at this point that the majority of these catastrophes are inflicted by man against man. To be sure, God is the ultimate source of the judgments, but He has a willing ally in the fallen natures of men. Ecologists tell us that man's selfishness threatens to pollute him off the planet, so God can't take all the blame when man finally succeeds in doing the job!

NINE

Holocaust from the East

The first four trumpet judgments were directed toward the *earth's* ecology, but the last three judgments are directed toward *man* himself. Each of these judgments increases in scope and magnitude as it unfolds. It appears that God is putting the pressure on man, a little more each time, to try to get him to repent and turn to Jesus for salvation.

Even the word "woe" which the angel pronounces on mankind is a solemn warning in itself. Webster defines the word as "sorrow, calamity, affliction." If only men would heed this somber pronouncement! But the indication is that most will not.

It may seem a little confusing at first, but let me try to make clear the order of the next judgments. The *first* woe that is set loose on man is actually the *fifth* trumpet judgment (Revelation 9:1–12). The *second* woe which man has to endure is synonymous with the *sixth* trumpet (Revelation 9:13–21). The *third* woe is the *seventh* trumpet, and this judgment contains the final and most awful catastrophes of all times, called the "seven bowl judgments" (Revelation 11:14, 15; 16:1–21). All of the woe judgments occur very near the end of the Tribulation.

DEMONIC LOCUSTS

(1) And the fifth angel sounded, and I saw a star fall from heaven to the earth; and the key of the bottomless pit was given to him. (2) And he

123

opened the bottomless pit, and smoke arose out of the pit, like the smoke of a great furnace; and the sun and the air were darkened by the smoke of the pit.

(3) And locusts came out of the smoke onto the earth, and power was given to them to sting like the scorpions of the earth. (4) And they were commanded that they should not hurt the grass of the earth, or any green thing, or any tree, but only those men who do not have the seal of God on their foreheads. (5) They were commanded not to kill them, but that they should be tormented five months; and their torment was like the torment of a scorpion when he strikes a man. (6) In those days shall men seek death, and shall not find it; and shall desire to die, and death shall flee from them. (7) The shapes of the locusts were like horses prepared for battle; and on their heads were something like crowns of gold, and their faces were like the faces of men. (8) They had hair like the hair of women, and their teeth were like the teeth of lions. (9) They have breastplates, that seemed to be breastplates of iron; and the sound of their wings was like the sound of chariots of many horses running to battle. (10) They had tails like scorpions, and there were stingers in their tails; and their power was to hurt men five months. (11) They had a king over them, who is the angel of the bottomless pit, whose name in the Hebrew tongue is Abaddon, but in the Greek tongue his name was Apollyon.   REVELATION 9:1–11

The "star" of Revelation 9:1 has to be a person rather than a literal star, since "he" is given a key with which he opens the bottomless pit. I believe this fallen star is none other than Satan himself, described in Isaiah 14:12 as "Lucifer" or "Star of the Morning." Satan receives the key from Christ Himself, since Christ is the possessor of the key of hell (Revelation 1:18).

The opening of the bottomless pit unleashes a judgment that is unparalleled in its torment. The "locusts" of Revelation 9:3 are said to be possessed by hell's worst demons—fallen angels so ferocious that God has kept them bound since the days of Noah (2 Peter 2:4, 5). Their leader is apparently a demon of almost the power and authority of Satan himself. He is described in Revelation 9:11 as "Abaddon" and "Apollyon," meaning "destroyer."

God permits the release of these vicious beings because men have failed to heed the judgments against their unbelief and have not taken advantage of the lull in the storm to cry out to God for mercy.

JESUS DEALT WITH DEMONS

Before you start saying, "I don't believe in any of that demon jazz," remember that Christ Himself talked with demons on several occasions. Luke describes one occasion in which Christ talked with hundreds of demons living in a single man! Later this same group of demons moved into a herd of two thousand pigs, plunging them to their death in a lake!

Although I wouldn't go looking for demons myself, I have on several occasions been confronted with people who through involvement in the occult have become demon-possessed or have been harassed by demons.

Recently while I was in the home of a United States congressman I had a very unnerving encounter with a demon. Several other Christians and I were visiting with the congressman, a new believer, and were urging him to renounce his past extensive involvement with occultic mediums. Just then a sudden and awful oppressive spirit was felt by all seven persons present.

The congressman said, "Do you feel the presence of this spirit too? He has come here on several occasions before and rapped on the walls at night. Sometimes this spirit has come while my dog is in the room, and the dog's hair stands up on his back and he begins to bark wildly."

At this point I asked all the people present to kneel with me and pray; then in the name of Jesus Christ I ordered the demon to leave and not come back. Immediately the room was relieved of the oppressive presence—the demon was gone!

This didn't happen in the wilds of Africa, but in Washington, D.C.! Nor were there any superstitious pagans present—only responsible and well-educated men!

A MUTANT LOCUST

The locusts described in this chapter are unlike any known to man today. It's very difficult to fully understand everything about these unnatural creatures, but we can make certain observations about them.

They are possessed by the especially malignant demons who have just been released from the abyss. They have a king over them named "the Destroyer," who is the mighty fallen angel who apparently ruled over the abyss. This is certainly unnatural for locusts, since Proverbs 30:27 says that "locusts have no king."

These "locusts" have a scorpionlike stinger in their tails

with which they relentlessly torment men for five months. The sting will be so painful that men will wish they could die. History records that the ancient Roman soldiers were famous for their ability to take pain without flickering an eye. But when several of them were bitten by scorpions in the desert of Egypt they screamed and writhed in pain. Scorpion stings are among the most painful wounds a person can endure.

The demon-possessed locusts are not permitted to kill anyone. As with the case of Job, God here grants the Devil authority to torment but not to kill.

They can't even touch believers, for they will all have "the seal of God on their foreheads." This bears out the power and faithfulness with which God protects His own.

There are diverse opinions among Bible teachers as to whether these creatures are actually going to be a supernatural, mutant locust especially created for this judgment or whether they symbolize some modern device of warfare.

I have a Christian friend who was a Green Beret in Vietnam. When he first read this chapter he said, "I know what those are. I've seen hundreds of them in Vietnam. They're Cobra helicopters!"

That may just be conjecture, but it does give you something to think about! A Cobra helicopter does fit the composite description very well. They also make the sound of "many chariots." My friend believes that the means of torment will be a kind of nerve gas sprayed from its tail.

THE SECOND WOE: 200 MILLION ORIENTALS ATTACK

(12) One woe is past, but now there are two more coming. (13) Then the sixth angel sounded, and I heard a voice from the four horns of the golden altar which is before God, (14) saying to the sixth angel who had the trumpet, "Release the four angels who are bound at the great river, Euphrates." (15) The four angels were released, who were prepared for an hour, and a day, and a month, and a year, to slay the third part of men. (16) The number of the army of the horsemen were two hundred million: I heard the number of them.

(17) Now this is how I saw the horses and those who sat upon them in the vision; the riders had breastplates of fire, and of jacinth, and brimstone; and the heads of the horses were like the heads of lions, and out of their mouths issued fire and smoke and brimstone. (18) A third of mankind was killed by these three things, by the fire, and by the smoke, and by the brimstone, which issued out of their mouths. (19) For their power is in their

mouth, and in their tails; for their tails were like serpents, and had heads,
and with them they do harm.   REVELATION 9:12–19

Verse 13 begins with the second woe (the sixth trumpet). It's a terrifying judgment. Four of the most wicked and powerful of all fallen angels are released to inspire the destruction of a third of all remaining mankind! Remember that one-fourth of the world population has already been destroyed by the judgments described in Revelation 6:8. The poisoning of fresh-water sources killed many more. Now the remaining population is reduced by still another 33 percent!

DOWN BY THE RIVERSIDE

These four angels at the River Euphrates are very significant. They were bound by God because they were tremendously powerful emissaries of Satan. Their confinement at the River Euphrates is especially momentous.

The first human sin was committed right at this Euphrates region, in the Garden of Eden. In this area the first murder and the first great revolt against God also took place. It was in nearby Babylon that the first world ruler set up his kingdom. The Euphrates region is truly the site of many significant events of human history!

The Romans, Greeks, and Babylonians always considered the Euphrates River the boundary line between the East and the West. Rudyard Kipling put it succinctly: "East is East, and West is West, and never the twain shall meet."

But they're going to meet in the Tribulation! The four angels of Revelation 9:14, 15 will mobilize an army of 200 million soldiers from east of the Euphrates. Revelation 16 will provide more details about this, but in essence I believe these 200 million troops are Red Chinese soldiers accompanied by other Eastern allies. It's possible that the industrial might of Japan will be united with Red China. For the first time in history there will be a full invasion of the West by the Orient.

200 MILLION STRONG

It has to be more than coincidence that an Associated Press article by John H. Hightower, dateline Washington, D.C., April 28, 1964, said, "The documents (secret Chinese military plans) make clear that the Red Chinese leaders believe they cannot be defeated by long-range nuclear weapons—such as U.S. missiles—and if they were invaded they would rely on their vast military manpower. One estimate is that in April, 1961, there were supposed to be *200 million* armed and organized militiamen" (emphasis mine).

If the armed militia of China was estimated at 200 million in 1961, what do you suppose it is now? The obvious significance of this fact is that for the first time in history there is an Oriental power that can do exactly what this prophecy foretells!

Consider also at this point that when John wrote this prophecy there were not yet 200 million people in the whole world! This is truly an amazing and terrifying prophecy.

THE YELLOW PERIL

It's also interesting to note that throughout history there's never been a great invasion of the West by the East. It's as if God put an invisible boundary line there, restraining the forces that could have mobilized the Orient for a full-scale invasion of the West. But with the releasing of these four mighty demons, all stops are pulled. There will be a full mobilization of "the kings of the East" (Revelation 16:12). The fabled "yellow peril" will become a horrible reality as they swoop across the dried-up Euphrates River into the Middle East, where war is already in progress.

The Apostle John describes the army's mounts as horses with heads like lions and with fire, smoke, and brimstone coming out of their mouths. My opinion is that he is describing some kind of mobilized ballistic missile launcher. This great army will apparently destroy one-third of the world's remaining population while en route from the Orient to the Middle East. This could mean the destruction of the great population centers of Asia, such as India, Japan, Pakistan, Indo-China, and Indonesia. It could also include a long-range strike at the United States itself. (This might explain why the United States is nowhere intimated in the Bible's prophecies of the last war of the world.)

THE CHINESE NUCLEAR THREAT

John describes the means by which one-third of mankind will be annihilated as "fire, smoke, and brimstone." All of these things are a part of a thermonuclear war: smoke represents the immense clouds of radioactive fallout and debris, while brimstone is simply melted earth and building materials.

Red China is not only a thermonuclear power at the time of this writing but the rapidity with which she became one is even more startling.

During President Reagan's recent trip to China, the U.S. (wanting to balance the scale of power, now heavily tilted toward the Soviet Union, which deploys one-third of its armed forces in the Far East and Western Pacific) agreed to supply nuclear technology and equipment to the Chinese for peaceful use in atomic reactors. This is viewed as a building block between our nations and a way to bring China more in line with today's technological developments. The theory is that as China grows more powerful economically, the leaders will see the benefits of capitalism for its people and be more of an Asian ally in offsetting Soviet aggression.

Of course, Red China balked at a U.S. law which claims "consent rights" over the use of atomic fuel once it has been spent in an American-built reactor. This law was designed to prevent the fuel from being used in nuclear weapons. The Chinese, however, said this law infringes on their sovereignty. Finally, on the eve of President Reagan's visit, the Chinese capitulated in order to receive the badly needed technology to supply electricity to factories that have been shut down due to lack of power. However, they spoke of their commitment only in verbal terms, and did not sign any formal treaty barring such activities on their part with the U.S. I believe that what they eventually intend to do with the reprocessed uranium is not hard to figure out. (Although the technology has been delayed the U.S. is seeking a compromise with China.)

In a revealing speech to a visiting delegation of the European Economic Community's Parliament, Peng Zhen, chairman of China's Parliament, showed just what Red China thinks of nuclear weapons. While denouncing the Soviet and U.S. arms race, Peng said it was essential that China maintain a strong nuclear deterrent if world war was to be avoided. Said Jacqueline Desouches, leader of the delegates, " . . . they said they hoped for a strong Europe—including a Europe that is militarily strong—and said they thought a nuclear deterrent force was necessary for themselves because it ensures war does not happen . . ."

China now deploys medium-range ballistic missiles capable of hitting every major city in Asia. What has the Soviets worried is that those missiles can hit Moscow, too!

I personally believe that the "four evil angels" who will be unbound at the River Euphrates will instantly mobilize a giant war machine made up of some of the Oriental countries, primarily Red China, and will be responsible for wiping out one-third of mankind.

This holocaust is again followed by an interlude. Once more God gives man a chance to repent and turn to Jesus, and once more man refuses.

The third and last woe (the seventh trumpet judgment) includes the final seven judgments which God pours out on the earth. These "vial" or "bowl" judgments are mercifully postponed by God until the events of Revelation 16. In the intervening chapters many of the central characters and events of the Tribulation period are introduced and explained.

AND THEY REPENTED NOT

(20) And the rest of the men who were not killed by these plagues still did not repent of the works of their hands, so that they should not worship demons, and idols of gold, and silver, and bronze, and stone, and wood, which neither can see, nor hear, nor walk. (21) Neither did they repent of their murders, nor of their sorceries, nor of their sexual immorality, nor of their thefts. REVELATION 9:20, 21

These two verses have got to be among the most incredible in the whole Bible. After all the foregoing supernatural events, men are still unwilling to repent and turn to Christ!

These two verses also reveal another remarkable prediction—that men will once again turn back to worshipping demons and idols. Ten years ago I couldn't imagine how people with today's education and enlightenment could do such a thing. But in the last few years we've seen the greatest turning to witchcraft, Satan worship, and occultism since the days of ancient Rome!

Some members of the academic community who were formerly agnostic in their religious views and opposed religion of any kind in the classroom now not only *accept the possibility* of the supernatural but actually *practice* various forms of it in private and in the classroom under the label of parapsychology!

Coupled with this introduction to the occult in our class-rooms, the rise of "heavy metal" rock music in the 1970's has brought this phenomenon to frightening heights. Rightfully called "the Devil's music," heavy metal has sprung such acts as Ozzy Osbourne, who began with the group Black Sabbath. At his concerts, his willing teenage audience shouts its approval as he bites the heads of birds and bats off. Other groups such as AC/DC (the letters denote that a person "swings both ways," meaning that he or she is bisexual) rode into the Top 10 music charts with songs like "Highway to Hell." These groups also do not fear displaying demonic album covers such as Motley Crue's "Shout at the Devil" album, which depicts an upsidedown pentagram (a satanic symbol and a favorite tool of these types of bands, especially onstage). Many groups are also blatantly blasphemous in their lyrical content. In fact, I wouldn't even consider repeating the offensive "artistic expressions" of these "songwriters."

The result of all this has been a generation of children who view the occult not as something harmful but as something powerful! In a March 18, 1984, front-page article on the growing resurgence of Satan worship, the *Los Angeles Herald Examiner* focused on a follower of the band Judas Priest. Describing a drug-induced vision, the 17-year-old was quoted as saying, "I was like on this highway, and all I saw was flames all around me, and at the end of the road the mighty Lucifer looked down upon me. It was a red, muscular body, with a sort of like a black jumpsuit on. This one didn't have a tail, but it had the goat's head for the head. And his eyes were glowing with hatred." The youth went on to say that he was being "demonized." "It slowly takes you over. It happens without you knowing it. It's slowly happening to me now."

Illuminating the fact that demonic possession is real, psychiatrist M. Scott Peck, author of the books *The Road Less Traveled* and *People of the Lie: The Hope for Healing Human Evil*, explains that demonization is not like what was depicted in the movie "The Exorcist." "In that movie," Peck told the *Los Angeles Times*, "the girl is possessed but we're given no idea of why. As if it were possible to walk down the street someday and the devil jumps out of a bush and into you. It doesn't happen that way. What happens is that every day of our lives, we've got all these opportunities to make decisions and, one by one, in order to avoid the inevitable pain and suffering of life, we keep selling out to the Devil. One day we've gone too far, and we're possessed. There's no going back. But it didn't hit us out of the blue. We've sold out in certain ways with the process."

Peck, by the way, was into Zen Buddhism until he started professionally investigating why some people remain evil despite attempts at rehabilitation. "At the time I began to work on the book, I was an atheist," he said, "or an 'a-devilist.' But as a result of these . . . cases [where he witnessed exorcisms], I became convinced. . . ." Now Peck considers himself a Christian.

In the 1960's, Anton LeVay founded the Church of Satan in San Francisco and published the "Satanist Bible." The "church" now has followers in Los Angeles, New York, and Amsterdam. Authorities are concerned that there is a link between LeVay's book, heavy metal music, and the rise in grave robbings, animal mutilations, murders, general antisocial behavior, and criminal activities on the part of young people. In the *Los Angeles Herald* article, Dave Gaerin, a detective in the San Diego County Sheriff's Department's juvenile division, said, "Satanism is all over the country. And California seems to be, from all indicators, the leader in the nation." Gaerin should know—he made those remarks after conducting a seminar for law enforcement officials outlining the rise of Satanism!

The Lord Jesus told His disciples that in the last days there would be many demons loosed upon the earth. A survey of heavy metal bands today might well show just how many have "sold out" to the Devil in order to obtain the riches of this world. I saw the beginning of this great and frightening change of attitude toward the supernatural on college campuses in the late 1960's. Since then it has become a worldwide phenomenon, multiplying at a geometric rate.

For more in-depth insight on this whole subject, I recommend Johanna Michaelsen's book, *The Beautiful Side of Evil*, as must reading.

Feature magazine had this to say about it (November 13, 1970): "One might say that we are living in a new 'Age of Faith,' but the kind of faith that people put into their astrologer's predictions, palmists, or clairvoyants. The revival of interest in witchcraft today is said to be due to our attempt to escape from the lunacy that we now live in. Societies in all civilizations have had some sort of faith, faith in the unknown, the supernatural. Witchcraft now appears to be man's answer as a replacement for their lost faith in Christianity."

MAN IS A "RELIGION FREAK"

History shows that man cannot live in a religious vacuum. Since modern secular man in general has rejected God's truth, he is now moving toward the occult to find a means of relieving his sense of fear about the uncertainty of the future and to find meaning for his existence. He is seeking to find some relief from his sense of powerlessness over his own destiny in the midst of a modern, computerized, and pressurized society.

Even Russia, which is officially atheistic in its national life and policy, has been exploring the strange world of the occult. A well-documented book entitled *Psychic Phenomena Behind the Iron Curtain* reveals that the U.S.S.R. is leading the world in experiments with clairvoyancies of all kinds. The Soviets have been enormously successful at contacting supernatural forces and spirits. However, since they don't accept the Bible, they are completely ignorant of the fact that these forces are demons.

According to the *New York Times*, the success of the Soviets in "psycho warfare" has forced the Pentagon to spend millions in research to close the "psychic arms gap." While the U.S. denies spending money in this field, three reports in 1983, according to the *Times*, show the superpowers waging a battle to master "ESP [extrasensory perception], telepathy [thought transfer], clairvoyance [seeing things out of sight], and psychokinesis [mental influence over objects]."

While some people might find this hard to believe, the Soviets in 1984 sent the first spaceman from India along on a mission to the Salyut spacelab, where yoga was practiced for the first time in space to see how it could aid the human body during weightlessness. Interestingly, one dictionary definition of yoga is: "A Hindu discipline aimed at training the consciousness for a state of perfect spiritual insight and tranquility." Just the type of situation demons know how to exploit!

This experimentation is setting the stage for a general acceptance by the atheistic Russians of an occultic-based religion—and it's just another step toward the one-world religion which will worship the Antichrist during the Tribulation! (See Revelation 17.)

THE BIG-FOUR SINS

Revelation 9:21 lists the four most prominent sins of the Tribulation. The significance of these particular sins is great in the light of present trends in the world. It's no coincidence that the four major sins listed here are four of the most serious problems facing law enforcement today.

The first of these characteristic sins is murder. Over a century ago, before America groaned under the present crime wave, Joseph Seiss, the author of *The Apocalypse*, predicted on the basis of Revelation 9:21 that capital punishment would have been largely abolished by the time of the Tribulation! He foresaw the day when murderers would be spared punishment because society rather than the individual would be held responsible for their crimes!

Many law enforcement officers, as well as private citizens, believe that the failure of the courts to use capital punishment is one of the reasons for the alarming increase in murders. Whether capital punishment is a strong deterrent to murder is perhaps debatable, but there are other factors which many *would* agree have contributed to the rise in crime.

First is the failure of parents and churches to teach children and adults the sinful nature of man and God's remedy for it— a new birth in Christ. I'm sure there have been murders committed by people who knew they were sinful, but I'm also sure that most of these people did not know how to deal with the dark, angry emotions that surged through them in the depths of their beings. No one had ever told them about a Savior who would come to live within them and cleanse their hearts of hatred, greed, and lust.

Another strong factor in the making of murderers is the rejection of absolute standards of right and wrong. This rejection came about partly because of the liberal theologians' stripping the Bible of its authority in the minds of men. Add to this the "situational ethics" and relative standards of morality fostered by certain nineteenth-century philosophical and psychological thinkers, and it's no wonder that men can explode with their passions and then somehow justify to themselves the taking of another's life.

The breakdown in the home and the failure of fathers to assume their roles of leadership have also been strong contributing factors to the increase of violent crimes. A child who is never taught discipline and respect for authority in the home will grow up with destructive anxieties and frustrations, and too often he takes out his hostilities on society.

DRUGS + WITCHCRAFT = NIGHTMARE

The second prominent sin of the Tribulation era will be drug-related occultic activities. The word "sorceries" in Revelation 9:21, comes from the Greek word *pharmakia*, which means "pharmacy" and refers here to the practice of the occult with the use of drugs. Even in Biblical times drug use often led to astrology, witchcraft, and outright demon worship.

In our day, drug addiction—touted and flaunted by many rock stars—has swelled into a flood across the nation. While the 1970's saw an abatement toward use of mind-altering drugs such as LSD, the punk and heavy-metal teenagers of the 1980's are once again experimenting with this dangerous drug, as well as heroin. While cocaine is still the "rich man's drug," its use has also rapidly spread, with many users combining it with heroin into what is commonly called a "speedball." With this has come an unprecedented tide of witchcraft and demonism.

Use of these drugs by unwitting youngsters has led to demon worship at heavy-metal concerts. Said Detective Gaerin in the *Los Angeles Herald*, "The biggest hook for Satanism is the music. The kids are getting all kinds of messages in the music. If you ask a lot of the kids, they wouldn't realize what those things are that are being said. We had a concert down here [in San Diego] where the band had 15,000 kids chanting, 'Natas!' " That, my dear brothers and sisters, is Satan spelled backward!

I've talked with people who've been on LSD for a long time, and they've told me, "Demons are no strangers to me!" Demons and drugs are very similar in their effect on the human mind. They can take over a man to the point where he's completely altered in personality and would think nothing of committing the crimes of grave-robbing and animal mutilation for sacrificial purposes—or even murder!

An article in *The International Journal of Social Psychiatry* (Spring, 1971) dealt with the reality of demon possession and how to diagnose it, and gave the following instruction: "There is a need to ascertain if there is any involvement in *drug addiction*, as it is common that addicts, especially with heroin and alcohol, become involved in black magic and vice versa. . . . (Some) have been known in some cases to have been very religious people who defaulted, and thus left themselves open to some power other than God to control their lives."

The interesting thing to me is that in many cases with which I am familiar the person first used drugs, then got into witchcraft. But when a deep involvement with the occult followed, drugs were eventually dropped in favor of the more powerful experience with spirits.

CASTANEDA'S STRANGE JOURNEY

A powerful writer of our time, Carlos Castaneda, has written of his own personal experiences along this line in his bestseller of the 1970's, *Journey to Ixtlan*. In this book and his two previous ones, he tells of his initiation into the practice of Indian sorcery in Mexico through such hallucinogenic drugs as peyote, Jimson weed, mushrooms mixed with other plants, and other natural drugs.

While Castaneda was on his "trips" he had all kinds of encounters with "beings" he couldn't understand. He was continually urged by an old Indian sorcerer named Don Juan to seek to really "see" the other world. Whether Don Juan really exists or is simply a creation of Castaneda's pen, no one knows for sure. But Castaneda has spent ten years of his life seeking to "see" by negating the routine use of the five senses and to experience firsthand the world of spirits and psychic phenomena. For his efforts in this field UCLA gave him a Ph.D. for *Journey to Ixtlan*!

One of the most important things that Castaneda discovered in his journey to becoming a sorcerer is that drugs are only necessary in the beginning. As a seeker becomes fully committed to sorcery, a "spirit entity" attaches itself to the seeker and gives him unimaginable power.

The reason I've taken so much space to mention Carlos Castaneda's writings is that these three books of his, *The Teach-*

ings, A Separate Reality, and *Journey to Ixtlan,* have sold in the millions and are now considered by many in the academic world as among the most important anthropological research of all time. And do you know what it is they are so excited and stimulated about? The Bible calls them *demons!*

According to the prophecies of the Book of Revelation, those who reject the truth about Jesus Christ will become so deceived that they will not only *believe* in the reality of demons, but they will actually *worship* them through the coming one-world religion called "mystery Babylon" (Revelation 17).

THE PLAYBOY PHILOSOPHY

The third prominent sin of the Tribulation will be rampant immorality. *Porneia,* the Greek word used in this verse, refers to all kinds of sexual activity outside of its Biblically-sanctioned function between a married man and woman. The marriage vow will be virtually unknown at this time, and there will be a complete breakdown in family relationships.

The *Futurist* magazine devoted the whole April 1973 issue to "Man-Woman Relationships in the Future." In the lead article Dr. Herbert Otto says, "A psychologist foresees a society in which men and women will explore new depths of intimacy, and the pursuit of joy will become an art form. . . . More people will indulge in group sex . . . and the ideal life will not be marriage, children, and a house in the suburbs, but rather the experiencing of a series of deep and fullfilling relationships in a variety of environments."

We live in a day when the impact of the rejection of Biblical morality and absolutes is beginning to be seen at every level of society, but especially in attitudes toward sex. While *Time* magazine reported in its April 9, 1984, issue that the sex revolution of the last two decades is over in the 1980's I would disagree with that assessment. The article pointed out correctly the economic and social factors contributing to the decline of "free sex," as well as the specter of sexually spread herpes and AIDS, which certainly cooled the trends of the 1970's. But even though many men and women have come to see the error of a casual sexual relationship with its unwanted moral dilemmas, including abortion, the sexual revolution has moved on toward the acceptance of an androgynous society.

This is most evident, once again, in the rock stars revered and idolized by a generation of children unaware of the dangers that their acceptance poses. This was brought home to me by the cover of *Newsweek's* January 23, 1984, issue. It portrayed the latest and hottest stars of rock, especially in the exploding world of music videos. The only problem posed by the picture of the two rock stars was, "Who is the man and who is the woman?" Boy George of Culture Club and Annie Lennox of the Eurythmics take delight in wearing the clothes, makeup, jewelry, and hairstyles usually associated with the opposite sex, while imitating a mixture of mannerisms. In Lennox's case, this includes overt sadomasochism—and that is the legacy they are leaving their fans.

When Boy George and his group received a Grammy Award for Best New Artists of 1983, his comment on nationwide TV and to the millions of teenagers watching was, "America, you know a good drag queen when you see one." Boy George has also started a revolution in clothes, wearing the Hasidic hat and coat that most people associate with Orthodox Jews! On the back of his coat he has been seen wearing the number 999! And the name of one of his biggest hits that propelled him to stardom? "Church of the Poison Mind"!

It is important to note that I am not accusing Boy George of intentional blasphemy, but when a person is ignorant of God's ways and the reality of Satan, it's hard to see who is manipulating the actions of this teenage idol. After all, Boy George stated in the *Newsweek* interview that he had been reared on the anarchy of the punk revolution, where anything is permissible, and he looked up to the punk group the Sex Pistols, who sang the lyrics "I Am the Antichrist" in the song "Anarchy in the U.K." It is also interesting to note that one of the Sex Pistols' members, Sid Vicoius, was accused of murdering his girlfriend/manager, who died of multiple stab wounds—but before he went to trial, Vicious did himself in by overdosing on drugs.

Another insidious attempt at moving our society toward an androgynous state is the National Council of Churches' "nonsexist" lectionary which they published in 1983. Here, in one great swell of blasphemy, the NCC has downgraded our Lord from the only Son of God to just a "Child" of God. Caving in to the voices of feminism, the NCC took it upon itself to correct God and the gender through which He chose to send His Savior to the world!

And we have yet to see the end of the NCC's blasphemous nature toward acceptance of all sexualities and the "utopia" of an androgynous society. In 1983 it came very close to accepting the membership of the Metropolitan Community Church, which is made up almost entirely of homosexual men and women. Although the group was not allowed admission, they were told that it was not quite time yet, but the decision will be reviewed. I believe this decision will constantly be reviewed until enough political and public pressure is found to permit the membership of this gay church. This is just another step in a long line of moves that are teaching our children today that any type of sex or sexuality is okay, no matter what the Bible says!

Couple this mentality with that of a magazine like *Hustler*, and it's no wonder that young people today find it hard to respect God. Publisher Larry Flynt, who at one time had the audacity to call himself a born-again Christian, permitted one of the most vile and gross covers on a men's magazine that I have ever seen. It depicted the body of a naked woman hung limply upon a glass cross in a mock imitation of our Lord's most precious sacrifice. Believe me, no self-respecting, God-fearing Christian would permit mockery of that kind pertaining to Jesus' sacrifice!

The world is in a headlong plunge *downward* to the morality of Sodom and Gomorrah and, unfortunately, to their same judgment as well!

CRIME ON THE INCREASE

The fourth characteristic of the Tribulation will be thievery of all kinds, including burglaries (theft by breaking into houses and businesses) and robberies (theft by threat of personal violence). I hardly need to convince you that these kinds of crimes are on the upsurge today!

When a society's family unit breaks down, the whole society falls apart. Many of our world's people are without moral conviction and natural affection because they have been set adrift on the sea of life with no compass, rudder or destination. The *Futurist* issue quoted above also reported, "Divorcing parents traditionally have battled to gain custody over their children, but in a growing number of broken families today *neither* parent wants custody."

Imagine what devastation that is to a kid! In a society with a growing number of unwanted children who are not given love, understanding, discipline, and a respect for authority, the predictable outcome is lawlessness and spiraling crime.

In 1984 the breakdown of the family unit was seen throughout the U.S. in our bulging prison population. A Justice Department survey released in April reported a record 438,830 inmates serving time in prisons around the nation. That represents a 115 percent increase in the prison population since 1974! Another 210,000 were in local jails awaiting trial or in for lesser offenses. That translated into the fact that 1 in every 350 Americans was a prisoner—an extremely high rate when compared with the rest of the world. And the cost to the taxpayers? A staggering 10 billion dollars a year! But what's worse is that most inmates are learning how to be more violent and cunning when they are released from prison. In fact, psychologist Stanton Samenow reported in his study, "Inside the Criminal Mind," that most ex-prisoners display a deep hatred and anger toward society which can erupt into violent, vicious attacks against innocent victims at any time.

By the time of the Great Tribulation, many more prisoners will have been imbued with this hatred toward society, blaming it for the lack of ever really knowing what family life was all about.

TEN

An Ambassador From Galaxy "H"

This chapter describes an interlude of peace between the sixth and seventh trumpets which occurs very near the end of the seven-year Tribulation. Up to this point we've considered twelve specific judgments which will have devastated the earth. Now God once again stays His hand of judgment in order to give man every chance to turn to Him for mercy and forgiveness.

GOD'S MIGHTY REPOSSESSOR

(1) Then I saw another mighty angel come down from heaven, clothed with a cloud; and a rainbow was upon his head, and his face was as though it were the sun, and his feet like pillars of fire. (2) He had in his hand a little scroll open; and he set his right foot upon the sea, and his left foot on the earth, (3) and cried with a loud voice, as when a lion roars; and when he had cried, the seven thunders uttered their voices.

(4) And when the seven thunders had uttered their voices, I was about to write; and I heard a voice from heaven saying to me, "Seal up those things which the seven thunders said, and do not write them."

(5) And the angel whom I saw standing upon the sea and upon the earth lifted up his hand to heaven, (6) and swore by Him who lives forever and ever, who created heaven and the things that are in it, and the earth and the things that are in it, and the sea and the things which are in it, that there

should be delay no longer; (7) but in the days of the voice of the seventh angel, when he begins to sound, the mystery of God will be finished, as He has declared to His servants, the prophets. REVELATION 10:1–7

This mighty and glorious being is placed in the same rank and order with the "strong angel" of Revelation 5:2. We know this because the Greek word used here for "another" means "another of the same kind."

As I've said before, the Bible sets forth many levels of rank, power, and authority among the angelic realm. The angels designated "strong" are apparently part of the supreme group that stand continually in the presence of God and partake of the authority of His throne. The angel that appeared to doubting Zacharias with the announcement that he would have a son named John (the Baptist) rebuked him for not believing his word because, as he said, "I am Gabriel! I stand in the very presence of God. It was He who sent me to you with this good news!" (Luke 1:19, *TLB*)

The angel here in this chapter is most likely Michael, who is called *the archangel* in Jude verse 9.

INSIGNIA OF HIGHEST RANK

The supreme authority of this mighty angel is clearly revealed by his uniform of cloud, rainbow, sun, and fire. Men probably won't be able to actually see this dramatic event taking place, for it will most likely occur in the spiritual realm. But while the angelic hosts of heaven as well as Satan and his demon legions look on, this angel will claim initial possession of planet earth for Jesus. The fact that Satan doesn't prevent the angel from accomplishing his mission bears witness to the angel's great authority.

CLOTHED WITH A CLOUD

Clouds are frequently the vehicle in which heavenly visits were paid to this planet by God. (See Psalm 104:3; Isaiah 19:1; Daniel 7:13; Matthew 17:5.) This strong angel has been given the dignity and honor of appearing in the same mode that God does, with a cloud as his robe.

CROWNED WITH THE RAINBOW

Surrounding the head of this majestic being is the rainbow. You'll remember that God said that the rainbow was His sign to remind everyone that He would never again destroy the world with water (Genesis 9:9–17). Its presence at this incident symbolizes that God remembers and keeps His covenants—and even more important, in judgment He remembers mercy.

AGLOW WITH "THE PRESENCE"

The angel's face glowed with the brilliance of the sun, reminding us of the glory of the One from whose presence he had just come. When Moses descended down Mount Sinai from the presence of the Lord, Scripture says "Moses didn't realize as he came back down the mountain with the tablets that his face glowed from being in the presence of God" (Exodus 34:29, *TLB*).

FEET OF FIRE

As already noted in Chapter 1, the "feet like pillars of fire" symbolize judgment. As the angel dramatically plants his fiery feet upon the land and the sea, it symbolizes the taking possession of the land and sea of this planet by divine judgment.

As I study this passage I stand in awe of this profound and dramatic sight. There's little in either sacred or secular literature to compare with this majestic account!

WHEN THE LION ROARS

The angel's voice is like that of a lion as he pierces the silence of a calm day. As the angel roars his message, it's answered by an even more awesome sound of "seven thunders." These "thunders" give some kind of electrifying message which the Apostle John immediately starts to record, but is prevented from doing so by a voice from heaven. Nowhere in the rest of John's vision is he ever given permission to reveal what he heard. There's been a lot of speculation through the years as to what this unrevealed message was. It must be something so potent that the world simply can't take it at this point. Whatever it is, I think it won't be long before we can ask the angel personally what this unmentionable message is!

No More Delay

The angel carried a small, open book in his hand. At the same time he planted one of his feet on the land and one on the sea and raised his right hand to heaven. This always brings to my mind a picture of two fighters, one standing with his foot on the back of the other and his right hand raised in a signal of conquest.

I believe the small book contained the title deed to the earth and that the angel's stance of conquest represents his claim to the earth on behalf of Jesus Christ. The words, "There shall be delay no longer," in verse 6 show that all these preceding acts of the angel occur just before the *end* of the seven-year Tribulation, and Christ will delay His coming no longer.

A big question in Chapter 10 is: What is the *mystery* of God which has been proclaimed to God's servants, the prophets? I personally believe that this mystery is the age-old enigma: "Why has God allowed evil to continue in the world and not put down His enemies and established His perfect Kingdom long ago?'

Second Peter 3:9 clears up much of this mystery. "He isn't really being slow about His promised return, even though it sometimes seems that way. But He is waiting for the good reason that He is not willing that any should perish, and He is giving more time for sinners to repent" *(TLB)*. God's patience through all these centuries has provided ample opportunity for all men to repent and receive Jesus Christ as their personal Savior.

God So Loved the World

Look at human suffering from God's viewpoint for a moment. Here are all these agonies caused directly or indirectly by human sin. God could wipe out all the sinners who cause all the suffering, or He could patiently wait for them to repent and turn to Christ. If you possessed the infinite love and mercy which God does, which course of action would you decide to follow? Well, that's exactly what God decided to do long before you and I were born!

God created people with freedom of choice. If He'd wanted robots He could easily have created them. Freedom of choice includes the freedom to defy God and reject His love.

When I was a teenager I often wished that I could hypnotize a certain girl into liking me. You know—"Come here and kiss me."

"Yes, master!"

What a cold fish that would be! I think the point is obvious— love can't be forced.

Despite mankind's wholesale rejection of God, He has graciously restrained the evil devices of men enough so that the human race has never *quite* succeeded in destroying itself. The gas chambers of Nazi Germany would have been multiplied a thousand times over through all of human history if God the Holy Spirit had not held back the full fury of godless men. Something of man's horrendously evil capabilities will be seen during the Tribulation period, when for a short time God will lift His hand of restraint from man.

The mystery of God's patient grace which He revealed long ago to His prophets will receive full vindication when Christ returns to earth in sweeping judgment. The patience of the centuries will finally give way to the justice of the ages!

Another facet of the "mystery of God" is that there will be a new world coming after a period of purifying judgment on the earth. The angel wants "no more delay" in bringing God's kingdom to the earth.

THE BITTERSWEET MESSAGE

(8) And the voice which I heard from heaven spoke to me again, and said, "Go and take the little scroll which is open in the hand of the angel who stands upon the sea and upon the earth." (9) And I went to the angel, and said to him, "Give me the little scroll." And he said to me, "Take it, and eat it up; and it shall make your belly bitter, but it shall be as sweet as honey in your mouth." (10) So I took the little scroll out of the angel's hand, and ate it up; it was as sweet as honey in my mouth, but as soon as I had eaten it my belly was bitter. (11) He said to me, "You must prophesy again about many peoples, and nations, and tongues, and kings." REVELATION 10:8–11

Here's an interesting phenomenon: John is told to "eat" the opened book in the hand of the angel. While it would taste good in his mouth, the book would turn bitter once it became digested. Tasting and eating are often used in the Bible to portray hearing and believing. More than one Old Testament prophet was commanded to "eat" a scroll containing the Hebrew Scriptures. How can the Word of God be both sweet and bitter? It's sweet when we learn of the love of God for man and His gracious provision for our eternal salvation. It's bitter when we discover that all who reject Christ will suffer God's holy judgment for their sins.

This was John's dilemma. He rejoiced when he saw the revelation of the final judgment which still awaited the unbelieving earth dwellers.

No doubt the enormity of the devastations that were about to fall on man gave John "indigestion and a bitter stomach." The only "Alka-Seltzer" John had was the sure knowledge of God's new world that was coming! That alone could sweeten his taste!

ELEVEN

Jerusalem Troubles the World

For sheer enormity of historical significance, no city can even approximate Jerusalem. Consider the following highlights of its tumultuous but glorious past:

- it was the city of the mysterious Melchizedek, "a priest of the Most High God," who pronounced a blessing on the noble Abraham nearly 4,000 years ago;
- it was captured and exalted as the national capital of Israel by David the King nearly 3,000 years ago;
- it was beautified under Solomon;
- it was established as the spiritual center of the life of Israel by the erection of the Temple of Solomon;
- it is the only city God ever called "My city";
- it was the site of numerous invasions, which occured each time the Israelis forsook their faith in God;
- it is the place where Messiah Jesus was crucified;
- it is considered holy by three major religions—Judaism, Islam, and Christianity;
- it has witnessed countless invasions by crusaders from these religions;
- it has been the place nearest to the hearts of its dispersed people in many lands for nineteen centuries. At the end of their Passover meal they yearningly pray, "Next year in Jerusalem!"

But what has happened there is only a prelude to the incredible events that will occur there in the future, events which will shake the whole world.

Revelation 11 focuses on some of those important events that may soon begin to unfold in Jerusalem.

THE TEMPLE RISES AGAIN

> *(1) Then I was given a measuring stick; and the angel stood, saying, "Rise, and measure the Temple of God, and the altar, and those who worship in it. (2) But the court, which is outside the temple, leave out, and do not measure it, for it is given to the nations. They shall trample the holy city under foot forty-two months."*   REVELATION 11:1, 2

The Apostle John wrote the Book of Revelation about the year A.D. 95. This means that the Temple which had been standing in Jerusalem in Christ's day—the so-called "Second Temple"—was non-existent for the twenty-five years preceding John's writing, since the Roman legions under Titus had leveled both the Temple and the Holy City in A.D. 70. What Temple, then, was John referring to? There can be only one answer—a yet-to-be-built structure!

In Daniel 9:27 the Prophet Daniel predicts that the coming Antichrist will make and later break a covenant with the Jewish people of the Tribulation period, allowing them to re-institute animal sacrifices. There is only one place where a God-fearing Jew would venture to offer a sacrifice—in the Temple in Jerusalem!

Since the first writing of this book, amazing archeological discoveries have been made concerning the Temple location. Dr. Asher Kaufman, a professor of physics at Hebrew University, has made the most exciting and important archeological discovery of modern times. From the standpoint of Biblical prophecy, it is one of the most crucial factors in a final alignment of predicted events that will precede the seven-year Tribulation.

Dr. Kaufman, a crack archaeologist, spent 16 years in intensive investigation on the Temple Mount before his findings were made known to the world in the March 1983 *Biblical Archaeology Review*. I am sure that it is not just coincidence that there have been three armed attempts by religious radicals to take over the Temple Mount and at least two attempts to blow up the Dome of the Rock since April 1983.

Although all of the extensive evidence upon which Dr. Kaufman bases his establishment of the Temple foundation's exact location cannot be given here, I am convinced after carefully checking his evidence personally on the Temple Mount that he is absolutely correct.

The most obvious evidence that the golden Dome of the Rock could not be over the Temple site (as had been almost universally believed) is its proximity to the Eastern gate. Every ancient document describing the Temple placed the Eastern gate exactly on the east/west centerline of the Temple itself. The Dome of the Rock is at least 150 meters south of that centerline.

A little domed cupola sitting inconspicuously on the northwest corner of the present Temple platform has turned out to be the most important structure on the Temple Mount. It is called the "Dome of the Tablets" and also the "Dome of the Spirits." It covers one of the only two exposed protrusions of bedrock in the ancient Temple area. This little piece of bedrock is exactly on the east/west centerline of the ancient Eastern gate. This, and many other reasons, has led scholars to believe that this is the actual place within the ancient Holy of Holies where the Ark of the Covenant rested.

Dr. Kaufman has laid out the exact Temple foundation location using other discoveries (such as a cornerstone of the inner court wall and an ancient subterranean water cistern). They all fit exactly with the present archeological discoveries and ancient descriptions of the Temple.

The most electrifying excitement came to me while I was on the Temple Mount checking Dr. Kaufman's measurements with the archaeological artifacts. As I stepped off the location of the Temple and its inner court wall, I discovered that there was a 26-meter clearance from the Dome of the Rock's nearest point. It was at this moment that the Holy Spirit brought to mind Revelation 11:1, 2. I had always wondered why the Spirit of God had put this passage in the Bible about measuring the Temple of God, its altar, and those who worship there—and also why it said not to measure the outer court of the Temple because it was given to the Gentiles. But as I looked at the Dome of the Rock from the line where the inner court wall was built—and will be rebuilt—I realized that the Holy Spirit anticipated the existence of this Moslem mosque and was prophetically previewing that they would both be on the Temple

Mount at the same time. Had the Spirit included in His measurements the outer Temple court, it would have excluded the possibility of the mosque's existence during the Tribulation.

This all means that the Temple could be rebuilt at any time without the destruction of the third-holiest shrine of the Moslem faith—the Dome of the Rock. I believe that the Antichrist and the Israeli False Prophet will so solve the Arab-Israeli conflict (at least for the first three-and-a-half years) that construction of the Temple and the reinstitution of Mosaic animal sacrifice will be permitted.

However, as I have said in other places, the last war of the world will begin because of disputes concerning who owns Old Jerusalem, and especially conflict between Islam and Judaism over the Temple Mount holy places (Zechariah 12:2, 3).

Right after the Six-Day War, Israel Eldad, one of Israel's famous historians, was interviewed by *Time* magazine (June 30, 1967). When he was asked about the possibility of rebuilding the Temple in Jerusalem, he replied, "When the Jewish people took over Jerusalem the first time, under King David, only one generation passed before they built the Temple, and so shall it be with us!"

Arabs would violently react to a Jewish Temple being rebuilt on what they consider "their" sacred spot. I believe this very problem may be the reason for the "strong covenant" which the Prophet Daniel says the Jewish people will make with the Roman Antichrist (Daniel 9:27; Revelation 13:1–10). In return for certain concessions from the Jews, he will guarantee protection for them so that they can rebuild their Temple and reinstate animal sacrifice. The religious Jews will push for this and accept the False Prophet as the Messiah because he helps to secure the rebuilding of the Temple (Revelation 13:11–18).

Present-day believers in Christ will probably not be here when the Temple is rebuilt. It will most likely be started after the Rapture. However, if you should begin to see work start on a new Jewish Temple on Mount Moriah, you'd better finish up your business fast, because things are winding down to a close!

WHAT'S THE POINT OF THE MEASUREMENT?

In Revelation 11:1 the Apostle John was told to measure this future Temple, including its altar and its worshippers. If you will study Ezekiel 40 and Zechariah 2 carefully, you will notice that when God takes measurements it's to evaluate the spiritual condition of His people.

His appraisal of this future Temple therefore determines whether it's truly fulfilling its intended purpose. Unfortunately, it turns out to be an apostate place of worship. Its reconstruction is not based on a recognition of Jesus as the Messiah, but on a nationalistic desire to once again possess a national religious symbol and draw the people back to a belief in their God. Even today a large number of Jews are agnostics, and by then the vast majority may be.

In all its architecture and furnishings the Old Testament Temple prefigured the Person and work of the Messiah. In a sense it was God's "Passion Play," dramatizing to the Jewish people what the Messiah would be like and what He would do when He came into the world. All of the various sacrifices spoke of the Holy One who was to come, picturing Him as a sinless substitute who would take upon Himself man's sin and bear the divine judgment due man, the sinner.

Because the majority of the Jews living during the Tribulation will not have heeded the truth about the Messiah that this Old Testament sacrificial symbolism portrayed, a precise period of judgment by the Gentile nations upon Jerusalem is measured out: "But the court, which is outside the Temple, leave out, and do not measure it, for it is given to the nations. They shall trample the Holy City under foot *forty-two months.*" (Revelation 11:2, *TLB*).

This prophecy of measurement not only speaks of Gentiles and Jews sharing holy places on the Temple Mount, but also predicts the awful last half of the Tribulation.

During this period of forty-two months (equivalent to three and one-half years) Jerusalem will see nothing but war; one Gentile army after another will invade the city of Jerusalem and march up and down its streets. In Luke 21:24 Jesus predicted, "Jerusalem shall be trodden down by the Gentiles until the times of the Gentiles be fulfilled." The "Times of the Gentiles" end with the return of Jesus the Messiah to the earth at the last battle of the Tribulation, the Battle of Armageddon.

TWO JESUS FREAKS WHO SHAKE THE WORLD

(3) But before this I will give power to My two witnesses, and they shall prophesy a thousand two hundred and sixty days, clothed in sackcloth. (4)

These are the two olive trees, and the two lampstands standing before the God of the whole earth. (5) Whenever any man tries to hurt them, fire proceeds out of their mouth, and devours their enemies; and whenever any man tries to hurt them, he must in this manner be killed. (6) These have power to shut up the sky, that it will not rain during the days of their prophecy; and they have power over the waters to turn them to blood, and to smite the earth with all kinds of plagues, as often as they will. REVELATION 11:3–6

The two witnesses that God will raise up at this time will preach so effectively that no one will be able to plead ignorance about the facts of salvation. The truthfulness of the two witnesses will stand in sharp contrast to the hypocrisy of the reconstructed Temple. The two witnesses will make it a point to prove that everything in the Temple has already been fulfilled by Christ, and that this magnificent new building is nothing but a nationalistic sham! As a result the Jewish people will rejoice when the Roman Antichrist kills these two prophets by a great demonstration of Satan's power.

Before God allows the murder of these men, however, they will have preached for 1,260 days. Using the Biblical year of three hundred and sixty days, this comes out to three and one-half years, or the first half of the seven-year Tribulation period. In addition to exposing the falsity of the new Temple and preaching the true way of salvation, the witnesses will identify the new world leader for what he really is—the long-prophesied Antichrist and dictator of the people. The two witnesses will show that his temporary peace will soon give way to the greatest war this world has ever known. This is why the "Beast" (Revelation 11:7) murders them.

IDENTITY OF "WITNESSES"

Now who are these two witnesses really going to be? I believe they will be Moses and Elijah! There are many reasons why, but I'll mention only a few. In Malachi 4:5, 6—God's very last words in the Old Testament—the coming of Elijah is clearly predicted: "Behold, I will send you Elijah, the prophet, before the coming of *the great and dreadful day of the Lord;* and he will turn the hearts of the fathers to their children, and the hearts of the children to their fathers, lest I come and smite the land with a curse."

"The great and dreadful day of the Lord" refers specifically to the last half of the Tribulation period. Note that Elijah will come *before* this time to "turn (restore) the hearts of the fathers to the children and . . . the children to their fathers." In other words, the long-dead Jewish "fathers" or patriarchs (who had believed in the one, true Jehovah) and the presently-apostate "younger generation" would now find mutual harmony in their true Messiah, the Lord Jesus Christ. These two great prophets will turn many Israelis to the truth.

Miracles of Drought and Blood

Notice in Revelation 11:6 that the two witnesses have the power to cause drought by withholding rain (Elijah's most famous Old Testament miracle) and to turn earth's waters into blood (one of Moses' most famous miracles). These two prophets will duplicate their Old Testament miracles during the Tribulation period!

Among all the prophets of the Old Testament era, two were removed from this world before their ministries were finished. Who do you suppose these two men were? They were Moses and Elijah!

Moses was removed prematurely because he disobeyed God at the rock which gave water. Instead of speaking to the rock in a self-controlled voice as God had commanded, he shouted at the people and pounded the rock twice with his staff. God graciously sent the water gushing out anyway, but He had some things to say to Moses.

Here's what God said: "Because you did not believe Me, to set Me apart with reverence before the sons of Israel, therefore you shall not bring this assembly into the land which I have given them" (Numbers 20:12). And Moses never set foot in the Promised Land! (God did allow him, however, to take a good long look at the land from the vantage point of Mount Nebo.) So Moses died with his ministry unfinished.

Elijah was a great Old Testament prophet, too—one of the greatest of all time. He stood up to four hundred leaders of the idolatrous Baal-worship cult and challenged them to a showdown. God answered Elijah with fire and overwhelmed the worshippers of Baal!

But on his way back to the capital city Elijah got a message from the heathen queen, Jezebel. The message was that Elijah would be murdered within twenty-four hours. What do you think the once-courageous prophet did? He ran for his life into the wilderness and asked God to kill him!

When God asked Elijah why he wanted to die, he responded with a "woe-is-me-I'm-being-persecuted" type of answer. Then God repeated His question and Elijah repeated his pessimistic answer.

So God told Elijah, "Elisha, the son of Shaphat . . . you shall anoint to be prophet in your stead" (1 Kings 19:16). A little later God took Elijah to heaven in a whirlwind and chariot of fire. So Elijah's ministry wasn't finished either.

But in the coming Tribulation both Moses and Elijah will get a chance to finish their ministries. The same Moses who couldn't set foot in the Promised Land will stand and preach right in the middle of Jerusalem! The same Elijah who ran from the heathen queen will shake his fist under the nose of the end-time dictator!

A SUDDEN END TO A STRANGE CELEBRATION

(7) When they have finished their testimony, the Beast who ascends out of the bottomless pit will make war against them, and will overcome them, and kill them. (8) And their dead bodies will lie in the street of the great city, which spiritually is called Sodom and Egypt, where also their Lord was crucified. (9) And the people of all the kindreds and tongues and nations shall see their dead bodies three days and a half, and will not permit their dead bodies to be put in graves. (10) Those who dwell upon the earth shall rejoice over them, and make merry, and shall send gifts one to another, because these two prophets tormented those who dwell on the earth. (11) After three days and a half the spirit of life from God entered into them, and they stood upon their feet, and great fear fell upon those who saw them. (12) They heard a great voice from heaven saying to them, "Come up here." And they ascended up to heaven in a cloud while their enemies beheld them. (13) In the same hour there was a great earthquake, and the tenth part of the city fell. The earthquake killed seven thousand men, and the remnant were terrified, and gave glory to the God of heaven. (14) The second woe is past; behold, the third woe comes quickly.   REVELATION 11:7–14

The "Beast that ascends out of the pit" refers to the coming Antichrist, a European who will set up headquarters first in Rome, then later in Jerusalem. While in Jerusalem the Antichrist will hear the preaching of the two witnesses. He'll become so infuriated at their straightforward gospel witness that he will "make war against them" and kill them!

Their bodies will lie in the street of "the great city which spiritually is called Sodom and Egypt, where also our Lord was crucified." This is a derogatory reference to the apostate city of Jerusalem. "Sodom" refers to its immorality and "Egypt" to its worldliness, while the reminder of its crucifixion of Jesus emphasizes its consistent rejection of witnesses.

For three and one-half days ungodly people from every nation on earth will gaze gleefully at the unburied bodies of God's great witnesses.

Some men who wrote commentaries on Revelation a hundred or more years ago used the most interesting arguments to discredit the worldwide viewing of the corpses. One writer questioned the truthfulness of the Book of Revelation by asking, "How can all the people in the world possibly look at the bodies of these men lying in Jerusalem?"

How will so many people be able to view the two corpses? Through Telstar television, of course!

SATANIC "XMAS"

The murder of the witnesses will be followed by a sort of Satanic Christmas celebration. Verse 10 says that people will celebrate and give gifts to each other. It'll be a big bonus day for Santa!

But after three and one-half days the joyride will be over, for all of a sudden the bodies come to life again! Right in front of the dumbfounded onlookers the resurrected men rise up to heaven in a cloud! Then an earthquake strikes the city of Jerusalem and kills seven thousand people. Those who live are terrified, and give glory to the God of heaven (verse 13). Finally many of the Jews in Jerusalem get the point about God and turn in faith to Him.

THE FINAL TRUMPET BLOWS

> *(15) And the seventh angel sounded; and there were great voices in heaven, saying, "The kingdom of this world has become the Kingdom of our Lord, and of His Christ, and He shall reign forever and ever." (16) And the twenty-four Elders, who sat before God on their thrones, fell upon their faces, and worshipped God, (17) Saying, "We give you thanks, O Lord God Almighty, who is, and was, and is to come, because You have taken up Your great power, and have begun to reign. (18) The nations were angry, and Your*

wrath has come, and it is the time to judge the dead, and that You should give rewards to Your servants, the prophets, and to the saints, and those who fear Your name, small and great. It is also time for You to destroy those who destroy the earth."   REVELATION 11:15–18

As the seventh angel sounds his trumpet, signaling the last swift and terrible judgments to begin, the people of God surrounding His throne in heaven can see the long-awaited Kingdom of God about to be established, so they burst into songs of praise.

This longing for a Kingdom of peace and prosperity on earth had been the dearest desire of all the Old Testament believers. It was the primary hope of Judaism, promised in hundreds of passages through their prophets.

The writers of the New Testament promised their readers a union with Christ in *heaven*, but the Old Testament saints were promised a perfectly-restored *earth* where there was peace, justice, and righteousness in the midst of a perfect environment with Messiah ruling over it. One thing we know for sure—God never breaks a promise, and this is one which He definitely plans to fulfill!

A MYSTERY CLEARED UP

It was concerning this Jewish hope of an earthly kingdom that the apostles inquired just before Jesus Christ's ascension: "Lord, will You at this time restore again the Kingdom to Israel?" (Acts 1:6). The apostles didn't realize that the Kingdom promised to Israel had been temporarily postponed until God could call out from among the Gentiles a people who would accept His Messiah and then be eligible to partake of the blessings promised to Israel.

This new people of God, called "the Church," was a mystery in the Old Testament. The apostles didn't seem to fully understand this until in Acts 15 James recalled a prophecy from Amos which showed that God would return to give the Kingdom to Israel at a time *after* Gentiles were brought into His family (see Acts 15:13–19).

TIME FOR REWARDS (VERSE 18)

The believers of the Old Testament and those who become believers during the Tribulation will be resurrected and rewarded at the *end* of the Tribulation, when Jesus returns to the earth as King of Kings. The Church-age believers (that is, those who have believed from the Day of Pentecost until the Rapture) will already be in their new, immortal bodies and will have received their rewards at the Judgment Seat of Christ in heaven sometime soon after the Rapture.

THE HEAVENLY TEMPLE OPENED

> *(19) And the Temple of God was opened in heaven, and there was seen in His Temple the ark of His covenant; and there were lightnings, and voices, and thunderclaps, and an earthquake, and great hail.* REVELATION 11:19

In the Epistle to the Hebrews, a big point is made concerning God's instructions to build everything in the earthly tabernacle according to the exact pattern of the heavenly Temple (Hebrews 8:5). Evidently there is a complete Temple in heaven of which the earthly one was only a replica. In Revelation 11:19 we see this heavenly Temple opened, revealing the ark of God's covenant.

The ark, as you recall, was the main piece of furniture in the Holy of Holies in the tabernacle in the wilderness and later in the Temple in Jerusalem. It had a golden throne on its top, which was the place where the blood of a spotless lamb was sprinkled on the Day of Atonement by the high priest. When this was done, symbolically this throne changed from a throne of judgment to a throne of mercy. It was called "the Mercy-seat." It was here that God met man's need for forgiveness in the Old Testament.

Every believing Jew knew that the ark was where God dealt with their national and personal problem of sin and separation from Him. Their understanding of all this wasn't perfect, but they understood enough to know that this sacrificial provision gave them acceptance and forgiveness with God.

The fact that God opens heaven's Temple and shows the Jews the ark is to remind them that He will be unconditionally faithful to His covenant of forgiveness that He makes with those who will accept the message of His Messiah Jesus.

This great chapter closes with flashes of lightning and violent peals of thunder—a warning to those who reject the Messiah that God's final climactic judgments are on the way.

TWELVE

The Mystery of Anti-Semitism

One of the grimmest recurrences of history has been the continuing irrational hatred and persecution of the Jewish people. Twice these people had their national homeland torn from them; twice they were led as captives into other lands and nations; twice they miraculously survived incomparable persecutions in foreign lands; and twice they miraculously returned to the land of their fathers to reestablish their nation, each time against such opposition that the world stood and watched in amazement.

The Jews' second dispersion from the land of Israel lasted from A.D. 70 to 1948. During that time the Jewish people endured some of the most inhuman treatment ever inflicted in human history, and yet they survived as a distinct race. Virtually every country in which they took refuge ultimately turned against them. From the holocaust of Titus and the Roman legions' destruction of Jerusalem through the Inquisitions and Crusades and on to the gas ovens of the Hitler era, anti-Semitism has kept rekindling into insane flames of hatred and slaughter.

One of the great motion pictures of our times, *Fiddler on the Roof*, shows the dilemma of the Jews in a little village in Russia about seventy-five years ago. What happened there has happened a thousand times in a thousand places to many hundreds of thousands of Jews.

Have you ever wondered why?

I believe this chapter answers the puzzling mystery of anti-Semitism. It shows that anyone who hates and persecutes a Jew is actually doing so at the instigation of a mighty spirit-being who hates all Jews.

As terrible as Jewish harassment has been in the past, anti-Semitism will reach its most feverish pitch during the last three and one-half years of the Tribulation. In Revelation 12 we're introduced to four of the main actors involved in the drama of this awful period of Jewish persecution: (1) the woman, representing Israel, (2) the great red dragon, representing Satan and a final world kingdom which he will control, (3) the male child, referring to Christ, and (4) Michael, representing the angels of God.

Around these main characters revolves the astounding drama of the Great Tribulation.

THE ACTORS ON STAGE

(1) Then there appeared a great wonder in heaven—a woman clothed with the sun, and the moon under her feet, and upon her head a crown of twelve stars. (2) She was with child and cried out with labor pains. (3) There appeared another wonder in heaven; and behold, a great red dragon, having seven heads and ten horns, and seven crowns upon his heads. (4) His tail drew along with him a third of the stars of heaven and cast them to the earth. The dragon stood before the woman who was ready to give birth, to devour her child as soon as it was born. (5) She brought forth a male child, who was to rule all nations with a rod of iron; and her child was caught up to God and to his throne. (6) The woman fled into the wilderness, where she has a place prepared by God, so that they might feed her there a thousand two hundred and sixty days. REVELATION 12:1–6

WHAT A WOMAN!

The key to the unfolding drama of this whole situation is the woman in celestial clothing. She is introduced in verse 1 as a "great wonder" or "great sign." In the original language the word means a miraculous signpost, something that should cause men to see the hand of God in history.

The identity of this "woman" can be partly established by the symbols that make up her unusual clothing.

In his famous prophetic dream, Joseph, the Hebrew patriarch, saw himself as a star shining brightly in the sky (Genesis

37:9, 10). The sun, moon, and eleven stars bowed down in homage to him. His father, Jacob, one of the founders of the Hebrew nation, indignantly pointed out that the dream meant that there would come a time when Joseph's family would bow down to Joseph, since in the dream the sun symbolized his father, Jacob; the moon stood for his mother, Rachel; and the eleven stars represented his eleven brothers.

Eventually Joseph's dream did come true, confirming the symbolizing of his family. Thus we can reason that these symbols of the sun, moon, and stars which the "woman" wears in Revelation 12:1 identify the woman as Israel and her adorning stars as the founders of her race.

The woman is further identified by the fact that she gave birth to a male child who is to rule all the nations with a rod of iron. This can only refer to an undisputed prophecy about the Messiah of Israel found in Psalm 2:9 and mentioned again in Revelation 19:15. It states of Jesus Christ, "He shall rule them with a rod of iron." This refers to Christ's reign on earth over all the nations for 1,000 years. This reign is still in the future and will be discussed more fully in Chapter 20. However, since it's clear that the male child represents the Jewish Messiah (who would of necessity come out of the Hebrew race), the woman who gives birth to this child must symbolically refer to the nation of Israel.

How Is Israel a Sign?

The story is told of Napoleon that one of his generals asked him what he believed to be the greatest miracle of all time. Without hesitation Napoleon answered, "The Jews." There's no question that Israel is one of the greatest phenomena that history has witnessed. What God has done *to* that nation, *for* that nation, and *through* that nation has done more to make men aware of a personal God and how to have a relationship with Him than any other factor in human history.

The Great Red Dragon, Satan

Because of God's selection of this nation to be the physical race through which He would allow His Son to be born into this world, Satan has a special hatred for the "woman" and her "child." In fact, he has a special hatred for *anyone* who loves the woman (Israel) or her child (Jesus Christ). Look at the names of this fiend that appear in Chapter 12. It starts out by calling him a "great red dragon." Everyone knows that the dragon is always the villain in horror stories, and here's where that reputation got started. I think this dragon in Revelation 12 is *red* because he's covered with the blood of all the wars and slaughters of history which he instigated!

The dragon has seven heads and ten horns, and we'll see in detail in following chapters that the many-headed dragon is symbolic not only of the person of Satan, but also of a great future revival of the Roman Empire, which will be made up of seven willing and three reluctant member-nations.

Like a vulture waiting for its prey, the dragon stands before the woman and waits to devour her child. There's no question that this refers to Satan's desire both to prevent the birth of Jesus and to seek to destroy Him after He was born. On several critical occasions in the history of Israel, Satan sought to annihilate the whole race of Jews in order to prevent the Messiah's birth. His final attempt was to inspire Herod, the embodiment of the Roman Empire in Israel, to murder all the baby boys two years and under at just the time of Jesus' birth.

SATAN IS A SNAKE

Another name aptly given to the Devil is "that old serpent." He first got this name in the Garden of Eden, and the connotation is that he's a sly tempter who twists the truth and maligns God and believers every chance he gets.

One of the names which suits Satan best is "the Devil," since this means "slanderer" or "accuser." Verse 10 says that he accuses the believers before God night and day. This is one of his favorite pastimes. I can hear him now at God's throne with his portfolio of accusations: "God, I'm sorry to have to bring this to Your attention, but one of Your children down on earth, Hal Lindsey, just blew it in his Christian life. Knowing how You hate sin, I'm sure You'll want to do something about it right away."

"Lucifer, you Devil, won't you ever give up? I *did* do something about it when I let My Son die on the Cross and take the penalty for Hal's sins. So get lost! You haven't got a case against Hal."

Little children love to recite a ditty which perfectly fits this accusing mania of the Devil: "Sticks and stones may break my bones, but names can never hurt me!" When the Devil can't make any headway at slandering you before God, he gets to working on your conscience and tries to tie you in knots with guilt. It's then that you need to realize that his other name, *Satan*, means that he's a vicious *adversary*, passionately dedicated to doing everything he can to foul up believers. He'll use every dirty trick in the book—lies, deceit, slander, accusation, hypocrisy, temptation, and much more—to neutralize God's children spiritually.

Verse 12 of this chapter explains *why* Satan is in such a frenzy to gain as much ground as he can: "The devil is come down to you, having great wrath, *because he knows that he has but a short time.*"

Misery loves company, and Satan wants as much company as he can get to spend eternity with him in his final place of judgment, the Lake of Fire.

THE IDENTITY OF THE MALE CHILD

As I have pointed out before, the reason for Satan's bitter hatred of Israel is that she was greatly responsible for his undoing. Moses outlined how this would be accomplished when he wrote of God's conversation with the serpent, Satan, in the Garden of Eden. God told the Devil that He was going to put "enmity" (hostility) between the woman's seed (offspring) and Satan's seed, and that the woman's offspring would eventually crush Satan's head (Genesis 3:15).

I don't believe it's mere coincidence that the first prophetic reference to a woman who will bear a child is found in the *first* book of the Bible, and the last reference to a pregnant woman is found in the *last* book of the Bible, and in *both* cases the child is to crush Satan. It seems likely to me that the woman and child in both of these passages are referring to Israel and her offspring, the Messiah Jesus.

The fact that Jesus did, in fact, crush Satan's aspirations of world dominion and seal his eventual doom is evident as you read the New Testament. The writer of Hebrews puts it this way: "He also Himself likewise partook of the same (*flesh and blood*), so that through death He might strip away the authority of the one who was holding the power of death, that is, the Devil" (Hebrews 2:14).

SEATED NOW, REIGNING SOON

The male child, Jesus, is destined to rule all the nations with a rod of iron (absolute authority) and He will do so during those great thousand years of God's kingdom on earth which is not far in the future. The Apostle John tells us in verse 5 that in the meantime the "child" was caught up to God and His throne. This obviously refers to Christ's ascension into heaven after His resurrection to sit at the right hand of God the Father. And that's exactly where we find Him in Revelation 4 and 5— the Lamb upon the throne!

MICHAEL'S WAR IN HEAVEN

(7) And there was war in heaven. Michael and his angels fought against the dragon, and the dragon and his angels fought (8) and did not prevail, neither was their place found anymore in heaven. (9) And the great dragon was cast out, that old serpent, called the Devil and Satan, who deceives the whole world; he was thrown down to the earth along with all his angels. (10) I heard a loud voice saying in heaven, "Now has come salvation, and strength, and the kingdom of our God, and the power of His Christ; for the accuser of our brethren has been cast down, who accused them before our God day and night." REVELATION 12:7–10

Satan is what I call a diehard! Here he is with his boys, making one last attempt to take over heaven. But God has a champion in the person of His archangel, Michael, and even though Jude 9 tells us of a prior dispute between Michael and Satan in which Michael handles him with kid gloves, we don't see any of that in this scene.

Satan and his angels are instead booted out of heaven *to* the earth, and from that point on he is never allowed to come before God again with accusations against God's children or for any other reason.

Since this conflict takes place at the middle of the Tribulation, I hate to think of the fury that Satan will unleash on the earth when he no longer has access to the heavenlies where he and his cohorts have resided since their original fall from heaven's good graces!

For the last three and one-half years of the Tribulation, Satan will have a field day with those still left on earth, both believers and unbelievers. Since he can no longer accuse Christians before the Father, he'll no doubt seek to accuse and torment everyone on earth who has believed in Christ.

THE VICTORY OF THE MARTYRS

> *(11) And they overcame him by the blood of the Lamb, and by the word of their testimony and by not loving their lives to the death. (12) Therefore rejoice, you heavens and all who dwell in them. Woe to the inhabitants of the earth and of the sea! For the Devil has come down to you, having great wrath, because he knows that he has but a short time.*
>
> REVELATION 12:11, 12

In verse 11 we see the secret of how our Tribulation brothers will defeat the Devil and how we ourselves can defeat him daily as he seeks to accuse and torment us.

"They overcome him by the blood of the Lamb. . . ." When you remind Satan about the blood of Jesus he gets an instant mental picture of the Cross, Christ's triumph over death and hell, and of his own bitter dethronement as the god of this world. He knows that we are more than conquerors over him because of Christ who loved us and gave Himself for us (Romans 8:37). The question is: Do *we* know it and live like it's a fact in our own lives? That's going to make the difference between those who *overcome* and those who *are overcome!*

A LIFE THAT WITNESSES

The second weapon believers have for defeating the "dragon's" attacks is the "word of their testimony." The Devil will use every clever device he has to keep us from being willing to share with others what God has done in our lives. A guy who may have been the life of the party and never at a loss for words before he trusted Christ can be intimidated by Satan to clam up like a shell when it comes to witnessing for Christ. Grown men will tremble in front of youngsters when asked to give a word for Jesus. Remember Peter in the Gospel of Mark and the young girl who asked him if he'd been a friend of Jesus; Peter not only denied it but swore at her also! (See Mark 14:69–71.)

Nothing can have a greater impact upon a seeking but unconvinced friend than a life that has been changed for the better by Jesus' inner power. The reason this is such a threat to Satan is that God has chosen to give His children the privilege of bringing men into His kingdom by their testimony—both by what they say and how they live. For this reason nothing gives Satan more pleasure than to foul up a believer's testimony in word and life.

To Die Is Gain

The greatest weapon a believer ultimately has against Satan is that he's prepared for death. The word "martyr" comes straight from the original Greek of the New Testament and means "a witness."

An experience which all Christians should have is to read *Foxe's Book of Martyrs.* It's a factual record of scores of believers who have been martyred for Jesus during the past nineteen centuries. To see how they went to their deaths with songs of praise to God on their lips has been a tremendously strengthening factor in my own life.

In some countries of the world today, believers are still being called on to give their lives for their testimony of Christ. The depth of commitment of Christians who have grown up under the shadow of martyrdom is something to be envied. Many Christian leaders today feel that what the Church desperately needs to purify and strengthen it is severe persecution that will cause men to count the cost of being a disciple of Christ.

Miraculous Protection for Israel

(13) When the dragon saw that he was cast to the earth, he persecuted the woman who gave birth to the male child. (14) And to the woman were given two wings of a great eagle, so that she might fly into the wilderness, into her place, where she is to be nourished for a time, and times, and half a time, from the face of the serpent. (15) And the serpent cast out of his mouth water like a flood after the woman, that he might cause her to be carried away by the flood. (16) But the earth helped the woman, and earth opened its mouth and swallowed up the flood which the dragon cast out of his mouth. (17) And the dragon was angry with the woman, and went to make war with the remnant of her seed, who keep the commandments of God, and have the testimony of Jesus Christ. Revelation 12:13–17

The last half of the Great Tribulation will be a time of unparalleled persecution of Jews. Satan will not only incite men on the earth to hound them, but he and his angels will give special attention to their destruction. He'll be particularly angry over Jews who have finally placed their faith in Jesus as their Messiah.

When this great outpouring of Satanic fury begins, the believing Jews will be reminded of the words of Jesus in Matthew 24:16, 17 where He forewarned those who would be alive at the time of the "abomination of desolation" to flee to the mountains, not even stopping to go back into their houses for their coats.

WHAT IS THE ABOMINATION?

During the Tribulation Satan will control a man who will rule the whole world and be known as the Roman Antichrist. When this man signs a covenant with the Jews allowing them to rebuild their Temple and reinstate worship and sacrifice, it will officially begin the seven years of tribulation.

He'll pretend to be a great friend of Israel for the first three and one-half years of the Tribulation, but then he'll turn on them at the time Satan is cast out of heaven. I believe *that* will be the point when Satan personally indwells the Antichrist. Since Satan does not have the powers of omnipresence and can only be in one place at a time (now that he is confined to earth by divine decree), he makes himself visible by clothing himself with the humanity of the Antichrist.

Satan has always wanted to be worshipped as God (read Isaiah 14), and now is his big chance. The Antichrist enters the newly-rebuilt Jewish Temple, places a statue of himself there in the Holy of Holies, and proclaims himself to be God. From that point on he demands that all people worship him and his statue. This is the ultimate sacrilege which could happen to the nation of Israel, and it was predicted by the prophet Daniel (Daniel 9:27; 12:11) and Jesus Himself (Matthew 24:15). In Jewish terminology this is what is called "the abomination of desolation."

When this happens there will no doubt be many Jews who will have their eyes opened and see that this Antichrist is evil and that his companion, the False Prophet, is *not* Messiah. These

Jews will then turn in faith to God's Messiah, Jesus, and when they do, they become the special objects of the Antichrist's wrath.

AN AIRLIFT CALLED "EAGLE"

"Two wings of the great eagle" are provided to fly this group of Jewish believers to a protective place in the wilderness. Many Bible scholars believe that this will be the natural fortress of Petra, the ancient "City of Rock" in the Jordanian wilderness south of the Dead Sea.

Some kind of a massive airlift will rapidly transport these fleeing Jews across the rugged terrain to their place of protection. Since the eagle is the national symbol of the United States, it's possible that the airlift will be made available by aircraft from the U.S. Sixth Fleet in the Mediterranean.

The Antichrist isn't going to stand for these Jewish believers getting out from under his dominion, and so he will send a flood of pursuers after them. These will probably be soldiers from the armies controlled by the Antichrist. As this great army seeks to trap and annihilate the believers, God will cause the earth to open and swallow them.

When the Antichrist realizes he has been checkmated there, he will inspire the unbelievers to hunt and try to kill everyone who has believed in Christ. He'll probably convince them that the believers are the reason for their present misery.

Thank God there will be a numberless multitude who will choose to die for their faith rather than worship the Roman dictator!

These won't be hurt by "the second death," but will live forever with God!

THIRTEEN

The Two Antichrists

"The streets of our country are in turmoil; the universities are filled with students rebelling and rioting; Communists are seeking to destroy our country, and the Republic is in danger—yes, danger from within and without. We need law and order! Without law and order our nation cannot survive!"

Who do you think uttered these words? An irate congressman? The mayor of a midwest farming community? A public-spirited citizen?

It was none of these. The words were spoken in 1932 by Adolf Hitler!

Dictators rarely take over nations by brute force. Almost always political or economic problems pave the way for tyranny. Even the notorious Roman Empire did not exercise dictatorial authority in its early years. The nations it conquered were customarily ruled by local dignitaries. Only the later Caesars played God over the people. How did the Roman Empire get started? What led to the ultimate outrage of Caesar-worship.

How Caesars Became "Gods"

When the Roman Empire first started taking over countries, the conquered people felt indebted to Rome for the law and order which it provided. The smaller countries in particular were grateful for the newfound stability which replaced their once-shaky political structures. In a number of cases, obnoxious little tyrants were replaced by temperate Roman rulers. So the people were happy.

In Asia Minor especially, the people became so enthusiastic about the Roman Empire that they came to regard it as an object of veneration. But, as historian Arnold Toynbee wisely pointed out, it's hard to worship an impersonal system! Eventually, therefore, the Roman subjects conceived the idea of emperor-worship. The first actual case of emperor-worship on record took place in Pergamum in 29 B.C. Here the local citizens erected the first known statue of a Roman Caesar.

But full-blown Caesar-worship took a number of years to develop. The first Caesars to be worshipped were actually somewhat embarrassed by all the public attention. Later Caesars, however, came to realize the important advantages of accepting public veneration. The first Roman Empire extended into the entire known world of the time, embracing dozens of cultures, languages, and religions. What the Roman senate was looking for was some strong unifying principle—something that would bind the entire Empire together. The mandating of Caesar-worship seemed to be the answer.

So late in the first century A.D. the worshipping of Caesar (whichever one happened to be ruling at the time!) became an official government requirement. At first the edict wasn't taken very seriously, but later, under Domitian, every Roman subject was expected to comply with the order. Once a year each person had to appear before an official "priest" and swear allegiance to Caesar. The oath would be witnessed by a signed certificate and would also often be accompanied by an animal sacrifice.

CAESAR-WORSHIP GOT OUT OF HAND

The Caesar-worship that was once kind of an inside joke among the government leaders was now turning into a Frankenstein monster. Nero came to believe that he actually *was* God in the flesh. Other Caesars had self-delusions almost as strong as Nero's. The whole episode turned out to be a nightmare for the Christians and Jews.

For most of the subjects of Rome, Caesar-worship was nothing more than an annoyance. In some cases it simply added another "god" to their list of deities. But for the Christians the picture was entirely different. No true Christian can acknowledge any Lord except one: the Lord Jesus Christ. So these early Christians refused to swear allegiance to Caesar, and instead quoted a little chant: "Jesus Christ is Lord, and none other."

In no time at all the believers were labeled as traitors. Soon the Romans invented a clever way to dispose of these "traitors to the Empire"—feed them to the lions! And so the Coliseum games began to feature half-time shows of lion feedings, with whole families of devoted believers as "one-time guest stars!" It's really a sickening tale of disgrace for the Romans. The blood ran so freely that to this day the floor of the Coliseum is stained with the blood of the saints.

THE LESSON LEARNED FROM THE CAESARS

Now remember how all this got started: nations in political or economic turmoil succumbed to the seemingly benevolent tentacles of Rome. For awhile there was unprecedented peace, justice, and order. The leader of this "domestic tranquility" came to be deified by many of the people. Then the leader took the veneration of his subjects to heart and proclaimed himself as the absolute and infallible monarch of the world.

Nazi Germany replayed the drama of dictatorship in the '30's and '40's.

In 1930 Germany was in desperate financial straits. Inflation was so severe that thousands of people were virtually starving. The Communists stirred up riots in the streets and created pandemonium in the universities. No one seemed able to create order out of the confusion. Germany was on the verge of collapse.

Then Adolf Hitler appeared. Suddenly a voice of authority spoke in the midst of chaos. With impassioned fury he proclaimed the glory of the nation of destiny. He wept as he rehearsed the past glories of the nation, and shouted as he promised the glories to come. Once again Germany would rule the world! The Roman Empire would live again, and Hitler would be its king!

The people acclaimed Hitler with shouts of joy: "Heil Hitler!" rang in the streets. Here indeed stood the super-leader of all time! Even true Christians plunged into the maelstrom of public acclamation. It has been said that as many as eighty percent of the evangelical believers in Germany voted for Hitler during the '30's! Not long ago I talked with an intelligent German woman who had grown to adulthood during Hitler's rise to power. Not until the middle of World War II did this devout Christian lady realize that Hitler was something less than a God-sent savior of the German nation!

Actually Adolf Hitler *was* something of a savior at first. The rioting stopped, men started working, people started eating, and Ferdinand Porsche designed the first Volkswagen! Most important of all, every citizen had a new sense of national purpose and pride. *Now* their new Fuhrer would lead them into the millennium of the Third Reich!

MANKIND NEVER LEARNS!

What a tragic way to relearn world history. The sad truth is, as Hegel said, "History teaches us that man learns nothing from history."

Adolf Hitler was but a "choir boy" when compared with the dictator that will take over the world during the Tribulation. I believe that this very man lives right now somewhere in Europe, inflaming his soul with visions of what he will be able to do for mankind with all his grand schemes and revolutionary ideas.

A biographical sketch of this man appears in this chapter. He's called by various names throughout the Bible. Here are just a few: *King of Babylon* (Isaiah 14:4); *Little Horn* (Daniel 7:8; 8:9); *Man of Sin, Son of Perdition* (2 Thessalonians 2:3); *Antichrist* (1 John 2:18); *Beast* (Revelation 13:1).

He will be a supreme humanist, believing passionately that man can solve his own dilemmas. He will not accept the Bible's evaluation that man is on the verge of chaos because of sin. In fact, he'll no doubt react violently to groups and individuals who analyze man's problem as sin. He'll feel that he is doing a good thing by bringing repressive measures against believers, whom he will consider "non-progressives." This Antichrist will be against every solution the Bible presents for the world's problems, and because he'll be so persuasive he'll turn the whole world against Christ and the believers and convince everyone that *he* has the answers to the human dilemma.

IS ANTICHRIST NEAR?

Chapter 13 of Revelation hints at the answer to the intriguing question, "Is the time ripe for the appearance of the Antichrist?" I believe that the present worldwide economic, political, and social disturbances will boil over into an unmanageable mess which will culminate during the rapidly approaching Tribulation period. Then the frantic populace will race to proclaim this powerful, smooth-talking peacemaker who will head the European Economic Community as the savior of the world.

One of the key factors that will set up the world for accepting the powers and supernatural aura of the Antichrist is the world's unprecedented acceptance of the occult and supernatural. Twenty years ago, if someone had appeared on the scene doing the supernatural things the Antichrist will do, he would have been thrown into jail or a mental institution. But now universities, governments, and think tanks are teaching people how to perform supernatural feats and make contact with beings from other realms.

Listen to this 1984 interview that *U.S News and World Report* had with Keith Harary, an experimental psychologist and co-author of the book *The Mind Race: Understanding and Using Psychic Abilities*. Harary, who spent the last decade researching the subject for Duke University and a prominent think tank, was quoted as saying, "The U.S. government is interested in psychic research and for more than a decade has been sponsoring a multimillion-dollar research program at SRI International, a West Coast think tank. Beyond that, I can't comment or speculate on Defense Department involvement in this field. I can say, however, that the Soviet Union is interested in psychic research. The Soviets take it very seriously at the highest levels—no doubt about it. My co-author, Russell Targ, and I have visited their remote-viewing laboratory in Soviet Armenia, and it appears the Soviets are also pursuing their interest in the theoretical possibility of behavior manipulation from a distance."

Sounds like one of the powers the Antichrist will exhibit!

THE ROMAN ANTICHRIST

(1) Then I stood upon the sand of the sea, and saw a Beast rise up out of the sea, having seven heads and ten horns, and upon his horns ten crowns,

and upon his heads the name of blasphemy. (2) The Beast which I saw was like a leopard, and his feet were like the feet of a bear, and his mouth like the mouth of a lion; and the dragon gave him his power, and his seat (throne), and great authority.

(3) I saw one of his heads as though it were mortally wounded; and his mortal wound was healed, and all the world wondered after the beast. (4) And they worshipped the dragon who gave power to the Beast; and they worshipped the Beast, saying, "Who is like the Beast? Who is able to make war with him?"

(5) There was given to him a mouth speaking great things and blasphemies, and power was given to him to continue forty and two months. (6) And he opened his mouth in blasphemy against God, to blaspheme his name, and his tabernacle, and those who dwell in heaven. (7) And it was given to him to make war with the saints, and to overcome them; and power was given him over all kindreds, and tongues, and nations. (8) And all who dwell upon the earth shall worship him, whose names are not written in the Book of Life of the Lamb slain from the foundation of the world.

(9) If anyone has an ear, let him hear. (10) He who leads into captivity shall go into captivity; he who kills with the sword must be killed with the sword. In this is the patience and the faith of the saints.
REVELATION 13:1–10

The Antichrist is called a "beast" because that's what he is in the sight of God—a ruthless, unfeeling dictator. His true, ruthless nature is exposed in wide-screen horror in the latter part of the Tribulation period, even though at the beginning he appears to be the most wonderfully benevolent leader of all time.

Now why does the Beast emerge from the sea? John explains the figure in Revelation 17:15. "The waters which you saw . . . are peoples and multitudes and nations and tongues." In Biblical usage the ocean pictures the restless strivings of the nations of the world. As Isaiah put it, "The wicked are like the troubled sea, when it cannot rest, whose waters cast up mire and dirt" (Isaiah 57:20). It's from this chaos of the nations that the Antichrist will rise.

HORNS, HEADS, AND CROWNS

What do the ten horns with crowns represent? In Biblical symbology horns almost always represent political power. In this case the Beast's ten horns picture ten nations that will form a confederacy which the beast will rule during the Tribulation. Daniel elaborates on this in Daniel 7 and 8.

The symbolism in Daniel's prophecies is rather elaborate, but the point he makes is that four successive world empires would rise and fall (Babylon, Medo-Persia, Greece, and Rome). Then, when God is about to climax world history on this planet, ten nations will emerge from the ancient people and culture of the fourth empire, Rome, and will form a tight confederation that will become a sovereign political entity.

At this point a scintillating personality will rise to world prominence and be proclaimed the head of this nation. Of the ten nations that confederate, seven will acquiesce willingly, but three will have to be brought into the union unwillingly. This will be accomplished by the Roman leader, who thereafter becomes a virtual dictator.

KEEP YOUR EYE ON EUROPE

One of the reasons I'm convinced we're living in the closing days of the world's history is because of the emergence of the European Common Market, also known as the European Economic Community. There is no doubt in my mind that it's the forerunner of the Revived Roman Empire which the prophet Daniel spoke about with such certainty. He predicted that the number of nations in it would be limited to ten. This is the very number which the Common Market has set as its goal for inner membership!

Daniel also said that this confederacy would be the greatest Gentile power to ever gain control of the whole world, and that it would acquire this worldwide control through its economic strength and its great leader. As of now, Europe has become the largest trading block in the world, and this is beginning to cause some alarm in the United States.

President Nixon expressed this concern in his February 1971 "State of the World" message: "For years . . . it was believed uncritically that a unified Western Europe would automatically lift burdens from the shoulders of the United States. The truth is not so simple. European unity will also pose problems for American policy which it would be idle to ignore."

In order for there to be an emergence of the superpower in Europe which the Apostle John and Daniel the prophet predicted, there must be a decline in American economic status in the world. Many world economists believe this is already happening, as evidenced by the devaluation of the American dollar and the growing prominence of Europe and Japan in the world markets.

What's happening in Europe today is not simply a cooperation of nations for economic relief. The European Economic Community is a full political union, with its own elected parliament, president, court, and economic system (called the European Monetary System). The EEC originally began in 1958 with six member nations, and now has grown to ten! All the nations which are EEC members were once part of the Roman Empire. The original six—Germany, France, Italy, Belgium, Luxembourg, and the Netherlands—have added the memberships of Britain, Ireland, Denmark, and Greece. The EMS is now five years old and awaiting the birth of its counterpart—a European central bank (which has been proposed but not yet established).

However, all of these actions show the strength with which the EEC has moved toward true unification of the continent and nations—a goal long sought throughout history. Included in this are two more significant developments. First, the trauma and debate in 1983 on placing U.S. Pershing and cruise missiles on European soil to offset Soviet aggression in the form of SS-20s gave rise to the cry from both sides of the Atlantic that Europe alone must be prepared to defend itself. Said European Parliament President Pieter Denkert, "The interests and objectives of the United States and the Western European countries are increasingly diverging. The sheer number of disputes between the United States and Western Europe has gradually eroded . . . mutual respect and confidence." This debate on the Euromissiles is still going in 1984 in the Netherlands, where, at the time of this writing, the government has decided to delay those missiles. Some had predicted the fall of the Dutch government if they had gone ahead with the deployment. With this decision, however, it may well be that we are witnessing the beginning of the end for NATO (North Atlantic Treaty Organization). If so, this would force Europeans to start banding together more, under the EEC's umbrella, in order to defend the continent from the ever-present and growing threat of Soviet aggression.

The second significant event for the EEC happened in early 1984 when Britain—under Prime Minister Margaret Thatcher's stubbornness—refused to compromise on reducing its contribution to the EEC budget. That led to fears of bankruptcy for the organization. Although the matter has not been resolved as yet, a summit meeting of the ten leaders is scheduled to take place, and I believe a compromise will be found to keep the EEC moving forward. Heads of state were revealing in their comments on the crisis. French President Francois Mitterrand answered critics sounding the EEC's funeral knell with, "We will start again. The Europe of the Ten isn't dead." West German Chancellor Helmut Kohl echoed that feeling by saying that despite the current setback he saw no alternative for his country's future except as a member of the EEC.

Perhaps unintentionally revealing in his analysis of the situation, Robert Bowie, a foreign affairs expert for Harvard Univerity, had this to say about the crisis. "Settling these disputed issues will keep the community afloat. But alone, that will not produce the necessary new initiatives. They will require political commitment and leadership which have been lacking. . . . Margaret Thatcher appears to be a little Englander at heart. . . ."

The one who will provide this political leadership and appear to be a peacemaker among all the nations with only the good of Europe at heart will be the Antichrist!

It is extremely important to note here that while there are ten nations in the EEC in 1984, applications for membership by Spain and Portugal are pending. However, that is not to say that the EEC can't undergo superficial changes such as this, including the possible expulsion of Britain as a means of settling the community's latest crisis. But once the confederacy includes the ten nations of God's choosing, the group will begin to look for a leader powerful enough to make this new nation the nucleus of a one-world government.

ONE-WORLD GOVERNMENT COMING

That the world is moving toward a one-world government is no longer being disputed by many knowledgeable men today. In an article in the *Honolulu Advertiser* of July 17, 1972, Dr. Saul Mendlovitz, professor of international law at Rutgers University, said, "It is no longer a question of whether or not there will be a world government by the year 2000. My own indication is that we are moving very rapidly toward this state."

Dr. Mendlovitz went on to say that there was a strong possibility of a complete and violent breakdown of world civilization by the year 2000, and that the most likely kind of government would involve the formation of an oligarchical and repressive world government run by technocratic elites.

A "technocratic elite" is an accurate description of this predicted world leader referred to by the Apostle John as the Beast. He will have a political genius that would have made him the envy of every great political giant of history.

By reconstructing a world government out of the ruins of the ancient Roman Empire, the Antichrist will have accomplished what no one else has been able to do since A.D. 476, the year the Roman Empire officially died. Charlemagne tried to put it together but failed. Napoleon did his best, but met his Waterloo! Bismarck dreamed of making Germany the capital of revived Rome, and did succeed in defeating France.

Then Hitler came along. He envisioned the Mediterranean Sea as a German lake and the whole world as his empire. He saw himself as the caesar of the third Roman Empire—the "Third Reich." His efforts resulted in the downfall of his own nation.

So fruitless were the efforts of men to reconstruct the Roman Empire that poets wrote sonnets about the futility of it all! Believe it or not, the children's nursery rhyme *Humpty Dumpty* was originally written about the fallen Roman Empire and all of the attempts to put it back together again.

A Strange-Looking Beast

In Revelation 13:2 the Antichrist-Beast is compared with a leopard, a bear, and a lion. He will, in other words, combine the distinguishing features of the three prominent world empires of the past which characterize these animals. The ancient Greek Empire struck its foes like a leopard. In no time at all one foe after another caved in to the brilliant attacks of Alexander the Great. The entire mighty empire of Medo-Persians fell to Alexander in a matter of two and one-half years! But the coming Antichrist will outperform Alexander the

Great. In a matter of *weeks* he will take over the ten-nation European confederacy and eventually subjugate the whole world to himself.

During its prime the Medo-Persian Empire was like a powerful, deliberate bear. The raw power of its ponderous army was almost unstoppable. Whatever nations the Medo-Persians attacked, they conquered. That's the way it will be with the Antichrist. During the first part of the Tribulation his satanic backing will assure him eventual domination of the whole world population without a fight.

The Babylonian Empire was famous for its regal splendor. Most of the ancient wonders of the world were conceived and constructed by the monarchs of this era.

Like the lion, the king of beasts, the Antichrist will outdo even the ancient Babylonian Empire with his bag of royal tricks! First he "rises from the dead" by means of the healing of a mortal head wound, then he takes over Europe and the world in a brilliant political and religious coup.

After that he uses Satan's super-human wisdom to solve (temporarily) earth's overwhelming crises—poverty, hunger, and war. For a year or two the world will revel in peace and prosperity! No wonder people will worship the Beast!

ANTICHRIST'S MORTAL WOUND HEALED

As brilliant as he is, notice where the Antichrist gets his power: "The dragon gave him his power and his seat (throne), and great authority" (Revelation 13:2). During the last half of the Tribulation, God will allow Satan to give the Antichrist tremendous supernatural ability. So great will be the Antichrist's influence over people that every "tribe and people and tongue and nation" will yield to his sway. For the first time in the history of the world Satan will get what he's been after all these years—the worldwide worship of earth's people!

He will gain this popularity either by performing a fantastic miracle or by simulating one which will fool the people into thinking it was real. In verse 3 John says that he saw one of the Beast's heads *as if* it had been killed. When this apparently mortal head wound is somehow miraculously healed by Satan, the whole world will follow after the Beast in amazement.

Once the Antichrist has the allegiance of the people, his

facade of peace and prosperity evaporates. For three and one-half years he blasphemes God and His worshippers, ultimately killing a great many of the Tribulation saints because these loyal believers are the only fly in Satan's ointment and the only resistance to his unanimous acclaim.

LAMB'S BOOK OF LIFE

In verse 8 John speaks of a book called "the Book of Life of the Lamb." In this book are written the names of every person who ever lived on the face of the earth. When a person rejects Jesus Christ as Savior, and God knows that he will *never* change his mind, that man's name is blotted out of the Book of Life. Those whose names are no longer in God's book will be the ones who will worship Antichrist.

Satan will be so furious with those whose names are still in the Book of Life because they've trusted in Christ that he'll stimulate the Antichrist to wage a war of attrition on them. By one means or another all over the world, believers will have to suffer or die for their faith (verse10). They won't resist, but will submit willingly just like the thousands of martyrs before them.

ANTICHRIST'S PAL, THE FALSE PROPHET

(11) As I looked, another beast came up out of the earth. He had two horns like a lamb, but he spoke like a dragon. (12) He exercises all the power of the first Beast before him, and causes the earth and those who dwell on it to worship the first Beast, whose mortal wound was healed. (13) He performs great wonders, so that he makes fire come down from heaven on the earth in the sight of men. (14) He deceives those who dwell on the earth by means of those miracles which he had power to do in the sight of the Beast, saying to those who dwell on the earth, that they should make an image to the Beast, who had the wound by a sword, and yet lived. (15) He has power to give life to the image of the Beast, so that the image of the Beast can both speak, and cause as many as will not worship the image of the Beast to be killed. (16) He will cause all, both small and great, rich and poor, free and enslaved, to receive a mark in their right hand, or in their foreheads.

(17) And no man can buy or sell unless he has the mark, or the name of the Beast, or the number of his name. (18) Here is wisdom. Let the one who has understanding count the number of the Beast; for it is the number of a man; and his number is six hundred and sixty-six.

REVELATION 13:11–18

Despite the merciless, sweeping tyranny of the first beast

(the Roman Antichrist), Satan will not be content to stop there. He'll raise up a conspirator who is an even more ruthless tyrant because he will enslave the *minds* and *souls* of men.

Basically the second Beast will be similar to the first one. The Greek word translated "another" in verse 11 specifically means *another of the same kind*. He will have the same scintillating personality, the same tireless dynamism, the same oratorical finesse as the first Beast. He will also have the same Satanic powers.

But there will be some differences too. While the first Beast emerged from the sea (the unrest of troubled nations), the second beast emerges from the *land*. ("Earth" in verse 11 could just as well be translated "land.") When the Bible uses the word "land" symbolically, it usually refers to the land that belongs to Israel. So the second beast will come from the region of the Middle East, and I believe he will be a Jew.

A RELIGIOUS BEAST

Like the first Beast, the second one wears horns. However, the second beast has only two *uncrowned* horns (not ten *crowned* ones, as the first Antichrist). What kind of power do these two horns symbolize? Not political, since the ten federated governments of the Tribulation are pictured by the ten *crowned* horns of the first Beast and crowns symbolize political kingdoms.

The second Beast wields *religious* power, and for that reason he is also called "the False Prophet." He'll amalgamate all religious systems into one counterfeit one. His two horns are *like* a lamb, showing that this personage will try to imitate the real Lamb, Jesus Christ.

Millions of people will fall for his deception and the movement toward a Gentile and Jewish messiah. Already the World Council of Churches is hard at work merging various religions and denominations together. And its U.S. counterpart, the National Council of Churches, as I mentioned previously, has already done its bit to help in this deception with its "nonsexist" lectionary of Bible studies. Through the denegation of our Lord's title "Son of God" to "Child of God," the NCC has brought more confusion and disrepute on the Bible, and more blasphemy into the Christian church, than the world has witnessed in quite some time. By the time the Beast tackles the project, liberal

Judaism (which is now ordaining women as rabbis) will probably be ready to join the merger too, since any true doctrine about Jesus Christ and the role of the rabbinate will have disappeared.

AN UNHOLY TRINITY

When the religious merger is complete, Satan will have accomplished one of the most fiendish deceptions of all times—a blasphemous imitation of the triune God!

The first Beast will proclaim himself *God.*

The second Beast will masquerade as the *Messiah.*

The liberated demons (Revelation 16:13, 14) will imitate the power of the *Holy Spirit!*

What a test for the discernment of the believers!

Though the False Prophet is a *religious* specialist, he'll have just as much power as the first Beast. Here are seven things that the False Prophet does:

(1) He exercises unlimited authority (verse 12).

(2) He forces people to worship the Roman Antichrist (verse 12).

(3) He performs great miracles (verse 13).

(4) He deceives the population (verse 14).

(5) He forces people to worship the Antichrist's image in the Temple (verse 14).

(6) He murders all nonconformists (verse 15).

(7) He forces people to receive "the mark of the Beast" (verse 16).

THE GREAT COUNTERFEITER

What kind of "great miracles" does the False Prophet perform? An example is given in verse 13. Through Satanic power he makes fire streak from the sky to the earth in the sight of astonished onlookers. Through this and other spectacular miracles the False Prophet will convince most men that he is the God-sent Messiah. Satan knows all too well what kind of showmanship will impress the curious crowds!

That's why we have to be extra alert in our present generation. We're seeing more and more "miracles" all around us, but not everything that is miraculous is from God. Read Merrill

Unger's book, *The Mystery of Bishop Pike* (Tyndale), and you'll
see documented evidence of supernatural phenomena by demons.

The increase in demonic miracles is just another sign of the
approach of the Rapture and Tribulation. People have been
anticipating the Rapture for so many years that it's hard to
believe we could actually be the generation that witnesses it,
but prophetic events are falling together so fast that we have
to heed what Christ Himself said: "When you see all these things
beginning to happen, you can know that my return is near,
even at the doors" (Matthew 24:33, *TLB*).

THE MARK OF THE BEAST

In verse 15 the False Prophet gives life to the image of the
first Beast, the Roman Antichrist. Then he forces people to worship the image under penalty of death! Where do you suppose
the image will be erected? Right in the middle of the reconstructed Temple! This desecration as noted in the previous
chapter is what Daniel meant when he predicted "the abomination of desolation" in Daniel 9:27 and 12:11.

The False Prophet will perfect a way to expose everyone
who believes in Jesus Christ. All Beast-worshippers will be
compelled to receive a distinguishing mark (perhaps a tattoo
visible only under ultraviolet light) on their right hand or their
forehead. Everyone who refuses the mark will be cut off from
economic survival. They will be forbidden to buy or sell anything.

NUMBERED FROM BIRTH TO DEATH

As farfetched as this may sound, the U.S. government may
right at this moment be inadvertently setting up the system by
which this monstrous outrage will be committed. Along with
the governments of France, Holland, and Norway, the U.S. is
testing what is known as the "Smart Card." This plastic credit
card contains a microchip feature which allows the card to retain and sort information. The cardholder, of course, has a secret code number to activate the card, which carries a "memory"
of past financial transactions and the sum of the person's account. Amazingly, France, according to *U.S. News and World*

Report, is testing the cards "for use as children's portable school records and for storage of vaccination and other personal health information." West Germany may be the next nation to try out the Smart Card.

In an article on the Smart card entitled "Your Life May Be Sandwiched in a Card," the Commercial Appeal of Memphis, Tennessee, stated, "It may well be the ultimate transaction vehicle of our consuming world. It could bring about the much-discussed cashless, paperless society. . . . And it may also end up as a national identification card—a prospect that chills many. . . ." The article pointed out the various functions the card could be used for, including:

—crediting and debiting
—all other banking functions
—computer data access
—medical information
—telephone access
—passport use
—Social Security information
—identification purposes
—security access.

The article stated that the cards would probably be extensively used throughout the U.S. by 1986!

Meanwhile, the Defense Department is eyeing the card for its security value. In seeking to think through all the possible problems that could arise from this, one of the first considerations has been the problem of theft of your card or loss of it in some other manner. Since your whole financial and personal history might be wrapped up in your card, a thief or spy could wipe you out overnight. The Apostle John says that the Antichrist will require everyone to have an identifying mark on either his forehead or right hand. Strangely enough, that is the same solution that's being talked about by some who have been wrestling with this problem for a decade. There's no way to lose your number or have your identification subverted if it's tattooed on you!

THE 'HIGH PRICE' OF THE NUMBER

What will happen to the millions of people who succumb to the False Prophet's threats and receive the Beast's number?

John gives us the answer: "If any man worships the Beast and his image, and receives his mark in his forehead, or in his hand, the same shall drink of the wine of the wrath of God, which is poured out without mixture into the cup of His indignation; and he shall be tormented with fire and brimstone in the presence of the holy angels, and in the presence of the Lamb" (Revelation 14:9, 10).

The number of the Roman Beast is 666. Down through the years Bible expositors have tried to figure out exactly what this means, but it's really no big mystery. Since the number 6 in the Bible stands for humanity, I believe the meaning of 666 is man trying to imitate the trinity of God (three sixes in one person). Anyone who acknowledges this blasphemous trinity by worshipping the 666 Beast will be separated *forever* from the true triune God.

FOURTEEN

To Believe Or Not To Believe — The Options

Revelation 14 is a sort of prophetic cameo—a series of short scenes that will take place toward the end the Tribulation. The theme that binds all the scenes together is Christ's ultimate truimph over all the forces of evil that run rampant during the Tribulation. This chapter reminds us that all of Satan's viciousness is strictly limited by what God will allow. Revelation 12 gave us a picture of Satan's fury toward the earth as he was cast down onto it from heaven. The diabolical maneuverings of the two Antichrists was the theme of Chapter 13. But Chapter 14 presents a refreshing interlude in the outpouring of divine judgment upon fallen man.

Here we have the adoration of the Lamb by his "sheep" on the pasture of Mount Zion; the pastoral calm of the scene provides welcome relief to the flashes of lightning and thunder which accompanied the angry judgments of God in prior chapters.

THE LAMB ON MOUNT ZION

(1) Then I looked and saw a Lamb standing on Mount Zion, and with Him one hundred and forty-four thousand, having His Father's name written on their foreheads. (2) I heard a voice from heaven, like the voice of many waters, and like the voice of a great thunder; and I heard the sound of

harpers playing on their harps. (3) And they sang, as it were, a new song before the throne, and before the four Living Beings and the Elders; and no man could learn that song but the hundred and forty-four thousand, who were redeemed from the earth. (4) These are they who were not defiled with women; for they are virgins. These are the ones who follow the Lamb wherever He goes. These were redeemed from among men, the first fruits for God and to the Lamb. (5) In their mouth no guile was found, for they are without fault before the throne of God.   REVELATION 14:1–5

Revelation 14 reminds us that there will be a large group of people who never gave in to the persuasions of the Beast. Among these are the 144,000 converted Jewish evangelists, first mentioned in Chapter 7. Because Christ gives them superhuman insight, they are able to recognize the personal magnetism and miracles of the two Beasts for what they really are—frauds from the Devil himself.

INDESTRUCTIBLE MEN

These 144,000 will be miraculously preserved by Christ through all seven years of the Tribulation period. This is a first-magnitude miracle, since more than half the earth's population, including many thousands of the evangelists' converts, will be wiped out during the horrors of the Tribulation period. The 144,000 evangelists will all be hunted men because of their refusal to bow to the Antichrist.

So persecuted will these evangelists be that they will have to depend on their converts to provide for their everyday needs. They'll be unable to buy or sell, they'll be unclothed and hungry, they'll be sick and imprisoned. When Christ judges the people still alive at the end of the Tribulation period, He will assign them to eternal life or eternal death on the basis of their treatment of His 144,000 evangelists, since that will reflect their attitude toward Christ Himself (Matthew 25:31-46).

A NEW SONG IN THE GLOOM

Verse 3 tells us that these 144,000 Jews will sing a new song before the throne of God and the Elders. (Remember that the Elders represent believers who lived during our age, the Church age.) No one could learn that song but the 144,000 because it's a joyous testimony of the miraculous and preserving grace of God through the horrors of the Tribulation. This song will be a hymn of praise to the mighty sustaining power of God for believers in times of great trial.

I have talked with Christians in many parts of the world, but there's something really different about a Christian who has gone through tremendous trials of life. A person like this is very grateful to God for holding him up during his testing, and radiates a joy that you just don't find in most other Christians. These joyful believers are able to share a message which really encourages you!

These 144,000 converted Jewish evanglists will sing an absolutely unique song, for they will have endured and been delivered through tribulation never before known to man.

Today we can experience something of the delivering power that these Jews will know because we're all called upon to go through tests in our daily living; God allows pressures, trial, and troubles to enter each one of our lives. It isn't always something we've brought on ourselves either—remember how much suffering Jesus had to endure!

The real reason our sovereign God allows unexplainable problems to come into our lives is to teach us to trust *Him* rather than ourselves. No doubt the favorite Scripture verse of the Tribulation believers will be, "*We* know that all things work together for good to those who love God . . . who are called according to His purpose" (Romans 8:28).

GOD'S VIRGINS

"These are they who were not defiled with women, for they are virgins (celibates)" (verse 4). Since a celibate is one who has taken a vow never to marry, it might almost seem as though God has something against marriage. However, most Bible commentators agree that the celibacy of these men refers not so much to *sexual* purity (although this is important) but to separation from *spiritual* fornication and adultery (James 4:4). This concept of spiritual virginity is used a number of times in the Bible.

To give an example, in Second Corinthians 11:2 the Apostle Paul yearns to present all believers as a pure virgin to Christ. If this referred to *physical* virginity, all married Christians would be left out of the picture! But we *can* be virgins in our spiritual relationship with Christ. And that'll be the issue dur-

188 *There's A New World Coming*

ing the Tribulation—steering clear of the Satanically-inspired religious system of the Antichrist who will prostitute the souls of men.

These 144,000 Tribulation celibates are "redeemed from among men as firstfruits to God and to the Lamb" (verse 4). In ancient Israel the Jewish people followed an agricultural practice which was commanded by God Himself. At the beginning of every harvest the people presented a token amount of the first and best fruits of the field as an offering to the Lord. This was known as the "first fruits" offering. This practice is used here to picture the conversion of the 144,000 Jewish witnesses. They will be the very first people saved during the Tribulation period. They in turn will lead millions all around the world to the only true Messiah, the Lord Jesus.

THREE ANGELIC EVANGELISTS

> *(6) And I saw another angel fly in the midst of the sky, having the everlasting gospel to preach to those who dwell on the earth, and to every nation, and kindred, and tongue, and people. (7) Saying with a loud voice, "Fear God, and give glory to Him; for the hour of His judgment has come; worship Him that made heaven, and earth, and the sea, and the fountains of waters." (8) There followed another angel, saying, "Babylon is fallen, that great city, because she made all nations drink of the wine of the wrath of her fornication." (9) The third angel followed them, saying with a loud voice, "If any man worship the Beast and his image, and receive his mark on his forehead, or on his hand, (10) the same shall drink of the wine of the wrath of God, which is poured out without mixture into the cup of his indignation in the presence of the holy angels, and in the presence of the Lamb; (11) and the smoke of their torment ascends up forever and ever; and they have no rest day nor night, who worship the Beast and his image, and whoever receives the mark of his name."* REVELATION 14:6–11

ANGELS GET INTO THE ACT

Toward the end of the Tribulation period this Jewish evangelization will be followed by a phenomenon never before seen in the history of the world—angels preaching the gospel to men! The phenomenon is described in verses 6 through 11. God will proclaim one last all-out offer of grace before He buries the world under an avalanche of final judgment. Three angels will fly through the atmosphere above the earth proclaiming the "everlasting gospel."

For centuries angels have wanted to get in on the act of

world evangelization. Peter tells us that the angels are intensely interested in the whole story of redemption (1 Peter 1:12). They have been itching to preach the gospel—but God has given that privilege to us. The angels would love to push us to one side and really get the job done right. First Peter 1:10–12 tells us that the angels are all excited about the grace that God is showing to us by letting us tell people about the eternal inheritance we have through Jesus Christ. Now at last the angels will have their chance!

The "everlasting gospel" (verse 6) emphasizes the fact that the people still living at the end of the Tribulation are on the very edge of eternity. Now the gospel is fundamentally the same no matter what era it's preached in. It's the good news that Christ took the penalty for every sin man would ever commit. But God has emphasized various facets of the gospel at different times down through history. The "gospel of the Kingdom," for example, will have been preached throughout most of the Tribulation period. It emphasizes that Christ will establish His millennial Kingdom when He returns to earth at the end of the Tribulation and that people can be part of it if they receive Christ as their Savior.

A SHOCKING BLOW TO EVOLUTION

Included in the proclamation of one of the missionary angels is a command to worship the God of creation (verse 7). The evolutionary theory that dominates the thinking of most men today will really sweep the world in the Tribulation era! It will take an angel from heaven to straighten people out on this atheistic nonsense.

"FALLEN, FALLEN IS BABYLON . . ."

Verse 8 looks ahead to another scene near the end of the Tribulation period and speaks of Babylon falling twice. Babylon as used in the Bible represents both a false religious system and the capital city of the one world government—Rome. Revelation 17 and 18 make both of these identifications. The false religious system is characterized by the ancient city of Babylon because it's a religion based on the black magic, witchcraft, and astrology which originated in ancient Babylon. This religion will have its headquarters in Rome during the first half of the Tribulation period.

As a religious system, Babylon will be destroyed about three and one-half years before Christ returns to earth. The Antichrist will get bugged with the system and destroy it because it takes the world's religious attentions off himself. That's the *first* fall of Babylon.

Then, during the great war that breaks out in the Middle East toward the end of the second half of the Tribulation, the city of Rome (which will be the capital city of the world and of Antichrist), will be completely blown to bits in a thermonuclear holocaust in one hour's time. This is the *second* fall of Babylon and is the destruction of the greatest economic and commercial center of all time. This is carefully discussed in Chapter 18.

The total destruction of both Babylons proves Christ's complete triumph over the evil Satanic system that tyrannizes the Tribulation world.

THE CLEAR OPTION

The message of the third angel (verses 9–11) is really a heavy one. Anyone who worships the Beast or receives his mark of allegiance will "drink of the wine of the wrath of God" forever. In other words, he will go to hell! The choice between Christ and the Beast will be so clear that no one will be able to plead ignorance. Those who worship the Beast will do so deliberately, recklessly disregarding all the warnings they have been given by God and His angels. The destiny for people who reject Christ during the Tribulation period is the same as that for people who reject Him at any other time. They will spend eternity in hell.

IS HELL FOR REAL?

Now, I don't like to talk about the subject of hell—it's such a horrible prospect. But the Bible has plenty to say on the subject, and it's an important thing for us to know about. The most familiar verse in the whole Bible, John 3:16, draws a sharp contrast between heaven and hell: "For God so loved the world that He gave his only-begotten Son, that whoever believes in Him should not perish, but have everlasting life." If there were no hell, Christ's death was a needless sacrifice and a tragic blunder.

It was Christ Himself who spoke more about hell than anyone else in the Bible. Most of what we know about the subject comes from His lips! In Matthew 25:41 Christ tells us that hell is a place of eternal fire, originally prepared for Satan and the angels who joined him in his primeval revolt against God.

In Mark 8:36, 37 Christ asked this question: "What shall it profit a man if he shall gain the whole world and lose his own soul? Or what shall a man give in exchange for his soul?" One human soul is worth more than the whole world!

When I was a teenager I used to give this saying to the gals I went with: "I'm gonna live fast, die young, and leave a good-looking corpse!" Little did I know what hell was all about! My buddies used to say, "Man, I'm going to hell. All my friends will be there and we'll all play poker together." And I used to laugh with them. Let me ask you one question, though—did you ever see anyone playing poker in a blast furnace?

A GLORIOUS ALTERNATIVE

(12) In this is the patience of the saints; these are the ones who keep the commandments of God, and the faith of Jesus. (13) I heard a voice from heaven saying to me, "Write: 'Blessed are the dead who die in the Lord from henceforth.'" "Yes," says the Spirit, "in order that they may rest from their labors, and their works will follow them." REVELATION 14:12, 13

"Blessed are the dead who die in the Lord" is the tremendous alternative of going to hell. Those who have received Jesus Christ into their lives need not fear death at all. For them death is just an entrance into the real destination of their lives on earth—heaven!

The time may be coming when Christians will be called on to suffer and die as never before. Some of you reading this book may someday die for your faith. Not too long from now men may kill you in the name of religion and feel that they have done a good thing.

When John mentions the perseverence of the saints, he's speaking of the Tribulation believers who will die for Christ rather than receive the mark of Satan's tyrant, the Antichrist. These will give their lives rather than worship the Beast.

PREVIEW OF TWO HARVESTS

> *(14) I looked and saw a white cloud, and sitting on the cloud was one like the Son of man, having on His head a golden crown, and in His hand a sharp sickle. (15) Another angel came out of the temple, crying with a loud voice to Him who sat on the cloud, "Thrust in Your sickle, and reap; for the time has come for You to reap: for the harvest of the earth is ripe." (16) And the One who sat on the cloud thrust in His sickle on the earth, and the earth was reaped.*

> *(17) And another angel came out of the Temple which is in heaven; he also had a sharp sickle. (18) Another angel came out from the altar, who had power over fire, and cried with a loud cry to him who had the sharp sickle, saying, "Thrust in your sharp sickle, and gather the clusters of the vine of the earth: for its grapes are fully ripe." (19) Then the angel thrust in his sickle over the earth, and gathered the vine of the earth, and cast it into the great winepress of the wrath of God. (20) And the winepress was trodden outside the city, and blood came out of the winepress, even up to the horses' bridles for two hundred miles.*   REVELATION 14:14–20

In this preview of the final events just prior to Jesus' return to the earth, the symbol of two kinds of harvest is used.

SEPARATION OF UNBELIEVERS FROM BELIEVERS

The first vision of a harvest (verse 14–16) uses terminology that would be applicable to the reaping of wheat. It's personally superintended by the "Son of man," who, as predicted in a parable by Jesus, is careful to gather in all the wheat and keep it separate from the tares. The parable reads as follows: "The harvest is the end of the age; and the reapers are the angels. Therefore, just as the tares are gathered and burned in the fire, so shall it be at the end of the age. The Son of man will send forth His angels, and they will *gather out* of His Kingdom things that cause stumbling, and those who practice lawlessness, and shall cast them into the furnace of fire; there shall be wailing and gnashing of teeth. *Then* the righteous will shine forth as the sun in the Kingdom of their Father" (Matthew 13:39–43).

This parable explains the first vision. Jesus does not do the dividing Himself but instead carefully *supervises* the separation of wheat and tares so that not one believer (wheat) is judged with the tares (unbelievers). This separating work is done by angels and happens just prior to the Lord's triumphant reappearance back to the earth at the end of the Tribulation. The day of grace is ended at this point. Fates are forever sealed; there is no more chance for the unbelieving.

This will be the saddest day in all of human history!

The believers will apparently be carefully protected from the final holocaust so that they can go directly into the Kingdom and repopulate the new world that's coming.

JUDGMENT OF THE ARMIES

The second vision which John the Apostle saw (verses 17–20) is very different from the first. The Son of man doesn't superintend this reaping. This harvest is done by an angel from the Temple of heaven. The symbol is that of a reaping for a vintage of wrath. All the clusters of grapes that are gathered in the harvest are cast into "the great winepress of the wrath of God." This indicates that there's no separation to be done here—all are unbelievers destined for destruction.

The place of this great judgment helps identify the ones being judged. God's great winepress of judgment is said to be "outside the city." "The city" could only be Jerusalem. So "ground zero" of God's most awful judgment is just outside Jerusalem. Zechariah gives us prophetic insight about this. As he predicts the last great war before the second coming of the Messiah, he gives us God's words: "I will gather *all nations* against Jerusalem. . . ." (Zechariah 14:2). Then he adds: "The Lord shall go forth and fight against those nations, as when He fought in the day of battle" (Zechariah 14:3).

MESSIAH TO JERUSALEM'S RESCUE

The armies of all nations will be gathered in the area of Israel, especially around Jerusalem. Think of it: at least 200 million soldiers from the Orient, with millions more from the forces of the West headed by the Antichrist of the Revived Roman Empire (Western Europe)! Messiah Jesus will first strike those who have ravaged His city, Jerusalem. Then he will strike the armies amassed in the valley of Meggido, or Armageddon. No wonder blood will stand to the horses' bridles for a distance of two hundred miles from Jerusalem! (Revelation 14:20).

It's grizzly to think about such a carnage, but just to check all this out I measured from the point where the Valley of Armageddon slopes down to the Jordan Valley. From that point southward down the Valley through the Dead Sea to the port of Elath on the Gulf of Aqabah measures approximately two hundred miles. Apparently this whole valley will be filled with war materials, animals, bodies of men, and blood!

Let the nations of the world be warned! Let those who attack the believing remnant of Israel in the last days take heed, for the Lord says of Israel, "After the glory He has sent Me (the Messiah) against the nations who persecuted and plundered you, for anyone who touches you, touches the apple of God's eye" (Zechariah 2:8).

FIFTEEN

A Gracious Interlude

Chapters 15 and 16 really go together because they describe two aspects of the same set of events—the seven final judgments of God upon the earth. Revelation 15 is the shortest chapter in the Book, but it is by no means the least important. It reveals a joyous yet solemn scene in heaven as preparation is made for the final, most dreadful judgments of the entire Tribulation.

GOD'S PATIENCE RUNS OUT

(1) Then I saw another sign in heaven, great and marvelous, seven angels having the seven last plagues; for in them God's wrath is finally finished. REVELATION 15:1

I personally don't know how the Apostle John held up under the awesome weight of all that he saw up to this point. One judgment after another has gotten successively more severe, and now he must reveal the final sign of coming punishment on the Christ-rejecting world.

When John speaks of the seven angels as "another" sign, it means *another of the same kind as before.* The other two great signs appeared in Chapter 12, where we saw that the *woman* represented Israel and the *great red dragon* represented Satan and the kingdom he would rule during the Tribulation.

Now we see the final sign. John describes it as great and glorious, and we'll see that these *seven angels* administer the divine judgment of God upon the Satanic kingdom and political power of the Beast.

The seven plagues brought by the seven angels finish the wrath of God on earth. This word "finished" in the Greek language of the New Testament is the same word that Jesus shouted from the Cross as He died: "It is finished!" As this triumphant cry came from Jesus it meant that the *debt of man's sin* against God was finished. Here, those who have rejected this finished work of Christ on their behalf find that God's *patience* is finished.

A VICTORY SONG OF MARTYRS

(2) And I saw, as it were, a sea of glass mixed with fire, and those who had won the victory over the Beast, and over his image, and over his mark, and over the number of his name, standing on the sea of glass, having the harps of God. (3) They sing the song of Moses, the servant of God, and the song of the Lamb, saying, "Great and marvelous are Your works, Lord God Almighty; just and true are Your ways, O You King of the saints. (4) Who will not reverence You, O Lord, and glorify Your name? For You alone are holy; for all nations will come and worship before You; for Your judgments are made manifest."   REVELATION 15:2–4

As John looks in awe at the seven mighty angels preparing to initiate things of such magnitude that they are without precedent in human history, his attention is shifted to a great crowd of people standing on a "sea of glass mingled with fire."

We encountered the same "sea of glass" in Chapter 4, and we saw there that it symbolized the mass of believers who came through the Rapture and are now at rest before God's throne. Now there is mixed with this sea of glorified Christians the symbol of judgment, which is fire.

I believe this judgment-fire is called forth by the believers in heaven on behalf of the martyrs who have come through the agonies of the Tribulation. It's as if these brother Christians smolder with outrage against the unbelieving world that has committed such unspeakable atrocities against the family of God.

TRIUMPH IN DEATH

John says that he saw a multitude who had obviously come out of the Tribulation by martyrdom, and that they were standing *on* the sea of glass. Here's a picture that comes to my mind: have you ever seen a mob of deliriously happy fans carry a coach and team off the field on their shoulders after they have just won the big game of the year?

That's what I see here—the Church-age saints carrying the Tribulation martyrs on their shoulders in triumph, since the big game of life is over and they're the winners!

All the believers who died during the Tribulation will have died horrible deaths and no doubt suffered unbearably before the release of death. But no one standing in this crowd before the throne bears any semblance of defeat or bitterness. There's nothing here but praise and worship and victory!

Perhaps nothing is more difficult for the natural mind to understand than how death can really mean victory, how submitting to injustice can ultimately produce triumph. But I like to think about what Jim Elliot, the dedicated young missionary to the Auca Indians, wrote shortly before he was cruelly martyred by those he went to minister to: "A man is no fool to give up that which he cannot keep to gain that which he cannot lose." Jesus said, "For what is a man profited, if he shall gain the whole world, and lose his own soul?" (Matthew 16:26)

Real victory is not found in seeking to avoid conflicts and living a don't-rock-the-boat kind of life. The cemetery is full of people who fit that category! The kind of triumph these martyrs of the Tribulation will experience will be deliverance *through* fire, not *out* of it.

There's no guarantee that any of us are going to be spared some fiery trials before we go to meet the Lord, but if we keep our eyes fixed on our destination, that sea of fellow believers rejoicing before the throne of our Lord, no testing will be unbearable, *not even death.* "For to me to live is Christ, and to die is gain" said one who suffered greatly, the Apostle Paul (Philippians 1:21).

A SONG OF PRAISE

Heaven echoes with the spontaneous singing of the martyrs as they praise the Lord, who has just made them victors over sorrow, pain, and death. All the heartache is behind them now, and they are just beginning to grasp the reality of what it's going to be like to spend eternity with all their beloved family of God and the Father Himself.

How fitting it is for them to sing the "song of Moses." This is a song the Jews have sung for thousands of years, and commemorates their great deliverance from Pharoah's army at the Red Sea.

Just as the Israelites looked back toward Egypt and realized that they were forever delivered from slavery and the taskmaster's whip, so these people will look back to their experiences of horror on earth and realize that they are forever delivered from the grasp of suffering and death. In this regard their song also becomes the "song of the Lamb," who brought about this great deliverance and made them joint-heirs in the eternal kingdom of God.

FROM PATIENCE TO WRATH

> *(5) After that I looked and saw that the Temple of the tabernacle of the testimony in heaven was opened. (6) And the seven angels came out of the Temple, having the seven plagues, clothed in pure and white linen, and having their chests clothed with golden vests. (7) One of the four Living Beings gave to the seven angels seven golden bowls full of the wrath of God, who lives forever and ever. (8) The Temple was filled with smoke from the glory of God, and from His power; and no one was able to enter into the Temple until the seven plagues of the seven angels were fulfilled.*
> REVELATION 15:5–8

From looking at the wonder of the victorious Tribulation saints, John's attention is drawn to another breathtaking sight. The heavenly tabernacle, of which the earthly tabernacle and Temple were patterned, was thrown open, and John was permitted to look into the Holy of Holies.

This concept of a tabernacle in heaven has been a hard thing for many people to understand. Remember that God gave Moses specific instructions on how to build the tabernacle in the wilderness and told him it was to be made from the same pattern as the one in heaven.

Now and then in the Bible we're given glimpses of what has gone on in the tabernacle in heaven. The Book of Hebrews in the New Testament draws many parallels between the function of the priests in the earthly tabernacle and Christ, our High Priest, in the heavenly tabernacle. It makes clear that the rituals and symbols of the earthly tabernacle worship were all

designed to portray things that would have an ultimate fulfillment in heaven's Temple.

As John tells us of his vision of the Temple in this chapter,
he emphasizes its function as a "tabernacle of testimony" or
witness. The Temple was both a witness *to* man and *against*
him. It was a witness *to* man in that its furniture and function
told of the way man must approach God. It witnessed *against*
him because the necessity of the rituals was a constant reminder that man was unworthy to come into the presence of a
holy God in his own merit.

A CLOSER LOOK AT THE TEMPLE

In order to better understand the scene which John is describing for us in Revelation 15, let's get a better picture of the
earthly tabernacle and its function.

The tabernacle itself was a portable building made of cloth
and skins and carried from place to place by the Jews during
their forty years in the wilderness and their first few years in
the Promised Land. Later they built their Temple in Jerusalem,
using the exact floor plan of the tabernacle. The main difference
was the opulence of the materials used in the Temple in Jerusalem.

There was only one gate in the fence that surrounded the
tabernacle. Squarely in front of the gate, inside the fence, was
the brazen altar of sacrifice. This showed man that there was
only one way to God, and that it was through an innocent sacrifice which would bear the guilt and death-penalty of the person making the sacrifice.

There was only one light inside the building, a candelabra
of God's design. It was by this light that all the divine services
of the priests were performed. This single light taught that only
God could provide illumination for the understanding of divine
truths and divine worship.

There was also the altar of incense, on which the priests
were to continually burn incense. The incense was symbolic of
the people's prayers. The fragrant aroma drifting into the rear
third of the tabernacle, called the Holy of Holies, was a picture
of our prayers continually coming into the presence of God.

DAY OF ATONEMENT

One of the greatest witnesses to man was the Day of Atonement. Once a year the high priest would select a spotless lamb and offer it on the altar for the sins of the people. He would then take some of its blood and go into the tabernacle.

Before entering the Holy of Holies the high priest would take a censer of incense and thrust it through the heavy veil that separated it from the Holy Place, which was the main room of the tabernacle. This symbolized his preparing the way into the holy presence of God by the people's prayers.

Then he would go into the Holy of Holies. In front of him he would see the ark of the covenant, a small gold-overlaid wooden chest with two angelic figures of gold standing upon its lid, facing each other and looking down at the box.

Between the two golden angels there was a radiant, dazzling, multicolored light called the Shekinah glory. This was the manifestation of God's presence on earth. No other spot in the world could boast of this special presence of God; only the Jews enjoyed this privilege, and only in the Holy of Holies of their tabernacle.

Atop the lid of the ark and beneath the blazing glory of light was a golden throne called the Mercyseat. It bore this name because it was here that the high priest obtained mercy for the people each year as he sprinkled the blood of a sacrifice on it.

THE ARK CONDEMNS

What was really significant about this golden box was that under the throne, inside the ark, were three unusual objects which God made the people put there. First were the second tablets of stone on which the Ten Commandments were rewritten by God. (Remember that Moses angrily broke the *original* tablets when **he** came down from Sinai and found the people steeped in gross sin.) These second tablets were put into the ark as a witness to *man's rejection of God's perfect moral law*.

Second, there was a pot of manna in the ark. This was placed there after the people complained about this heavenly food that God had provided. They were tired of manna for breakfast, lunch, and dinner even though I'm sure someone must have come up with a cookbook on *100 Best Ways to Prepare Manna*. Anyway,

God had them put a pot of the stuff in the ark to show *man's rejection of God's provision for daily needs.*

Thirdly, there was Aaron's staff which had miraculously sprouted leaves. This had occurred when a rebel group tried to take over the leadership of the nation from Moses and Aaron. God told the two groups of leaders to stand before the tabernacle and hold out their wooden staffs or rods—the symbols of their leadership. God proclaimed that whoever's rod sprouted leaves was the one He had chosen to be the leader. The rod of Aaron sprouted. God then instructed the people to put this rod into the ark as a witness of *man's rejection of God's chosen leadership.*

UTTER REJECTION OF GOD

These three articles taken together were a symbol of man's utter rejection of God. You can't reject someone more decisively than letting him know you reject the moral law he stands for, his attempts to provide your daily needs, and his authorized leadership. So these symbols were placed in the ark as a continual witness to the fact that man was sinful and rightfully deserving of God's judgment.

Once a year the high priest would sprinkle blood seven times on the golden throne. This blood of an innocent substitute symbolically covered the symbols of man's sin from the sight of God. As God looked at this blood His justice would be satisfied, for the penalty of man's sin, which was death, had been paid. He could then change His throne from one of judgment to one of mercy, since the blood of the innocent sacrificial substitute was the loving provision which He Himself had ordained to provide a way of escape for sinful men.

The name given to the lid of the ark was "the Mercy-seat" because this is where God's mercy was displayed toward man. All who came by faith in the atonement (sin-covering) provided by God were forgiven and accepted by God. All of this was intended to prefigure Jesus Christ, the "Lamb of God" whose blood would not merely cover but actally *take away* the sin of the world, thereby turning the throne of God in heaven's tabernacle to one of mercy for all who come by faith in Jesus.

MEANWHILE, BACK AT THE TABERNACLE

I've gone into all this detail about the tabernacle so that you can understand the shock that John, a good Jewish boy, must have received when he saw that there had been a sobering change in the very character of the sanctuary in heaven. It had become a place from which the seven final plagues were sent forth. No longer was it a place where men were reconciled to God. The throne of mercy had now become a throne of judgment against those who rejected God's Lamb.

The three reminders of man's sin in the ark were now uncovered and were witnessing *against* him. Because man had refused God's offer of salvation and had murdered God's messengers, the angel priests were handed seven bowls of holy outrage to pour upon the world.

TOO LATE TO PRAY

As the angels went forth to execute their awesome mission, the heavenly sanctuary was closed until the judgments were finished. The smoke of God's glory and power billowed forth from the building, and no one could enter God's presence until the vengeful holocaust had passed.

I believe this indicated that God closed His ears to the cries of those who had had ample light and yet had rejected it. Now they are about to be judged. In Chapter 14 we saw the last harvest of those who would believe. Now it's too late! The day of grace is over. The destiny of everyone on earth is settled.

The Bible tells us that a man may keep hardening his heart to God's gracious invitation until he has had his last chance . . . slipping out into eternity into the place of hopelessness, isolation, darkness, and torment. But God has never *sent* anyone to this kind of eternity. Men go there because they refuse the alternative!

SIXTEEN

The Seven Vials of Armageddon

---

(1) Then I heard a great voice out of the Temple saying to the seven angels,
"Go your ways, and pour out the bowls of the wrath of God upon the earth."
REVELATION 16:1

In Chapter 15 we saw God's reluctant but final decision near the end of the Tribulation to close the gates of heaven to any further entrants. In His great foreknowledge God knows that every unbeliever still alive on earth at that time will have hardened his heart to the gospel and will never turn to Him. Therefore He prepares to release the seven final climactic "bowl" judgments on the earth. They are sent forth by the mighty voice of God booming out of the smoke-filled heavenly Temple.

The seven angels who administer this solemn work are dressed in the uniform of priests—white robes and golden vests. Since it was as priests that they had presented the prayers of the martyred saints before God, it's fitting that they should carry the bowls (actually golden censers used in the Temple for carrying incense, the symbol of prayers) of retributive judgment in answer to those prayers.

MASS MALADY

(2) And the first went, and poured out his bowl upon the earth, and there fell a malignant, painful sore upon the men who had the mark of the Beast, and upon those who worshipped his image. REVELATION 16:2

Even though we live in the age of miracle drugs, there are many diseases for which we still have no cure. Many doctors have expressed concern that the indiscriminate use of antibiotics has made many people immune to their effectiveness. If a truly serious epidemic broke out, these people might not be able to resist infection—much like AIDS affects its victims. There is also a growing concern over the development of "superbacteria" which can't be stopped by any of the drugs presently being used. Several strains of flu have fallen into this category. Bubonic plague has had a remarkable resurgence in recent years. In Micronesia, leprosy has increased at an alarming rate.

One of the most dreaded diseases of our age is cancer. Nothing can so strike terror to a person's heart like the words, "I'm sorry, but the biopsy showed malignancy." However, the malady which the first angel pours out onto the earth will produce such intense suffering that cancer would seem like a welcome relief by comparison! There will be no cure for this malignancy, and it will afflict all unbelievers who have sworn allegiance to the Antichrist.

This rash of malignant sores could easily be caused by the tremendous radioactive pollution in the atmosphere. After the bombings of Nagasaki and Hiroshima thousands of people developed hideous sores because of the radioactivity.

Whatever the sores are, God will supernaturally protect the believers from this horrible plague, as He did when a similar plague was inflicted on Egypt in the days of Moses (Exodus 9:8–11).

THE DAY THE OCEANS DIE

(3) The second angel poured out his bowl upon the sea, and it became like the blood of a dead man; and every living soul that was in the sea died.   REVELATION 16:3

Another judgment follows rapidly on the heels of the terrible malignancy. The second angel poured his bowl into the sea, and it became blood like that of a dead man. Every living thing in the sea died. *Everything!*

Throughout the Book of Revelation God has been taking carefully measured steps of judgment against the world. You may have been thinking: "Isn't God cruel to bring such terrible judgments on the world!" But you know, one of the reasons the Book of Revelation describes the terrible things which God will allow is to so shake up man that he will see his need for God right now. The judgments all through the Revelation have increased gradually in measured progression; but now all the stops are pulled out.

The reason I say the judgments are carefully measured is because the same type of judgments take place in a less intense form earlier in the Book of Revelation. For example, the judgments of Revelation 8 are similar to those of Revelation 16, except less harsh. In Revelation 8:8, 9 only a *third* of the sea became blood and only a *third* of the marine life died. But in Revelation 16 *all* marine life is going to be wiped out.

We can only speculate as to whether a direct judgment of God, a tremendous nuclear exchange, or perhaps some unknown weapon that will be a result of the Stars Wars research will affect all marine life to this extent. We don't know which it will be, but whatever it is, it's going to destroy all living things in the sea.

ALL FRESH WATER POLLUTED

> *(4) The third angel poured out his bowl upon the rivers and fountains of waters, and they became blood. (5) I heard the angel of the waters say, "You are righteous, O Lord, who are, and was, and shall be, because You have judged in this way. (6) For they have shed the blood of saints and prophets, and You have given them blood to drink; for they deserve it." (7) I heard another out of the altar say, "Even so, Lord God Almighty, true and righteous are Your judgments."* REVELATION 16:4–7

As if the bloodied sea wasn't enough, the third angel poured out his bowl of judgement into the rivers and springs of waters, and they became blood also. It gets pretty grim when there is no fresh water to drink anywhere on earth. There's going to be a big run on Coca-Cola, but even this will give out after a while!

In verse 6 we're told why God inflicts this horrible judgment on the earth: "They have shed the blood of saints and prophets, and You have given them blood to drink. They deserve it."

As we've seen in previous chapters, the most vicious and bloody time of slaughter of believers which the world has ever seen is going to take place during these seven years of Tribulation horror. It's going to be done, *not* by *irreligious* men but by *religious* men, men who are part of a great one-world religious institution which we'll look at in detail in the next chapter.

INTOLERANT RELIGIONISTS

There's nothing more vindictive than a religious person who rejected the truth of the Bible and wants to get rid of a few contenders. Religion has been very hard on its competition. There's never been much tolerance for someone who says that Jesus Christ is the only way to God. Many people who are proud of their broad-mindedness get all uptight when someone quotes Jesus as saying, "I am the Way, the Truth, and the Life. No one comes to God except through Me." These people will be ready to spill the blood of Christ's believers during the Tribulation. It will be instigated by apostate religion.

There'll be worse bloodletting during the latter part of the seven-year Tribulation period than the medieval Inquisition. All the churches who still have their pastors after the "Great Snatch" takes place will take part in it! They will take out their revenge on believers who expose their falsity. They'll pour out the blood of the saints, and God in turn will give them blood to drink! God often renders "poetic justice" this way.

A GLOBAL HEAT WAVE

(8) And the fourth angel poured out his bowl upon the sun, and power was given to him to scorch men with fire. (9) And men were scorched with great heat, and blasphemed the name of God, who has power over these plagues; and they did not repent so as to give Him glory.
REVELATION 16:8, 9

Eleven years ago I wrote in the first edition of this book, "I believe that in a full-scale nuclear exchange, the balance of the atmosphere will be radically upset and this could be one of the things implied here." On October 30, 1983, Dr. Carl Sagan wrote in the aforementioned *Parade* magazine article, "Scientists initially underestimated the effects of nuclear explosions. . . . In 1973, it was discovered that high-yield airbursts will chemically burn the nitrogen in the upper air, converting it into oxides of nitrogen; these, in turn, combine with and destroy the protective ozone in the earth's stratosphere. The surface of the earth is shielded from deadly solar ultraviolet radiation by a layer of [tenuous] ozone. . . . Partial destruction of this ozone layer can have serious consequences for the biology of the entire planet."

As the clouds from the nuclear exchange begin to dissipate, holes in the ozone layer will let in deadly radiation, heating up the planet's surface until it becomes unbearably hot. This will be one of the worst judgments that man will experience, since there will be no water to drink to gain any relief.

But the most startling thing about the whole chapter is that men will go through all of this and still not repent! One of the reasons I don't believe in purgatory is this: when men reject Jesus Christ, even a foretaste of hell doesn't make them change their minds! People still remain set against Him. With all this fantastic phenomena taking place on earth, these men still refuse to repent and throw themselves upon the mercy of God.

CLOUDS OF DEATH OVER ROME

> *(10) And the fifth angel poured out his bowl upon the throne of the Beast, and his kingdom was full of darkness; and they gnawed their tongues for pain, (11) and blasphemed the God of heaven because of their pains and their sores, and did not repent of their deeds.*   REVELATION 16:10, 11

When John talked about this judgment falling upon the *throne* of the Beast and his *kingdom,* he was talking about the Revived Roman Empire which the Beast would lead, and its capital city, Rome.

Another important detail is added to this scene: tremendous darkness came upon the Beast's kingdom. This same thing happened in Egypt during the plagues; the whole land was enveloped in a darkness so oppressive that Moses said you could actually feel it! That's the sort of thing that will come upon the kingdom of the Antichrist.

I believe there's a reason for God's blackout of this Revived Roman Empire: the darkness will allow the movement of 200 million Oriental soldiers into the area of the Middle East, the subject of the next judgment.

THE YELLOW TERROR

> *(12) The sixth angel poured out his bowl upon the great river, Euphrates, and its water was dried up, in order that the way of the kings of the East might be prepared. (13) And I saw three unclean spirits, like frogs, come*

> *out of the mouth of the dragon, and out of the mouth of the Beast, and out of the mouth of the False Prophet. (14) For they are the spirits of demons, working miracles, going forth to the kings of the earth and of the whole world, to gather them to the battle of that great day of God Almighty. (15) "Behold, I am coming as a thief. Blessed is he who watches, and keeps his garments, lest he walk naked, and they see his shame." (16) And he gathered them together into a place called in the Hebrew tongue Armageddon.*
>
> REVELATION 16:12–16

The sixth bowl judgment is a horrible extension of the judgment of the sixth trumpet recorded in Chapter 9. You'll recall that the sixth trumpet revealed the vast hordes of the Orient mustered to *prepare* to march into the Middle East under cover of what appeared to be a limited nuclear strike. In this present situation of the sixth bowl, the terrifying army of 200 million Orientals has reached the banks of the Euphrates, the ancient boundary between the empires of the East and West.

This great army is designated as "kings of the East." This tells us that there will likely be a coalition of powers from the Eastern countries and it will probably be led by Red China. Their way is cleared for a rapid forced march and "banzai charge" by the drying up of the Euphrates River. This sort of thing has been made technically possible by the Russians' recent construction of a dam near the headwaters of the Euphrates.

The way for this great Oriental invasion has literally been paved by a road recently constructed from China through the Himalayas of Kashmir to Pakistan. India lodged a protest in the United Nations, calling this "a threat to peace in Asia." I'm sure that neither India nor any other nation realizes just how great a threat this will prove to be in the future.

THE WEST MOBILIZES FOR WAR

Satan (the dragon), the Roman Antichrist, and the False Prophet will be the unholy trinity of the Tribulation. John describes demon spirits that will proceed first from the mouth of Satan and then from the two world leaders. These three personalities act virtually as one, setting into action demons who perform miraculous signs in front of the leaders of the whole earth. Since the Eastern leaders are already massed at the Euphrates in readiness for war, these miraculous signs must be performed for the benefit of those world leaders from the West which the unholy trinity is trying to mobilize to fight against the Eastern hordes.

I believe that a great display of occultic miracles will be used to dazzle and mesmerize these nations into converging on Israel and squaring off against the kings of the East. Some 2,700 years ago the Prophet Joel foresaw this terrible day: "Let the nations be awakened, and come to the valley of Jehoshaphat (the place of Armageddon), for there I will sit to judge all the nations surrounding you. Multitudes, multitudes in the valley of decision; for the day of the Lord is near in the valley of decision" (Joel 3:12, 14).

SEQUENCE OF WORLD WAR III

In my book, *The Late Great Planet Earth*, I documented very carefully how the various political powers named here are found in the prophecies of the Bible, so because of limited space I won't repeat the documentation here. But I do want to show the stages involved in the military maneuvers of the four great political empires who will be involved in the last military conflict of the world, of which the Battle of Armageddon is the very last battle.

In order to help keep all of this in order in our minds, I'll refer to all of the battles fought during the major part of this military conflict as the *War* of Armageddon. But when I speak of the final conflict of this war, I'll call it the *Battle* of Armageddon. The entire campaign covers three and one-half years, the last half of the Tribulation. This period is usually referred to as the "*Great* Tribulation."

ARAB CONFEDERACY STRIKES

The *first stage* of this war begins when the Arab-African Confederacy (called "the king of the South" in Daniel 11:40) launches a massive attack against Israel. The *second stage* is an immediate full-scale invasion against Israel and the middle East by Russia (called "the king of the North" in Daniel 11:40–45) and her satellites. (See also Ezekiel 38:14–17 and Joel 2:1–10, 20.)

The first two stages of the War of Armageddon commence with the opening of the second seal (Revelation 6:3, 4) when the red apocalyptic horseman goes forth and takes peace from the earth. According to the Hebrew prophet, Daniel, the Russians will sweep down to join the Arabs in an attack on Israel and will then continue right through Israel to Egypt and take it over. Apparently they come into the conflict originally as allies of the Arabs but end up double-crossing them.

RUMORS FROM THE EAST

While the Russian commander is in Egypt preparing to attack and consolidate the African continent under his control, "rumors from the East and the North will disturb him. . . ." (Daniel 11:44). As the commander looks eastward from Egypt he hears of the Oriental army beginning to mobilize its troops. This was disclosed in the sixth trumpet judgment which tells us about the four vicious angels bound at the Euphrates river but now loosed to kill one-third of mankind (Revelation 9:13–16).

As the Russian leader looks northward from Egypt, he hears that the Revived Roman Empire is preparing to enter the war. The Roman Antichrist will rush to Israel's defense after she is attacked by the Arabs and Russians, since the False Prophet and Israel have signed a defense pact with the Antichrist which commits him to protect Israel (Daniel 9:27).

The *third stage* of the war begins when the Russians quickly return from Egypt to regroup their forces in Israel. Their command post will be set up in the Jerusalem area (Daniel 11:44b, 45).

THE GRAND RED ARMY THAT WAS

The *fourth stage* of the campaign finds the Russian army completely annihilated in Israel and its environs by the European forces of the Roman Antichrist (Daniel 11:45b; Ezekiel 38:18—39:5). Zechariah 14:12 predicts the plague that will inflict the soldiers who attack Jerusalem. He predicts that "their flesh will be consumed from their bones, their eyes burned out of their sockets, and their tongues consumed out of their mouths while they stand upon their feet."

For hundreds of years students of Bible prophecy have wondered what kind of plague could produce such instant ravaging of humans while still on their feet. Until the advent of the atomic bomb such a thing was not humanly possible. But now everything Zechariah predicted could come true instantly in a thermonuclear exchange! Nuclear weapons will surely be used in any warfare in the future. The major powers of the world aren't stockpiling nuclear weapons for nothing, and even an effective arms control agreement between nations wouldn't do away with existing weapons.

Ezekiel the prophet adds a further descriptive note to this martial exchange between Russia and the Revived Roman Empire in his prediction of "a torrential rain of hailstones, fire, and brimstone" (Ezekiel 38:22).

Part of the consequences of this confrontation will be the devastation of the USSR and many of her satellites. Israel will also suffer greatly from the bombings. Ezekiel 39:5–8 predicts this and adds that "fire" will fall upon many of the great population centers of the world, described as "those who inhabit the coastlands in safety." "Coastlands" was a term used for the great Gentile civilizations of Ezekiel's time.

A recent article which described Red China's nuclear strength revealed that China now has missiles capable of hitting most of the population centers of Russia and Asia. In all probability China will unleash some of her nuclear weapons on Russia at this time. The Roman Antichrist will also use tactical weapons against this great Northern Confederacy.

RED CHINA AND COMPANY

The *fifth stage* of the war is when the 200 million-man army from the Orient reaches the Euphrates and prepares to attack the Antichrist, who will be in Israel at that time (Revelation 16:12).

If anyone doubts that Red China will be part of this Biblical scenario (because historically they have never been involved in Mideast affairs), they should pick up their newspaper and read the statements of that nation's leaders. Right after President Reagan's trip to China, the next "head of state" to visit was Palestine Liberation Organization Chairman Yasser Arafat. According to an article in the *Los Angeles Times'*, May 8, 1984 edition, one unnamed senior Arab diplomat was quoted as saying, "China is responsible in many ways for Arafat's survival today as PLO chairman (after being forced to abandon Lebanon by Syrian-backed PLO rebels in 1983). Very quietly, but very quickly, China made sure he had enough arms (and food) to equip those who left Lebanon for Tunisia and South Yemen, because without weapons, he would have lost everyone. A guerrilla without a gun feels like a fool and hates the man who leads him."

Most revealingly, the diplomat added, "Arafat owes China a lot because of this—and even more because China does not demand he become 'Chinese' like the Soviet Union has demanded that he become 'Russian' and follow Kremlin orders."

Said a Chinese official, also quoted anonymously, "The Middle East is far away, but the conflict there still affects China in many ways. It has become an arena for the two superpowers to play out their rivalry, and that undermines peace throughout the world. The Arab countries are Third World countries, the issues are Third World issues and there must be solidarity with them. . . ." I think you can see which side China will be on! Another unidentified Chinese official added, "We honestly think that we can bring something to this problem, if only to remind everyone of the impact it has even as far away as China."

Officially, Arafat was greeted as a hero by the Chinese leaders. Said Premier Zhao Ziyang, "China will always firmly support the Palestinian people in their just struggle, firmly support the PLO as the sole legitimate representative of the Palestinian people and firmly support the revolutionary leadership of Brother Arafat."

I believe that China is unwittingly setting itself up to fit into its Biblical pattern predicted by John in Revelation. Let no one be unaware of the crucial role this nation plays, nor the warning that time is indeed growing short as all the nations fall into their prophesied scenario.

The *sixth stage* is the mobilization of all the rest of the world's armies to fight under the command of the Antichrist against the "kings of the East" (Revelation 16:12). At this point all the armies move into the Middle-East and spread out along the entire length and breadth of Israel, with the greatest concentration poised for the fiercest and final battle on the Plains of Armageddon (Revelation 16:13, 14).

THE FINAL HOUR

It's almost impossible for us to imagine the magnitude of what is predicted here. Just imagine—at least 300 million soldiers strung out across the entire Middle East and poised for the final mad act in man's most finely-developed art—war! The human waves of the East are pitted against the superior weaponry of the West. Then it happens—the final battle begins! The horrible carnage of the Valley of Armageddon (Revelation 16:16) . . . the indescribable clashes around Jerusalem and Judea (Zechariah 14:1–15). No wonder John predicts that blood will stand to the horses' bridles for two hundred miles in the Jordan Valley! (See Revelation 14:20.)

15 ON THE RICHTER SCALE

(17) The seventh angel poured out his bowl into the air, and there came a great voice out of the Temple of heaven, from the throne, saying, "It is done." (18) And there were voices, and thunders, and lightnings; and there was a great earthquake, such as was not since men were upon the earth, so mighty an earthquake, and so great. (19) And the great city was divided into three parts, and the cities of the nations fell; and great Babylon came in remembrance before God, to give to her the cup of the wine of the fierceness of His wrath. (20) And every island fled away, and the mountains were not found. (21) And there fell upon men a great hail out of heaven, every stone weighing about one hundred pounds, and men blasphemed God because of the plague of the hail; for the plague was exceedingly great.

REVELATION 16:17–21

While this great battle is raging, every city in the world is going to be leveled. This will take place by what is called an "earthquake" (Greek *seimos*), but that's not the only meaning. The word itself simply means "a great shaking of the earth." The earth could be shaken either by a literal earthquake or by a fullscale nuclear exchange of all remaining missiles. I lean toward the nuclear conflict; I believe that when these powers lock forces here, there will be a full-scale exchange of nuclear weapons, and it's at this time that "the cities of the nations fall." Just think of the great cities of the world—London, Rome, Paris, Berlin, New York, San Francisco, Los Angeles, Mexico City, and Tokyo—all of these great cities are going to be judged at that time!

WHAT ABOUT THE UNITED STATES?

Many people have wondered what the United States will be doing during this conflict. We've already seen that the U.S. is destined to lose its role as the leader of the West. This leadership will instead fall to the European confederacy which the Antichrist will rule.

There's no Scriptural indication that the United States will have been wiped out before this time, so we can only deduce that she will be part of the Western Confederacy which unifies nations against the great Asian power. However, in this last outpouring of judgment no nation will escape—every city in the world is going to be leveled.

Apparently the devastation will be so tremendous that not only will all the cities be destroyed, but the land itself will be ripped apart. The coastlines and continents will be changed and all the mountains will be shifted in elevation.

"And there was an incredible hailstorm from heaven; hailstones weighing one hundred pounds fell from the sky onto the people below, and they cursed God because of the terrible hail" (Revelation 16:21, *TLB*). I've been in West Texas when hailstones as big as golf balls fell, and let me tell you they really tear things up! But no one has ever laid eyes on hundred-pound hailstones, except the Apostle John. Wow! That will level what's left of any building still standing!

WHOLESALE SLAUGHTER

This chapter closes with multiplied millions of soldiers slaughtering each other in and around Israel. In the process, the cities of the world will have been reduced to rubble. The world will look just as you'd expect the "end of the world" to look.

With all of this, you would expect some people to consider the possibility that the things the martyrs had declared about God and His offer of deliverance through Jesus might be true. You'd expect many people to cry out for mercy and forgiveness. But look at what they will do instead: "Men blasphemed God because of the plague of hail. . . ."

Though all this may sound like the end of global life, we'll see in Chapter 19 that the personal return of Jesus Christ to earth will halt man from destroying all life on the planet and will bring a new world.

SEVENTEEN

How Rome Becomes Babylon

In this chapter and in Chapter 18 John deviates from his chronological unfolding of future history and pulls back the curtain to give a flashback to the development of the two great dynamics behind the Revived Roman Empire's meteoric rise to world dominion.

Many symbols used in the Book of Daniel and previously in Revelation are explained throughout this chapter. There are some very heavy concepts in this chapter because some of the principal personalities symbolize two different yet similar things.

In order to make the most sense of this material, you should read the whole chapter first, and then we'll consider the main subject topically.

THE HARLOT AND HER PARAMOURS

(1) Then there came one of the seven angels who had the seven bowls, and talked with me, saying to me, "Come here; I will show to you the judgment of the great whore who sits upon many waters; (2) with whom the kings of the earth have committed fornication, and the inhabitants of the earth have made drunk with the wine of her fornication."

(3) So he carried me away in the Spirit into the wilderness and I saw a woman sitting upon a scarlet-colored beast, full of names of blasphemy, having seven heads and ten horns. (4) The woman was clothed in purple and scarlet color, and lavished with gold and precious stones and pearls,

having a golden cup in her hand, full of abominations and filthiness of her fornication;

(5) upon her forehead was a name written, MYSTERY, BABYLON THE GREAT, THE MOTHER OF HARLOTS AND ABOMINATIONS OF THE EARTH.

(6) I saw the woman drunk with the blood of the saints, and with the blood of the martyrs of Jesus; and when I saw her, I wondered in amazement.

(7) And the angel said to me, "Why are you so amazed? I will tell you the mystery of the woman, and of the beast that carries her, which has the seven heads and ten horns. (8) The beast that you saw was, and is not, and shall ascend out of the bottomless pit, and go into perdition; and they who dwell on the earth (whose names were not written in the Book of Life from the foundation of the world) shall wonder when they behold the beast that was, and is not, and yet is.

(9) Here is the mind which has wisdom. The seven heads are seven mountains, on which the woman sits. (10) And they are seven kingdoms: five are fallen, and one is, and the other is not yet come; and when it comes, it must continue a short while. (11) And the beast that was, and is not, is himself the eighth, and yet is out of the seventh: and he will lead into perdition.

(12) And the ten horns which you saw are ten kings, who have received no kingdom as yet, but receive power as kings one hour with the beast. (13) These have one mind, and shall give their power and authority to the beast. (14) These shall make war with the Lamb, but the Lamb shall overcome them; for He is Lord of Lords, and King of Kings, and those who are with Him are called, and chosen, and faithful."

(15) And he said to me, "The waters which you saw, where the harlot sits, are peoples, and multitudes, and nations, and tongues. (16) The ten horns which you saw upon the beast, these shall hate the harlot, and shall make her desolate and naked, and shall eat her flesh, and burn her with fire. (17) For God has put in their hearts to fulfill His will, and to agree, and give their kingdom to the beast, until the words of God have been fulfilled.

(18) And the woman whom you saw is that great city, which reigns over the kings of the earth."   REVELATION 17:1–18

WHO'S WHO IN PROPHECY

In order to grasp the colossal things explained and predicted in this chapter, we'll need to firmly identify at the outset the symbols which are used. Many mysterious symbols used in both

Daniel and Revelation are clarified here. The two main figures
are a Harlot and a weird, seven-headed, ten-horned beast.

THE GREAT WHORE

Sometimes things that are evil are both fascinating and
repugnant. As John was shown the vision of a great Harlot he
was both spellbound and repulsed. He couldn't take his eyes off
this woman who was the epitome of evil. She was lavishly decked
out in jewels and luxurious garments of royalty. The cup she
held in her hand was of rich gold on the outside, but inside it
was filled with putrefying things. She looked like she'd just
come from a Halloween party, for she had a bizarre name gar-
ishly written on her forehead: "Babylon the Great, Mother of
Harlots and the Abomination of the Earth." The most disgust-
ing and horrible thing about her was that she was drunk—but
it wasn't alcohol that got her that way. It was blood—the blood
of believers!

When John gets his first glimpse of this Harlot, she's sitting
on a weird creature that looked like it was the "monster from
twenty thousand fathoms." The monster was just as repulsive
to John as the whore. It had seven heads and ten horns. Blasphemous names were written all over it and it was scarlet, the
color of blood. It was a fitting companion for the whore.

WHAT'S IT ALL ABOUT, JOHN?

As John stood there scratching his head and wondering what
this nightmare was all about, the angel begins to unravel the
mystifying sight. He begins by exposing just how gross this
whore really is. All the kings of the earth have committed adultery with her, and she is so immoral that she has intoxicated
the majority of people on the earth. She is said to "sit on many
waters," which is another way of saying that she has control
over vast numbers of people whom she has seduced in one way
or another (verse 15).

A SHORT HISTORY OF "HOOKERS"

The worst name a woman can be called is a whore. For the
angel to label this particular woman with that name must have

great significance. How can the kings of the earth commit adultery with her and all the people become drunk with her immorality?

In the Bible, the terms "whore", "harlot" and "adultery" are frequently used to symbolize a spiritual departure from God and His truth by an individual, a city, or a nation. The word "harlot" is especially used to connote a religion that is counterfeit. Isaiah the prophet lamented over Jerusalem, "How is the faithful city (Jerusalem) become a *harlot* . . . ?" (Isaiah 1:21) Jeremiah rebuked the nation of Israel for indulging in the demonic religions of her neighbors: "You (Israel) have lain down as a *harlot*." Ezekiel also chastized Israel with God's words: "I signed a covenant with you, and you became mine . . . . You took the very jewels and gold and silver ornaments I gave to you and made statues of men and worshipped them, which is adultery against Me" (Ezekiel 16:8, 17, TLB).

It is of special relevance to this chapter that the word "harlot" was connected with the practice of witchcraft when the Prophet Nahum pronounced judgment upon the great ancient city of Nineveh: "Because of the multitude of the harlotries of the charming *harlot*, the mistress of witchcrafts, that sells nations through her *harlotries*, and families through her witchcrafts" (Nahum 3:4). Isaiah also called the ancient city of Tyre a *harlot*.

DON'T PLAY AROUND WITH THE WORLD

James, the brother of Jesus, spoke of this spiritual prostitution when he warned, "You adulterers and adulteresses, don't you know that friendship with the world-system is enmity with God? Whoever therefore desires to remain a friend of the world-system is an enemy of God" (James 4:4).

The world-system is the organized system of world attitudes that excludes God's way and is under Satan's control. To be a friend of this system in the sense of compromising God's viewpoint of life and letting the world squeeze you into its mold is to commit adultery, spiritually speaking.

In a true relationship with God through Jesus Christ, believers are viewed as being the "Bride" of Christ (2 Corinthians 11:2). To play around with false religion is viewed throughout as spiritual adultery, since the true believer is already betrothed to Christ.

That Old Intoxicating Spell

In all the references we just looked at in Israel's history of seductions, each time she was lured away from her Jehovah God it was by a perversion of religion. And so it is with the great Harlot which John sees. She symbolizes an enormous false religious system that is so appealing that she has been able to seduce all the kings of the earth with her deceptions. Not only will this seductive religious prostitute wield control over the leaders of the nations, but even the common man will be intoxicated with her.

What kind of religious system will this Harlot be? What secret will lie behind her ability to bring under her power such unlikely subjects as an atheistic Russian, a Buddhist, a Moslem, a Hindu, or a liberal professing Christian? Most interpreters of this chapter have simply updated the thinking of the Protestant reformers who believed that the Pope was the Antichrist and the Roman Catholic Church was the whore of Babylon. In my opinion this is inaccurate. The Catholic Church has been steadily declining in popularity, and there would have to be a radical change in its appeal before it could amalgamate all these diverse people within it.

The main question is this: How could any false brand of *Christianity* get all the other religions to join it? Naturally, *professing* Christians who have all the outward form but no spiritual reality will be left behind when Christ takes the true believers, and they will become part of this ecumenical religion. But the religious system itself will have to offer something immensely more alluring than some watered-down brand of false Christianity in order to muster an appeal on the broad scale described here. Many churches today have already learned through their declining attendance that watered-down Christianity bores people to death!

Babylon the Great

The answer to this dilemma is unveiled in the "mystery" of the whore's name on her forehead—*"Babylon the Great, the*

Mother of Harlots and the Abominations of the Earth." This great Harlot is associated with an ancient city that immediately brings to mind sinful, lustful, depraved religion and life—Babylon!

What is it about Babylon of old that this great false religion will emulate?

A cardinal rule for interpreting symbols in the Bible is to examine their first Biblical usage and every successive occurrence. When we do this carefully with the concept of Babylon, the meaning is both clear and startling.

THE BIRTH OF BABYLON

The historical drama of Babylon began on the plains of Shinar, where the first world dictator established the world's first religious center. The dictator's name was Nimrod, which means "We will revolt." He's described literally as "a mighty hunter of men in defiance of the Lord."

The beginning of his kingdom was Babel, or Babylon (Genesis 10:8–10). Under this leader the first united religious act was performed—the building of a tower "whose top would reach into the heavens" (Genesis 11:4).

These people were smart enough to know that they couldn't build a tower through which they could climb up to where God lives. That wasn't of interest to them at all. You see, they were already studying the stars and the moon and were codifying the first system of astrology. The tower was to aid them in better observation of the stars. It was in essence an astrological observatory. Many centuries later, when God pronounced future judgment on Babylon, He said that, "she had labored with sorceries and astrology from her youth," indicating that these were practiced in Babylon from her very beginning in history. (Isaiah 47:12, 13).

DANIEL IN BABYLON'S DEN

In the seventh century B.C. the Prophet Daniel, while captive in Babylon, was made a member of the king's special advisors. These were all steeped in the religion of Babylon, which had now reached a very sophisticated stage. When the king had a nightmare one night, he called for his advisors to interpret what it meant. "Then the king commanded to summon the magicians, the astrologers (conjurers, incantationists), the sorcerers, and the Chaldeans, to reveal to the king his dreams. . . ." (Daniel 2:2).

What a motley crew this was! The *magicians* practiced black magic and performed various supernatural feats through contact with demon spirits. The *conjurers* were specialists at séances and at making objects miraculously materialize. By calling on the spirits of the dead, they made contact with demons, who then impersonated the dead person being summoned. The *sorcerer* specialized in witchcraft. The *Chaldean* was the highest of all the advisors. He was a part of a special priestly caste which was perpetuated by inheritance, a race that could trace its family history back to the originators of astrology. A Chaldean was a master astrologer!

BABYLON AND THE HARLOT

When the angel told John that he would tell him the *mystery* of the woman, he meant that this Harlot, the false religious system, would have as its main teachings the same occultic practices as ancient Babylon. It would include black magic, demon contact, séances, miraculous materializations, witchcraft, astrology, and sorcery. Her luxurious external appearance of jewels and royal clothes meant that she would have a great appeal to the sensual nature of men, but her gold cup filled with abominations represented her corrupt and perverse teachings. Her drunkenness with the saint's blood showed how she had successfully eliminated all who opposed her.

Just as Wall Street is synonymous with the whole investment world and as Madison Avenue brings to mind slick advertising, so the name Babylon symbolizes occultism in every form.

FROM EMPIRE TO EMPIRE

We know that the ancient city of Babylon was ruled by this occultic influence, but not many people are aware that the religion of Babylon passed from empire to empire until the days of ancient Rome.

The mystery that John was seeking to unveil for his readers

was that *religious* Babylon would be revived to control the last great world power in the last days of history. This religion will be an occultic amalgamation of all the world's religions. For the first three and one-half years of the Tribulation, it will enjoy a position of great power and influence over the Revived Roman Empire and its leader, the Antichrist.

THE WEIRDO BEAST

Keeping in mind what I've just said, let's take a look at the riddle of the beast with seven heads and ten horns (the monster which the woman is sitting on). Verses 9 and 10 of this chapter tell us that the seven heads represent *two things*: seven mountains and seven kingdoms (literally). I believe the seven mountains refer to the seven hills of the city of Rome. Rome has been associated with her seven hills throughout Roman literature and on coins of her day. What's being said here is that the Babylonish religious system was controlling the Rome of John's day, and indeed was synonymous with Rome itself. Rome was the center of pagan worship.

However, John tells us that the seven heads *also* represent seven kingdoms; five have fallen, one is, and the other is still to come. Here he is referring to those great world empires from the time of the original Babylon of Nimrod's day which have been dominated by the false occultic religion of Babylon.

"BABYLONISH" INFLUENCE OVER EMPIRES

The first kingdom was *Assyria*, with its occult-mad capital city of Nineveh (see Nahum 3:4). The second was *Egypt*, which devoted much of its total wealth to the construction of pyramids, all built according to astrological specifications. Egypt was also given to black magic (see Exodus 7:11, 22; 8:7, 18; 2 Timothy 3:9). The third was the *neo-Babylonian* empire of Daniel's day, which really perfected the black arts. The fourth was *Medo-Persia*, which conquered Babylon but was in turn enslaved by the Babylonian religion. The fifth was the *Greek* empire. One visit to Greece and her ancient temple sites will convince you of the sway which idolatrous religions held there!

Running through the culture of all these great past empires was an underlying belief in astrology. This was the cohesive force which bound together all the witchcraft, sorcery, and magic. Kings would seldom make a move without consulting advisors steeped in the ancient art of Babylonian religon. The ancient priests enjoyed royal stature and power, especially in Egypt.

When John speaks of the "five kingdoms that have fallen" he means the five I just mentioned. But then he says, "One is." This *has* to refer to the great empire of his day, Rome, which was filled with the same occultic beliefs that had originated on the plains of Shinar in ancient Babylon. This was the sixth kingdom of John's vision.

John looks to the future when he says of the seventh head (kingdom) that ". . . the other is not yet come; and when it comes, it must continue a short while" (Revelation 17:10c). This refers to the future *revival* of the Roman empire.

This seventh head is different from all the other six because it has ten horns on it. This indicates that this seventh kingdom will be made up of ten nations from the old Roman Empire (the sixth head) which will have confederated. In my opinion, this unquestionably refers to the European Economic Community, which I believe is destined to bloom into the last great world empire represented by the seventh head with the ten horns. This Revived Roman Empire will become dominated by the same Babylonish religious system that has ridden herd on the past great world empires.

A CLOSER LOOK AT THE BEAST

After having given John a panoramic view of all the past world powers and their seduction by the Harlot of Babylon, the angel now narrows his focus to the "beast" in its final form. Looking from this perspective, he says the beast *was* and *is not*, and then *will exist again* and be destroyed. He must be referring to the fact that Rome existed in his day, but that a day was coming when it would no longer exist. Then it would rise again and be destroyed.

As you review the history of Rome you recall that it was never conquered by anyone; it fell from within because of its own decadence. For nearly fifteen centuries Rome has not existed as a viable world political power. But the move in Europe today is destined to put the old Roman Empire back together again, whether the EEC realizes it or not. All the nations who are banding together in the European Economic Community have roots in old Roman culture and civilization. This is the "beast" that will rise up and then be destroyed.

Thus the Revived Roman Empire is referred to as a beast, as is the scintillating world leader who will control it and is also known as the Roman Antichrist. Although the "beast" we are looking at in this chapter has only seven heads, John says that it briefly sprouts another, an eighth head, but this head is really only an outgrowth of the seventh (the Revived Roman Empire) and is quickly destroyed. It's sort of like a *wart* that grows out of the seventh head of the beast and is cut off.

THE WART

This "wart" speaks of both the Antichrist himself and his kingdom, which will emerge full-bloom during the last half of the Tribulation. It will be an extension of the Revived Roman Empire which comes into existence when the Rapture takes place and seems for three and one-half years to be the answer to the hopes and dreams of the world for peace and prosperity. When the Antichrist becomes indwelt with Satan at the *middle* of the Tribulation, his kingdom from that point on will take a different tone. The whole world will worship the *Beast* instead of the Harlot. He will rule with force and deception, but the people will be completely spellbound by his clairvoyant abilities. Apparently they'll be mesmerized to the point where they won't even realize how repressive the goverment has become.

On the basis of John's prophecy of the rise of Babylon the Great and on the basis of the latest evidence of current events, I believe the stage is very nearly set for the resurrection of this great, occultic religious system. Eastern culture has always been open to various forms of the occult but now the West is also experiencing a great fascination with the black arts and dark religions.

This truth really threw me for a jolt when I saw how prevalent the occult has deeply penetrated the lives of our children—the future leaders of 1990's—when I walked into the local 7-Eleven store. A commercial enterprise that seems as American as mom, pop, and apple pie was sporting a new coin—operated video game for the local kids to play with. What was so frightening, however, was the artwork and name of the computer-operated game: "Satan's Hollow." With deep red-and-black colors, Lucifer was depicted as a powerful being waiting to snatch those who are not fast enough to escape the treacherous terrain and demons of the game. Long fingernails, horns, and tail beckoned those who would play.

My courage is such that I would not even dare expose myself to these subliminal images as one plays out the fantasies of the game. "Nothing but a fantasy and child's play—no danger to it"—that's what those who manufacture and rent such machines and allow their use would have us believe. But this is all overt preparation for the acceptance of the dark days and forces which lie ahead. It would appear that if there is a buck to be made, it matters not what the images and games are made out of for some Western businessmen today.

And that is true also in the popularity of the game "Dungeons and Dragons," another occultic setup that is feeding our children lies and allowing them to engage in dangerous role-playing. So much could be said about the effects of this game on children that it would be voluminous. Law enforcement officials throughout the U.S. have constantly pointed to this game as a cause behind some of the most perplexing and disturbing crimes that children in our society have committed. Yet no store has taken it off its shelves, and the manufacturer has certainly derived great financial reward from marketing this "game."

The Lord Jesus warned us that what we sow we reap. There will be no reward for those who lead others—whether in ignorance or through uncaring—down a path of doom and destruction. These games which fascinate the unprotected child can also lead them to an easier acceptance of the occultic heavy metal bands as they grow into teenagers and to mimic the antics that these bands champion.

BABYLON'S DOOM

To bring into focus what we've said so far, Babylon the Harlot symbolizes the great religious system which seduces and dominates the government of the world with her black arts. The seven-headed beast represents the six great powers which have had dominion over the world, and a seventh kingdom which has not yet risen. When it comes it will be a ten-nation revival of the sixth head (the old Roman Empire), and is pictured by the beast's ten horns.

For the first three and one-half years of the Tribulation the Antichrist of Rome finds it expedient to go along with the Harlot. He's her biggest paramour, but they are strange bedfellows. Each is trying to use the other, and there's no love lost between them. The fact that the Harlot *rides* the beast indicates that the religious system dominates the kingdom.

THE "WART" TURNS

But at the middle of the Tribulation the Roman Antichrist, working with the Jewish False Prophet, finds that he no longer needs the support of the religious system. He is now a clairvoyant and wonder worker himself. Possessed by Satan, he proclaims himself God in the Temple in Jerusalem. One of his next acts will be to turn on the great Harlot and destroy her.

God's judgments are all so poetic: since this great religious whore becomes drunk with the blood of true believers, God put it in the hearts of her paramours to turn on her and destroy her!

EIGHTEEN

The Last Days
of the Common Market

Do you remember how Chapter 16 of the Book of Revelation closed? All the cities of the world were destroyed, and the Battle of Armageddon was about to trigger the personal appearance of Jesus Christ back to this earth to restore it to its original beauty. This important event, which we call "the second coming of Jesus Christ," is described in detail in Chaper 19 of Revelation.

Between Revelation 16 and 19 we are given a parenthetical description of the destruction of two cities, each called Babylon. One is a religious system and the other is an economic metropolis. As we saw in Revelation 17, the religious system was not really a city at all in the sense that it had a specific geographical location. It was instead a *religious influence* which had attached itself to *many* cities during its long and blasphemous history since the days of its origin in ancient Babylon. The point that John makes in Revelation 17 is that this occultic religious system will attach itself to the last world empire during the Tribulation. For approximately three and one-half years "Babylon" will be synonymous with the kingdom of the Antichrist, until he finally rises up, throws off its control, and destroys it.

WHERE WILL THE HARLOT DIE?

The question that logically comes to mind is, "When the Antichrist destroys this Harlot in the middle of the Tribulation, does he destroy some *geographical location* from which she rules? I personally don't think so, since that would mean destroying his *own* kingdom, for it is in the Antichrist's kingdom that the Harlot has dominated. For example, if someone today wanted to break the power of the Roman Catholic Church, he wouldn't have to blow up Vatican City or the city of Rome. Assassinations of the Pope and the cardinals and bishops of the church, plus a destruction of some of the major seminaries and church buildings, and a confiscation of church property and wealth would finish the organization. The same is true of the Mormon Church. You wouldn't need to demolish Salt Lake City to do away with Mormonism!

I believe something like this will happen when the Antichrist destroys the false ecclesiastical system that seeks to smother him. He will purge its leaders and confiscate all its wealth. Then he will establish himself as the religious leader of the world and consolidate all worship in himself.

In Revelation 18, however, we see an entirely different picture. *This* Babylon is indeed a specific location. It's the center of fantastic commerce, trade, and industry in the last half of the Tribulation. In fact, I suspect there has never been a city in history that can rival the wealth, luxury, whirl of society, and moral decadence of this coming city! It will be so vital to the economic and cultural life of the whole world that when it's destroyed in one hour's time the whole will be plunged into mourning!

WILL BABYLON BE REBUILT?

The question of paramount interest at this point is, "Where will this great commercial Babylon be located? Is it some now-existing city which will be catapulted into world prominence, or will the ancient City of Babylon on the Plains of Shinar be rebuilt?" No question has tantalized Bible students more or given rise to more fanciful speculations.

There are many reputable Bible scholars who firmly believe that this Babylon is going to be an actual rebuilt city at the site of ancient Babylon on the Euphrates River. One of their main reasons for believing this is a prophecy of Isaiah about the ultimate destruction of Babylon. He said it would be destroyed *by the Lord Almighty* when the day of the Lord was near (Isaiah 13:6, 7). "The day of the Lord" refers to the period which immediately surrounds the coming of Christ.

Since the city of Babylon has not existed historically since the days of Alexander the Great, it would have to be rebuilt in order for God to destroy it in "the day of the Lord."

Another line of reasoning that seems to point to the rebuilding of Babylon is a prophecy by Zechariah about the last days. He speaks about a temple being built in the land of Shinar, which is Babylon. In order for a temple to be built there, it seems reasonable to assume that a city would have to be built as a site for the temple (Zechariah 5:5–11).

A NEW TOWER OF BABEL

In the *Los Angeles Times* of December 2, 1971, a very interesting article pointed out: "The tower of Babel, Biblical source of the world's languages, soon may rise again over the dusty plain once known as Mesopotamia. The Iraqi government is considering a plan to construct part of the ruins of Babylon, including a two hundred and ninety-five foot tower which probably inspired the author of the Book of Genesis."

Those plans are probably bogged down now because of the Gulf War between Iran and Iraq. But as the Arab world becomes wealthier from its oil revenues, other countries will probably assist the Iraqi government in its project to rebuild the ancient city and return it to its former glory. This would provide tourism and a national image they could look upon with favor in this age of technological marvels.

Although I and some other Bible students lean strongly in the direction of a rebuilt Babylon, other men believe with equal conviction that this Babylon represents a secular system of commerce and culture which is basically alienated from God. They feel it could be a great city of world acclaim in America, Europe, or Asia.

WHY REBUILD BABYLON?

If Babylon is actually to be rebuilt, what would be the purpose and function of the city? Would it be the economic giant we see in this chapter? I don't think so. It's hard to imagine how any city located in the hostile Arab world could rise to such world prominence with *all* the kings of the earth free to go in and out and conduct their business! Also, with the possible exception of Brasilia, the new capital of Brazil built in an uninhabited area in about ten years' time, it's very hard to imagine how a city of such predicted prominence could arise in the short period of time we have left and dwarf in importance such cities as New York, Los Angeles, London, Tokyo, and Rome.

No, I believe Babylon will be rebuilt, but *not* to be the commercial and economic center of the world. I believe it will be the center of the "Harlot" religion for a short while, until the religion is destroyed by Antichrist. Zechariah the Prophet affirms this reason for its rebuilding and the means by which it will be rebuilt with these words:

"Then the angel who talked with me went forth, and said, 'Lift up your eyes now, and see what this is that is going forth.' And I said, 'What is it?' And he said, 'This is an ephah that is going forth.' Again he said, 'This is their appearance throughout the land.' As I beheld, there was lifted up a talent of lead; and there sitting in the midst of the ephah was a woman. And he said to me, 'This is wickedness!' And he cast her down into the middle of the ephah; then he cast the weight of lead over its opening.

"Then I lifted up my eyes and looked, and two women were coming out with the wind in their wings; for they had wings like the wings of a stork, and they lifted up the ephah off the earth into the sky.

"Then I said to the angel who talked with me, 'Where are they taking the ephah?' And he said to me, 'To build for her a temple in the land of Shinar (Babylon); and she will be established there upon her own base' " (Zechariah 5:5–11).

THE EPHAH

An ephah was a symbol of commerce in Zechariah's day. It was a unit of dry measure which symbolized commercial and economic affairs. In fact, the symbol of two winged women holding an ephah and a balanced scale has for centuries been the recognized symbol of commerce. You can still find medallions with this picture on it, and many chambers of commerce still use this symbol.

Here in this prophecy the ephah represents the whole Satanic world system, including all the godless commercialism and hedonistic worship of luxury and pleasure which economic success permits. Zechariah also introduces a *woman*, who is at first seen sitting comfortably in the middle of this ephah (the godless commercial system). Here she is in intimate contact with all the worldy wealth and commerce by which she is supported and in which she delights.

But then Zechariah tells us that the angel pronounced an indictment of wickedness on the woman and threw her down into the middle of the ephah, restraining her there by means of a lead covering.

WHAT HAPPENS TO THE WOMAN?

The question that needs to be answered is, "How can the woman sit *contentedly* in the middle of this economic and commercial system (the ephah) and yet want to escape from it so badly that she has to be restrained?" I'll answer that in a minute, but first let's see what happens to this woman. She is picked up while still in the ephah and transported by two sympathetic women companions to the land of Shinar, the site of ancient Babylon. There the ephah (symbolizing the commercial and economic system) was to build a temple for the woman and to establish her in it.

Let me unscramble this prophecy for you now and tell you why I believe Babylon will be rebuilt, though *not* to be the great commercial-economic center of the world described in Revelation 18.

I believe that the *woman* which Zechariah speaks of in his prophecy is the religious Babylonish system which we saw in Revelation 17. It had its roots in the dark religion of ancient occultic Babylon. The *ephah* which this woman settles down in refers prophetically to the Revived Roman Empire and its capital, which I believe is Rome. For awhile this ecclesiastical Harlot is content to dwell in Rome. But sometime before the middle of the Tribulation she begins to get the idea that she isn't too popular with the Antichrist and his kingdom anymore, and so her religious system seeks to move her headquarters out of the clutches of the Antichrist. She casts about for the right spot to move to, and then decides on the location of her origin, Babylon. This is where all the magic, sorcery, and astrology began, and since all of this is such an important part of her worship and appeal, it's only natural that she would want to have Babylon looked to by the whole world as her religious headquarters.

Using the wealth she has accumulated by her stay within the "ephah" of Rome, she flees to Babylon and with the support of the Antichrist sets up shop. This is about midway through the Tribulation. Shortly after this the Roman Antichrist, much like Pharaoh of old, regrets that he let such wealth and power slip out of his grasp; so, realizing that he no longer needs the favor of this Harlot, he destroys her! It's possible that he also destroys what was rebuilt of Babylon, but I tend to think that God reserves that privilege for Himself at the end of the Tribulation.

For the next three and one-half years the Antichrist reigns as God on earth, killing the saints and coercing men to worship him. Then *his* great capital city, which I believe is Rome, is destroyed by the true God of heaven. This is the subject of Revelation 18.

I suggest that you now read all twenty-four verses of this chapter, keeping in mind that the chapter is describing the destruction of the most influential city in all of history (with the exception of Jerusalem). This "Babylon" must be located near a large body of water, since the smoke of its burning is seen by all kinds of ship personnel. It's also a great center of commerce, culture, and luxury and has a history of persecuting God's saints.

I believe this city is Rome! It's inconceivable to me that the Antichrist could be the most powerful ruler of the world, controlling a kingdom which surpasses all previous world empires in power and wealth, (and which is made up of people out of the old Roman culture) without having as his capital city the great economic center described in this chapter. And how could Rome not be the capital of the Revived Roman Empire? That this great city is called "Babylon" is no surprise either. It's synonymous with all the evil, corruption, dissoluteness, sensuality, and perversion of ancient Babylon and its reprobate child, religion.

CHAPTER 18

(1) After these things I saw another angel come down from heaven, having great authority, and the earth was made bright with his glory. (2) He cried mightily with a strong voice, saying, "Babylon the Great is fallen, is fallen, and has become the habitation of demons, and of every foul spirit, and a cage of every unclean and hateful bird. (3) For all nations have drunk of the wine of the wrath of her fornication, and the kings of the earth have committed fornication with her, and the merchants of the earth have grown rich through the power of her luxuries."

(4) I heard another voice from heaven, saying, "Come out of her, my people, in order that you may not be partakers of her sins, and that you do not receive her plagues; (5) for her sins have reached to heaven, and God has remembered her iniquities. (6) Reward her even as she rewarded you, and pay her back double according to her works; in the cup of torture which she filled for others, fill to her double. (7) As much as she has glorified herself, and lived luxuriously, so much torment and sorrow give her, for she said in her heart. 'I sit as a queen, and am no widow, and shall never see sorrow.' (8) Therefore shall her plagues come in one day, death, and mourning, and famine, and she shall be utterly burned with fire; for strong is the Lord God who judges her."

(9) And the kings of the earth, who have committed fornication and lived luxuriously with her, shall weep over her, and lament for her, when they see the smoke of her burning, (10) and they will stand afar off for fear of being involved in her torment saying, "Woe, woe the great city, Babylon, the mighty city! For in one hour your judgment has come."

(11) The merchants of the earth shall weep and mourn over her; for no man buys their merchandise any more; (12) the merchandise of gold and silver and precious stones, and pearls, and fine linen, and purple, and silk, and scarlet, and every kind of citron wood, and all kinds of vessels of ivory, and all kinds of vessels of most precious wood, and of bronze, and iron, and marble, (13) and cinnamon, and incense and perfumes, and ointments, and frankincense, and wine, and oil, and fine flour, and wheat, and cattle, and sheep, and horses, and chariots, and slaves, and souls of men.

(14) And the fruits that your soul so desired have departed from you, and all things which were luxurious and sumptuous have departed from you, and you will not find them anymore. (15) The merchants of these things, who were made rich by her, shall stand a distance away because of the fear of her torment, weeping and wailing, (16) and saying, "Woe, woe, the great city that was clothed in fine linen, and purple, and scarlet, and adorned with gold, and precious stones, and pearls! (17) For in one hour such great wealth has been destroyed."

And every shipmaster, and all the ship companies, and sailors, and as many as trade by sea, stood a distance away, (18) and cried when they saw

*the smoke of her burning, saying, "What city is like this great city?" (19)
They cast dust on their heads, and cried, weeping and wailing, saying, "Woe,
woe, the great city, in which all who had ships on the seas were made rich
by reason of her wealth! For in one hour she has been destroyed." (20) Rejoice
over her, you who dwell in heaven, and you holy apostles and prophets; for
God has avenged you on her.*

*(21)And a mighty angel took up a stone like a great millstone, and cast
it into the sea, saying, "In this same violent way that great city, Babylon,
will be thrown down, and will not be found again. (22) And the music of
harpers, and minstrels, and flute players, and trumpeters will not be heard
anymore in you; and no craftsman, and whatever craft he may be, will be
found any more in you; and the sound of a millstone will not be heard
anymore in you; (23) and the light of a lamp will not shine anymore in you;
and the voice of the bridegroom and the bride will not be heard anymore in
you; for your merchants were the great men of the earth; for by your sorceries
all nations were deceived." (24) And in her was found the blood of prophets,
and of saints, and of all that were slain upon the earth.*

REVELATION 18:1–24

PANIC SETS IN

Notice who it is that weeps the loudest over the fall of Babylon, the great city which is Rome. It's the merchants. These
businessmen have come from all over the world to do business
in this city. It's very possible that this will be the *capital* of the
world, since it's the city from which Antichrist will rule. That's
why it's the center of banking, finance, trade, culture, government, agriculture, industry, and the arts.

Everything these men hold dear—all their fame and for-
tunes—are wrapped up in this city and its continued growth.
No wonder they're so crushed at its fall. It's not often that you
see grown men weeping and wailing, at least not in public, but
at this time there will be no pride left in any man! Everything
they have will be lost. The panic will be a hundred times greater
than that which followed the U.S. stock market crash of 1929!

THEIR SOULS FOR A MESS OF POTTAGE

This superpower will deal not only with commodities, but
also with the *souls* of men (verse 13). How this is possible is
revealed in verse 23: "For your merchants were the great men
of the earth; for by your *sorceries* all the nations were deceived."
Evidently through the religious system, the Antichrist, and the

False Prophet (that unholy trinity!), men will be drawn under the hypnotic power of demons through sorcery and will actually sell their souls to Satan in exchange for his favor. Since no one will be able to buy or sell without the mark of the Beast, this represents his total control of every facet of the lives of those who've sworn allegiance to him. He literally becomes "Big Brother" of George Orwell's 1984!

THE FALL OF THE COMMON MARKET

The reason I call this chapter "The Last Days of the Common Market" is because I believe definitely that the present European Economic Community, also known as the Common Market, is the forerunner of the Biblically predicted Revived Roman Empire. The capital city of this Empire will be Rome, and it will become the unparalleled economic and commercial giant as described in this chapter of Revelation.

The "Harlot" religion of Chapter 17 is *not* a city. It's an occultic religious system and influence which exists in a spiritually adulterous relationship with the city of Rome and the kingdom of the Antichrist for the first half of the Tribulation. It then moves to new headquarters in a rebuilt city of Babylon on its ancient site, and after a brief reign from there is destroyed by Antichrist. At the end of the Tribulation, *Babylon the Great*, the capital of the Revived Roman Empire (Rome) and the subject of Chapter 18, is destroyed by God *Himself.* How He disposes of the Antichrist and the False Prophet is part of the subject of the next chapter.

NINETEEN

The Creator Repossesses
Planet Earth

For sheer drama it would be difficult to find any literature to compare with Revelation 19. Unparalleled contrasts are made in this chapter.

There are two suppers—one of sublime purity and joy as the Lamb takes his beloved bride, and the other of utter repugnance and horror as vultures come to devour the mountains of human bodies killed in the last mad battle on earth!

There are two responses to Jesus Christ—one a spontaneous thunder of praise about the rightness of God's judgments, and the other a hail of blasphemy and bullets to resist the King's return to His earth!

There are two rewards—one a dazzling robe of white linen given to each believer as he enters heaven, and the other a blinding flash of the naked power of Jesus Christ as He reduces to a sea of blood all those who wave their fists in defiance with their last ounce of strength!

WHAT TIME IS IT?

This chapter resumes the chronological picture of the future at the point where it left off at the end of Chapter 16.

In that chapter we saw the final acts of a godless world

coming to a roaring crescendo: millions of troops deployed along a battle line from Turkey to the Arabian and Sinai Peninsula are attacking each other with an insane frenzy. Cities are leveled, hundred-pound hailstones pulverize the earth, and the planet itself reels under the force of the greatest earthquake in the history of mankind!

These are the days about which Jesus had warned, "For then there will be great tribulation, such as has not been from the beginning of the world until now, no, and never will be. And if those days were not shortened, no human being would be left alive...." (Matthew 24:21, 22).

The *earth* will be on the precipice of self-annihilation, but in *heaven* it will be "the beginning of the end" for all human suffering.

THE JESUS RALLY WE'LL NEVER FORGET

> *(1) And after these things I heard a great voice of many people in heaven, saying, "Praise the Lord! Salvation, and glory, and honor, and power, belong to the Lord, our God; (2) For true and righteous are His judgments; for He has judged the great Harlot, who corrupted the earth with her fornication, and has avenged the blood of his servants at her hand." (3) And again they said, "Praise the Lord!" And her smoke rose up forever and ever. (4) And the twenty-four Elders and the four Living Beings fell down and worshipped God that sat on the throne, saying, "Praise our God, all you His servants, and you that fear Him, both small and great." (6) And I heard something like the voice of a great multitude, and like the voice of many waters, and like the voice of mighty peals of thunder, saying, "Praise the Lord! For the Lord our almighty God reigns."* REVELATION 19:1-6

This glimpse at the heavenly preparation for Jesus' return to earth reveals the most spirited Jesus Rally of all time. The scene revolves around five thunderous, resounding shouts of "Praise the Lord!" (the meaning of "hallelujah") which is sung in unison by angels, Old Testament saints, Tribulation saints, and Church saints.

I can really relate to this great scene because I've been in many Jesus rallies and worked with large numbers of young Jesus people in various countries. One of their favorite expressions is to shout in unison, "Praise the Lord!"

This is music to my ears. After growing up in a generation of timid and unexpressive Christians who felt like they had fulfilled their witnessing obligation if they told someone they didn't go to movies, it's beautiful to see the uninhibited way these young believers praise the Lord in public!

GOD'S JUSTICE IMPUGNED

In the eyes of unbelieving man, God is never fair in what He does. When men suffer the just consequences for flaunting God's grace, rejecting His love, and despising His law, they always blame God and call Him unjust! This willful blindness is reflected in Revelation 9:20, 21 and 16:21, where men blaspheme and curse God even though He has given warning after warning of impending judgment in an effort to get men to turn to Him in faith.

What a contrast with the scene going on at the same time in heaven! The vast multitude of redeemed men *praise* the triune God for His completed salvation, for His glory and power, and especially for His true and righteous judgment of the great religious system of the Harlot.

A CHORUS OF HALLELUJAHS

With the twenty-four Elders and four Living Beings on their faces before God's throne and the heavenly choir joining in the five great "Praise the Lord's," all creation gratefully extols the virtues of Christ their Creator!

All these beings rejoice at Christ's going to take His rightful reign over the earth. You see, Christ purchased the title deed to the earth at the Cross, but He hasn't yet exercised His *right* to the rulership of this earth. He'll do that when He comes back.

The saints in heaven break into the great "Hallelujah Chorus" of the Bible as Christ rises and prepares to return to the earth as King of Kings and Lord of Lords. They sing about how qualified Christ is to judge the world. Since He died for everyone, He has the right to judge those who turn down the love-gift He offers them.

You and I will be singing the Hallelujah Chorus too if we've received Christ as our personal Savior. You know, I'm really looking forward to finally getting to sing in a choir! Usually when I sing loudly in a song service before I speak, they tell me to save my voice for the message! But here's one time when we're *all* going to be singing, and I mean at the top of our voices, and it will sound like heaven itself!

INVITATION TO A WEDDING RECEPTION

> *(7) Let us be glad and rejoice, and give honor to Him; for the time of the marriage of the Lamb has come, and His bride has made herself ready. (8) And it was granted to her to be clothed with fine linen, clean and white; for the fine linen is the righteous acts of the saints. (9) And he said to me, "Write, 'Blessed are they who are called to the marriage supper of the Lamb.' " And he said to me, "These are the true words of God." (10) And I fell at his feet to worship him. And he said to me, "Don't do that! I am your fellow servant, and one of your brothers who declares the testimony about Jesus. Worship God; for the testimony about Jesus is the spirit of prophecy."*
>
> REVELATION 19:7–10

As I mentioned in Chapter 17, the Church is the bride of Jesus Christ. Nothing is more descriptive of the mystery of the Church than the Apostle Paul's sublime comparison of Christian marriage with the marriage of Church-age believers to the Lord.

Ephesians 5:25–32 reveals that each person who believes in Christ becomes a member of *His* body, of His flesh and bones. Then Paul writes, "For this cause a man shall leave his father and mother and be joined to his wife, and the two shall become one flesh. This mystery is a profound one, but I am speaking about Christ and the Church."

In order to better understand this *marriage* relationship with Christ, we need to examine the customs of the ancient world when Paul wrote these words. Although marriage customs varied, usually three steps were involved from the initial approach until the marriage union.

First, a marriage contract was negotiated between the parents, usually when the children were still too young to assume their adult roles. This contract was a binding agreement: it meant that the two parties were legally married even though they would have no sexual contact with each other for perhaps years. This condition was known as a "betrothal," but it was a much stronger tie than our present-day engagement period. It gave the two betrothed parties a chance to grow in their relationship before the actual consummation of their marriage vows.

The second step in the marriage process took place when the couple had reached a suitable age of maturity. The groom, accompanied by his friends, would go to the home of the bride and escort her to the house which he had prepared for both of them to live in. No doubt there would be an exchange of gifts as the bride presented her dowry and the groom gave gifts to his new bride.

Finally would come the consummating event, the wedding feast. To this gala event would be invited many guests to share the celebration of the union of the happy bride and groom.

THE CHURCH IS THE BRIDE OF CHRIST

What a beautiful picture of the union of a man or woman with Jesus Christ! When a person accepts the gift of forgiveness provided in Jesus' death on the Cross, he enters into a legal contract of union with Jesus. The Holy Spirit gives new life to the man's dead human spirit, and a beautiful, growing relationship develops between Christ and the new believer. This growth is called *maturing in your faith.*

When Christ returns at the Rapture for the Church, He is the Bridegroom coming to take His beloved bride to the home He has been preparing for her. There they joyously consummate their marriage vows, and the two who were previously *declared* one are now one in actual experience.

The bride eagerly lays her dowry at Jesus' feet—that dowry of crowns which she has won for faithfulness during her betrothal period on earth. Then the Bridegroom, Jesus, gives her the rewards of a well-pleased Groom.

This consummating phase of the believers' union with Christ takes place simultaneously with the Rapture and the immediately following Judgment Seat of Christ (the event in which rewards are given for faithful service on earth). Although it doesn't say so explicitly in any one passage of Scripture. I believe that the *friends of the Groom* who will attend this phase of the marriage service in heaven include both the Old Testament saints and the Tribulation saints who've died before the end of the Tribulation.

THE MARRIAGE SUPPER OF THE LAMB

The final step in the marriage of Christ to the Church is the wedding feast. While Revelation 19:9 pronounces a blessing on the guests at this supper, it doesn't indicate the time or place of it. One clue about where the supper will be held is Jesus' statement in Matthew 26:29 as He drinks the cup of wine at the Last Supper. He said He would not drink wine again until the day He drank it new with His disciples in His Father's *Kingdom.*

His "Father's Kingdom" is that thousand-year reign of Christ on earth following the Tribulation and the Battle of Armageddon. It's my feeling that the wedding feast of the Lamb and His bride will take place *on earth* at the very beginning of the millennial Kingdom of God. The special guests of honor will be those saints who survive the Tribulation and go into the thousand-year Kingdom as mortals. All those who return to earth with the Groom (including the bride, the Church) are *immortal* beings.

For the next thousand years the wedding guests join the bride and Groom in fellowship with one another on an earth that's been restored to its original beauty. This is one wedding where everybody goes home with the bride and Groom and they all live happily ever after!

A New Wardrobe for the Bride

One of the most exciting parts about a wedding is deciding what the wedding gown will be like. It's customary for the bride to wear white, symbolizing that she is pure. The Apostle Paul reminds us that Christ has given us His Word as a means of continual cleansing, so that He might bring us to Himself as a holy bride, without any spot or wrinkle or blemish (Ephesians 5:27).

John tells us here in Revelation 19 that the Lamb's bride has been given a wedding garment that would be the envy of every Paris designer! The unlimited imagination and skill of the great Designer of the universe have gone into the making of these gowns. They are to be made of fine linen, and this linen symbolizes the righteous deeds done by the saints while they lived on earth.

I think the point being made here is that *everyone* who is part of the bride will have a linen wedding gown, but the amount of yardage in the gown will be determined by how many deeds the bride did in dependence upon the Holy Spirit's power while she was still on earth.

TUNIC AND TOGA

To help appreciate this imagery we need to understand the standard clothing in John's day. Men wore a long, robelike undergarment called a tunic. This was usually plain white linen. Another loose, dressy robe was worn on top of this. In Roman times this was called a toga.

This clothing illustrates a very important truth. The linen undergarment represents the righteousness of *Christ*, which is given to every believer as a free gift when he believes in Christ as his Savior. Without this robe, no one would make it to heaven. On the other hand, once you've received the righteousness of *Christ* no one can ever take it from you. It's yours both for this life and for all eternity.

However, the robe which John speaks of is made up of the *believer's* righteous deeds and is analogous to the outer garment, the toga. The lavishness of this robe will be determined by the deeds we did while walking in communion with the Spirit. It will be woven with gold and silver and studded with precious stones to the degree that we performed our works by the power of the Spirit and *not* the flesh.

No one will stand "naked" at the Judgment Seat of Christ to have his works evaluated, but some will have garments with the smell of smoke on them from the fire that burned up their fleshly deeds of "wood, hay, and stubble" (see 1 Corinthians 3:10–15).

WE'RE SEWING FOR ETERNITY

We need to realize that we're preparing our "garments" for eternity *right now*. From the shabby Christian lives that some people live, it looks like there will be some "heavenly hippies"! It's better to be a hippy in heaven than not to be there at all, but it's better still to be a bride adorned to her fullest with a garment that befits the bride of a royal King!

WATCH OUT WHOM YOU KNEEL TO

A most educating incident occurred after John witnessed the breathtaking wedding scene of the Son and the joyous praise session. He was so awestruck by what the angel had showed him that he fell down at the angel's feet and worshipped him (Revelation 19:10).

Now this was no ordinary angel. He's described in Revelation 18:1 as having great authority and illuminating the earth with his glory. Yet look what he told John about worshipping him: "Don't do that! I am your fellow servant, and one of your brothers who declares the testimony about Jesus. Worship God: for the testimony about Jesus is the spirit of prophecy" (Revelation 19:10).

Since this mighty angel refused to accept worship, how much less should any other created being be worshipped or prayed to! Yet a common denominator of many of the religions of the world is that the person who founded the religious system eventually ends up being adulated or worshipped by his followers. (Christ is of course *worthy* of all the worship He receives since He didn't lead people in the quest *for* God but came to *show* us God, for that's who He claimed to be and who He is!)

PROPHECY IS A PERSON

The angel also reminded John that every aspect of *prophecy* is ultimately a testimony about Jesus. His Spirit permeates it.

That's one reason I love to preach prophetic messages. I'm sure that thousands have received Christ through the message of prophecy in my book, *The Late Great Planet Earth.* I've sat by the hour reading letters from people who've committed their lives to Christ through this message of Christ's return. It's also one of the strongest motivations to believers to get their priorities in life straightened out and to mean business for the Lord in their Christian lives.

Woe to the Christian who minimizes or rejects prophecy in the light of this statement by the angel! It's the same as rejecting Christ Himself.

BEHOLD, A WHITE HORSE!

(11) And I saw heaven thrown open, and a white horse charged forth; and He who sat on it was called Faithful and True, and in righteousness He judges and makes war. (12) His eyes were like a flame of fire, and on His head were many crowns; and He had a name written upon Him, which no man understood, but He Himself. (13) And He was clothed with a uni-

form dipped in blood; and His name is called the Word of God. (14) And the armies that were in heaven followed Him upon white horses, clothed in fine linen, white and clean. (15) And out of His mouth goes a sharp sword, so that with it He might strike the nations, and He shall rule them with a rod of iron; and He treads the winepress of the fierce wrath of Almighty God. (16) And He has on His uniform and on His thigh a name written, KING OF KINGS, AND LORD OF LORDS.   REVELATION 19:11–16

Think of how many Old Testament prophets and how many millions of saints have longed to see the moment when Jesus would return to earth as King of Kings and Lord of Lords and establish His kingdom of justice, equity, and peace, forever putting down those who oppose Him! It's overwhelming to realize that we are going to be a part of the group that experiences this glorious event depicted here!

It's always amazed me that so many professing Christians and ministers doubt that Jesus Christ will literally, visibly, and personally come back to this earth. And this in spite of the fact that one out of twenty-five verses in the New Testament says something about Christ's return to earth!

CHRIST PREDICTS HIS OWN RETURN

In Acts 1:8 Christ spoke His final words to His disciples before He physically left this earth. (I say *physically* because Christ is still in the world *spiritually*.) This is how Luke describes the events surrounding Christ's ascension from the earth: "And, when He had spoken these things, while they looked on, He was taken up, and a cloud received Him out of their sight. And while they were looking intently into the sky as He went up, behold, two men in white robes stood beside them" (Acts 1:9, 10).

Here's the scene. Christ had just given His disciples their final briefing, and then He started rising up into mid-air and disappeared into the sky. And there they all stood gaping. The disciples had just asked Jesus if He would give the kingdom to Israel at this time, and He had replied, "No." Then He told them there would be an interim program before the kingdom of God was to be set up.

The disciples stood there, startled by the fact that Jesus had gone, and in a very sensational way, to say the least. While they stood there dumbfounded, two angels appeared to them in the form of men, clothed with dazzling white garments. Verses 11 and 12 continue: " 'You men of Galilee, why are you standing looking into the sky? This same Jesus, who was taken up from you into the sky, will return in exactly the same manner as you saw Him go into heaven.' Then they returned to Jerusalem from the mount called Olivet, which is near Jerusalem, a Sabbath day's journey away."

When Jesus physically left the earth, angels immediately promised that He would come back *exactly* as He left. And how did He leave? Bodily, physically, and visibly! He was received up into a cloud. And He's going to come back the same way to the same place.

The Prophet Zecharaiah predicted five hundred years before Christ was born that His foot would first touch the earth at the Mount of Olives (Zecharaiah 14:4–8). Now that's the very place He left from! So He's coming back in the same way and to the same place.

Zecharaiah goes on to tell us that the Mount of Olives will be split in two by an incredible earthquake the moment Christ's foot touches it. A geological fault has been discovered which runs in exactly the direction this prophecy predicts! The main reason it hasn't split open until now is that it's waiting for the "foot"!

THE LION OF JUDAH

The description of Jesus given here in Revelation 19 reveals Him as the fierce warrior executing judgment upon those who have rejected Him and His offer of redemption. What a contrast between this role and Christ's role at His first coming, when as the "Lamb of God" He came to take away the sins of the world!

Jesus dramatically charges forth from heaven on a white stallion. A white horse has always been the symbol of conquest in the ancient world. The hands that hold the reins of this horse still bear the great scars of His crucifixion, a mute reminder to everyone being judged that He had died for their sins!

Zecharaiah 12:10 and Revelation 1:7 predict that the scars of Christ's crucifixion will be visible to the whole world, and that all the people, and especially the Jews, will mourn over Him.

Christ's eyes flash with vengeance as He righteously judges

those who slaughtered His people. He will be faithful and true to every promise and warning in the Bible!

A NAME ABOVE ALL NAMES

Jesus wears the many crowns of His royal and divine titles. These indicate that He's supreme in all things. He has a name written on Him that's so glorious, so much a part of His infinite character, that no man can understand it. The finite can never comprehend the infinite!

All the clothing of King Jesus is stained with the blood of His enemies. This fulfills a prediction which the Prophet Isaiah received after he asked the Lord about a vision he had seen: "Who is this who comes from Edom, with garments of crimson from Bozrah? . . . Why is your apparel red, and your garments like one who treads in the winepress?"

The Lord answers Isaiah, "I have trodden the winepress alone, and of the people there was none with Me; for I will tread them in My anger, and trample them in My fury; and their blood shall be sprinkled upon My garments, and I will stain all My raiment. For the day of vengeance is in My heart, and the year of My redeemed is come" (Isaiah 63:1–4).

THE WORD OF GOD IN FLESH

In Revelation 19:13 John tells us that Jesus' name is still "The Word of God." A few years later when this same John wrote the Gospel which bears his name, he explained fully what it meant for Jesus to be called "The Word."

Just as my words reveal my invisible self to you, so Christ is the visible expression of the invisible God. God clothed all His thoughts toward man in the Person of Jesus. In that sense Jesus is the ultimate communication of God to man. He's called "The Living Word" because in His person Jesus embodies everything God has to say to man about how to obtain eternal life.

THE KING AND HIS ARMY RIDE FORTH

What a sight this great army and its Leader will make! The King's clothes are stained with red and His troops are uniformed in pure white. The soldiers are all the redeemed in heaven, and as they follow behind their Leader they appear as a great cloud in the heavens.

When Christ appears at the Rapture seven years prior to this, He doesn't set foot on the earth; instead, He comes in the air, and only the believers see Him. But at *this* coming as King of Kings and Lord of Lords, *every* eye will see Christ and His army as they descend upon the earth!

With a sword coming out of His mouth, He'll destroy all His enemies and deliver the Tribulation believers who are still living.

God will at last send His Messiah to earth as King. Millions of people have said that they could never accept a suffering servant as their Messiah. So here He comes as a conquering King, and it's too late to fall at His feet and call Him Lord!

Oh, the blindness of men who *will* not see!

THE SUPPER OF FOOLS!

> *(17) And I saw an angel standing in the sun; and he cried with a loud voice, saying to all the fowls that fly in the atmosphere: "Come and gather yourselves together to the supper of the great God, (18) that you may eat the flesh of kings, and flesh of captains, and the flesh of mighty men, and the flesh of horses and of those who sit on them, and the flesh of all men, both free and enslaved, both small and great." (19) And I saw the Beast, and the kings of the earth, and their armies, gathered together to make war against Him who sat on the horse, and against His army. (20) And the Beast was seized, along with the False Prophet who performed miracles before him, with which he deceived those who had received the mark of the Beast, and those who worshipped his image. These were both cast alive into a Lake of Fire burning with brimstone. (21) And the rest of the Beast's followers were slain with the sword of Him who sat upon the horse, whose sword proceeded out of His mouth; and all the fowls were filled with their flesh.*
>
> REVELATION 19:17–21

The hardness of men's hearts reaches its zenith at the sight of Christ's return. The forces of the Antichrist and False Prophet and the great Oriental army apparently forget their animosity toward each other and join forces against their common enemy—the Lord Jesus Christ.

What insane folly!

But it does vindicate one thing. Every person who is condemned to hell will go there because he has deliberately chosen to reject Christ and heaven.

ANTICHRIST AND THE PROPHET JUDGED

Both the False Prophet who mesmerized unbelievers with his sorcery and miracles from Satan and the Roman Antichrist (the Beast) are now judged immediately by the Lord Jesus. They are cast directly into the Lake of Fire, while still conscious in their mortal life.

The difference between their judgment and that of all other unbelievers is that these false leaders are sent *directly* to the place called in the next chapter "the second death." In this horrible place there isn't even a further audience with Christ at the Great White Throne Judgment (which occurs at the end of the thousand-year Kingdom of God on earth). The evil of these two is so great that their guilt is beyond dispute!

Immediately after the disposal of the Antichrist and the False Prophet, Christ turns to judge all those still alive on earth who have rejected Him. This judgment is described in Matthew 25:31–46.

THE SHEEP AND GOATS SEPARATED

Jesus predicted in Matthew 25 that when He came the second time as Judge of the Universe He would separate the sheep from the goats. The sheep would be those people who had evidenced their faith in Him by the way they treated a group He called "these brothers of mine." As I mentioned in Chapter 7, I believe that "these brothers" refers to the 144,000 Jewish evangelists who will minister during the Tribulation. Each one of these preachers will have a price on his head, and anyone who helps one will do so at the risk of his own life.

Jesus calls these benevolent helpers "the righteous" and "sheep," and invites them into the Kingdom of God as mortal beings. Along with the 144,000 Jewish evangelists, these will be the only *mortal* (unglorified) persons to live on earth during the thousand-year Kingdom period.

The "goats" are those kings, captains, mighty men, and slaves who opposed the returning Christ and persecuted His evangelists during the Tribulation. They are now judged and sentenced to eternal fire and then slain with the sword of the Lord. For the next thousand years they suffer in a place called "torments" (Luke 16:19–31). Then, at the time of the Great White Throne

Judgment at the end of the Millennium, their bodies are resurrected and they are cast into the Lake of Fire.

The carnage of men and beasts at Christ's return is so great that God calls forth all the vultures in the air to come and dine at this revolting supper. What a needless tragedy! All of these who are slain could have had eternal bliss and happiness. But now they have become a feast of fools!

TWENTY

1000 Years of New Management

This chapter is one of the greatest and yet one of the most controversial in the Bible. It continues the chronological history of Jesus Christ's final judgments immediately after His return to earth.

In Revelation 19 the Antichrist and the False Prophet were cast alive into the Lake of Fire. Then all the armies that followed them were destroyed. And now at the beginning of Chapter 20 Satan, the arch-fiend of the universe and public enemy number one, is finally judged.

I recommend that you read this whole chapter before we examine the various themes of prophecy John records here. Keep in mind that the events of this chapter cover a period of 1,000 years.

THE KINGDOM OF GOD ON EARTH

(1) And I saw an angel come down from heaven, having the key of the bottomless pit and a great chain in his hand. (2) And he seized the dragon, that old serpent, who is the Devil and Satan, and bound him a thousand years, (3) and cast him into the bottomless pit, and shut him up, and set a seal upon him, so that he could not deceive the nations anymore, till the thousand years were fulfilled; and after that he must be released a little while.

(4) And I saw thrones, and they sat upon them, and judgment was given to them; and I saw the souls of those who had been beheaded because of

witnessing for Jesus, and standing for the Word of God, who had not wor-
shipped the Beast, or his image, or received his mark upon their foreheads,
or in their hands; and they lived and reigned (on earth) with Christ a thou-
sand years.

(5) But the rest of the dead did not live again until the thousand years
were finished. This is the first resurrection. (6) Blessed and holy is he who
has part in the first resurrection; over these the second death has no power,
but they shall be priests of God and of Christ, and shall reign with Him a
thousand years.

(7) And when the thousand years come to an end, Satan shall be loosed
out of his prison, (8) and shall go out to deceive the nations which are in the
four quarters of the earth, Gog and Magog, to gather them together to battle;
the number of whom is as the sand of the seas. (9) And they went out onto
the broad expanse of the earth, and surrounded the camp of the saints, and
the beloved city; and fire came down from God out of heaven, and devoured
them.

(10) And the Devil who deceived them was cast into the Lake of Fire
and brimstone, where the Beast and the False Prophet are, and shall be
tormented day and night forever and ever.

(11) And I saw a Great White Throne, and Him who sat on it, from
whose face the earth and the heaven fled away, and there was found no place
for them. (12) And I saw the dead, small and great, stand before God, and
the books were opened; and another book was opened, which is the Book of
Life. And the dead were judged out of those things which were written in
the books, according to their works. (13) And the sea gave up the dead that
were in it, and death and hades delivered up the dead that were in them;
and they were judged every man according to their works. (14) And those
from death and hades were cast into the Lake of Fire. This is the second
death. (15) And whoever was not found written in the Book of Life was cast
into the Lake of Fire.

A QUESTION OF FAITH

There is a certain amount of theological dispute about this
chapter, and it centers around a theme mentioned six times in
the chapter, namely, whether there will be a literal thousand-
year period of history during which mortal and immortal men
will live in an earthly Kingdom ruled by Jesus the Messiah
after His return to earth. This Kingdom is usually referred to
as the *Millenium*, from the Latin words *milli* (one thousand)
and *annum* (year).

The real issue at stake is whether God ever promised such

an earthly Kingdom, and if He did, will He keep His promise literally.

There are more prophecies in the Bible about this Kingdom and its significance to the believing Jew than any other theme of prophecy. The heart of the Old Testament prophetic message is the coming of Messiah to set up an earthly Kingdom over which He would rule from the throne of David. The only important detail which the Book of Revelation adds concerning this promised messianic Kingdom is its duration—one thousand years.

ARE YOU A PRE-, A-, OR POST-MILLENNIALIST?

Most readers of this book probably have no idea which view of the Millennium they hold—and couldn't care less! However, since this is a controversial issue as well as one of the most important themes in the Book of Revelation, I feel it's necessary to briefly discuss the three most popular interpretations of this Kingdom period.

PRE-MILLENNIALISM

The oldest interpretation is called *pre-millennialism*. This view holds that Christ will literally and bodily return to earth *before* the thousand-year Kingdom begins. He will set up this Kingdom and reign from the throne of David out of a rebuilt city of Jerusalem. At the end of the thousand years He will turn the Kingdom over to His Father, at which point it will merge with God's *eternal* Kingdom.

Pre-millennialists also believe that God made many unconditional promises and covenants with Israel, and that regardless of Israel's past history of spiritual failures, God will *literally fulfill* all His promises during this thousand-year Kingdom period.

Church-age believers and Tribulation believers will also be the recipients of these promises as the adopted sons of Abraham.

I believe the apostles and early Christians unanimously expected Jesus to set up a literal, earthly Kingdom of God. In Acts 1:6, just before Jesus ascended into heaven, the disciples asked Him, "Lord, will you at this time restore the Kingdom to *Is-*

rael?" In His answer Christ didn't try to set them straight by telling them there wouldn't be an earthly Kingdom for Israel. He simply told His disciples that it wasn't for them to know *when* it would come to pass, for this was something which only God the Father knew.

In the Lord's Prayer, Jesus again emphasized this anticipated earthly Kingdom when He told His followers to pray, "Thy *Kingdom* come. Thy will be done *on earth* as it is in heaven." His will can't be done on earth in the same way it is in heaven until all of Christ's enemies have been put down and Satan hindered from tempting men!

One of the major tenets of pre-millennialism is that the earth is getting *worse* rather than better, and that the Kingdom age can't begin until Christ returns to destroy those who've led the world in its downward spiral.

A-MILLENNIALISM

A-millennialism teaches that there will be *no* thousand-year reign of Christ on earth and *no* earthly Kingdom of God. According to this view, when Christ returns to earth He will take all the believers out, condemn all the unbelievers, and eternity will begin right then. This is what they believe is meant by the dividing of the sheep (believers) from the goats (unbelievers).

This view tends to allegorize all the prophecies about the promised Kingdom. It also teaches that Israel forfeited all God's promises to her because of unbelief, and that the Church will inherit all the promises originally intended for Israel. A-millennialists teach that the Church is the fulfillment of the millennial Kingdom, and that Christ presently reigns through the Church in peace and righteousness.

This interpretation allegorizes the chaining of Satan in this chapter and teaches that he was instead bound by Christ at His first coming, so that each time Christ gives a believer victory over a temptation it's a kind of reaffirmation of that binding of Satan. A-millennialism optimistically sees the Church moving triumphantly to victory.

POST-MILLENNIALISM

This view teaches that there will be a literal thousand-year Kingdom on earth, but that Christ will claim His Kingdom only *after* the thousand years have expired. Post-millennialists believe that the world will get better and better through the spread of the gospel and this will be the millennial age. Then, *after* the Millennium Christ will take the believers to heaven and condemn those who reject Him.

However, this teaching suffered a severe reversal in the past sixty years because of two world wars and "police actions"! The world is obviously *not* getting better and better, even though the gospel has had its widest hearing of any era!

WHAT'S REALLY AT STAKE?

I've only briefly outlined the basic tenets of each of these three interpretations, and there are countless variations of the positions I've described. But as I study the Scriptures and consider the various views on this question, I'm convinced that the most important issue at stake is that of *consistency* in Bible interpretation.

For instance, in Chapter 20 of Revelation there is absolutely no basis for saying that the narrative should be taken nonliterally. There's no way it could have been written more forcefully as objective, historical fact rather than subjective allegory.

By the same principle of interpretation which the a-millennialist uses to make the thousand-year kingdom non-literal, I could say that the last judgment isn't literal either. But there's an obvious danger in this: how can you interpret a passage nonliterally when there's no evidence of allegory in the passage? Your only authority for doing this is your personal, subjective opinion of God's truth or a deeply ingrained tradition of theology. This divests Scripture of its objective and evident truth. This highly-questionable method of interpretation has led some people down the primrose path to liberal theology!

THERE REALLY IS A NEW WORLD COMING

For thousands of years men have sought to escape the pressures and trials of this life in some Utopia or Shangri-la. But these have only been illusive dreams, and denial of their fulfillment has only served to frustrate man still more.

But the Kingdom which Christ will bring and reign over

will be a world marvelously beyond man's wildest dreams. John in his vision in Revelation doesn't give us many details about this Kingdom. He merely emphasizes the fact and duration of it. It's the Old Testament prophets who paint the picture that has whetted the appetite of every heaven-bound traveler for centuries.

They tell us of a Kingdom where there will be peace and tranquility, where men will "beat their swords into plowshares and spears into pruning hooks and learn war no more" (Isaiah 2:4). The wolf will lie down with the lamb, and a man will be a child when he's a hundred years old (Isaiah 11:6; 65:20). There'll be justice for all, the wicked will be immediately punished and the whole world will be filled with the knowledge of God (Isaiah 11:9). Jesus Himself will rule from the capital city, Jerusalem, and there will be a perfect, one-world government (Zechariah 14:9, 16–21).

In order for man to inhabit the ravaged earth during the Millennium, it will first have to be restored by Jesus. That means that the whole animal and vegetable worlds will be at their highest state of development. Man won't have marred it with the refuse of his selfish activites. The sky will be bluer, the grass will be greener, the flowers will smell sweeter, the air will be cleaner, and man will be happier than he ever dreamed possible!

Four important phases of this Millennium are described in Revelation 20.

PHASE ONE — THE DECEIVER IS JAILED

(1) And I saw an angel come down from heaven, having the key of the bottomless pit and a great chain in his hand. (2) And he seized the dragon, that old serpent, who is the Devil and Satan, and bound him a thousand years, (3) and cast him into the bottomless pit, and shut him up, and set a seal upon him, so that he could not deceive the nations anymore, till the thousand years were fulfilled; and after that he must be released a little while. REVELATION 20:1–3

John tells us here about a powerful personage who comes down from heaven with a most unusual key and chain. He heads straight for Satan and does six things to him: (1) he lays hold on him; (2) he ties him up for a thousand years; (3) he casts him into a place called the bottomless pit or abyss; (4) he uses the key to lock him up; (5) he sets a seal on him that keeps him from continuing to deceive the nations; and (6) he lets him loose after the thousand years is over.

I said that the key and chain were unusual, and they would have to be in order to hold a creature such as Satan, who has such enormous power of his own. I don't really have any problem believing that God could make such a key and chain, since Satan has never really been free anyway. He's only been able to do what God has permitted. God has had him on a long leash, and now the time has come to pull it in!

WHY BIND SATAN?

Why does God finally put Satan under lock and key? So that Satan can't go around deceiving the nations during the thousand-year Kingdom. For thousands of years he has deceived the nations of the world into thinking that they can build a better world without Christ. Sometimes he convinced the nations that the only way to solve their problems was by war. At other times he deceived them into thinking that education, environment, and religion could save the world! He sponsored any program that left Christ out.

The Messianic Kingdom promised throughout the Old Testament is to be a period of universal righteousness and peace. But this couldn't be possible if Satan were free to incite men to follow the inclination of their lower natures. Even with Satan not active, there will still be a certain amount of sin during the Millennium. The Tribulation believers still in their physical bodies will have sinful natures, they and their children can choose to rebel against God, and some will.

PHASE TWO — THE FIRST RESURRECTION

(4) And I saw thrones, and they that sat upon them, and judgment was given to them; and I saw the souls of those who had been beheaded because of witnessing for Jesus, and standing for the Word of God, who had not worshipped the Beast, or his image, or received his mark upon their foreheads, or in their hands; and they lived and reigned on earth with Christ a thousand years. (5) But the rest of the dead did not live again until the thousand years were finished. This is the first resurrection. (6) Blessed and holy is he who has part in the first resurrection; over these the second death has no power, but they shall be priests of God and of Christ, and shall reign with Him a thousand years. REVELATION 20:4–6

Although many religions promise their followers a resurrection, they generally have in mind a spiritual resurrection—something that lets the spirit of the person live on in some way but leaves the body to decay and return to dust, never to live again.

Not so with the Judeo-Christian teaching. Both the Old and the New Testament speak of a bodily resurrection of the righteous and unrighteous dead. Four thousand years ago Job, God's suffering servant, said, "I know that my Redeemer lives, and that He shall stand in the latter day upon the earth; and after my skin has been destroyed, yet *in my flesh* I shall see God" (Job 19:25, 26).

One of the most treasured subjects in the whole Bible is its dogmatic presentation of life after death. Practically all men dream of waking from death to an eternal state of bliss. It forms a definite part of practically every ancient culture. The Egyptian Pharoahs were buried with gold, jewels, food, and their favorite things so they could use them in that next world. Even the American Indian was buried with his bow and arrows that he might hunt in the happy hunting ground.[1]

In the New Testament the word *resurrection* is used about forty times and almost always speaks of a *bodily* resurrection. Paul and Peter speak of it with certainty, and Jesus Himself made the strongest statement about it: "Marvel not at this, for the hour is coming in which all that are in the grave will hear His voice and will come forth" (John 5:28).

WHERE DO THE DEAD GO?

I've been to funerals of people who made no profession of interest in God or spiritual things and heard well-meaning ministers eulogize the dead person with, "He's gone on to his eternal reward."

I always wince when I hear this because I fear what his eternal reward is going to be—it's not what the minister has in mind!

Let me say first that while the *body* of everyone who dies eventually disintegrates, the soul leaves the body at the point

---

[1]Tim LaHaye, *Revelation Illustrated and Made Plain*, Family Life Seminar, 1973.

of death and continues on in a conscious state either with the Lord or separated from Him. The factor that decides where a person spends eternity is his faith in God and His provision of sacrifice for sin.

Both the Old Testament place of the dead (*sheol*) and the New Testament *hades* are often referred to as "hell," and many people have the idea that it's strictly a place of punishment. That's not the case, however. The fact is that *sheol* and *hades* are the same place, the place where *all* departed dead spirits went before Christ's resurrection, both good and bad people.

Hades had two compartments to it: *Paradise* (sometimes called "Abraham's bosom"), where those who had faith in God and His sacrifice for sin went, and *Torments*, the place where all unbelievers went and still are.

There was a great gulf fixed between these two places, so that even though people could look across it, they couldn't cross it. We're told that when Christ died on the Cross, he descended into hell (hades). It's certain that He went into the Paradise side of hades and announced that the promised redemption these saints had looked forward to with the faithful offering of sacrifices was now a completed fact.

He may also have entered Torments and preached to the spirits imprisoned there (1 Peter 3:19). The Greek word which Peter uses for *preached* means to *announce* something rather than to "seek to convert." For all the people in Torments it was too late for conversion-preaching. Evidently Christ announced to them that God's plan for legally breaking Satan's power over men was now accomplished, and that Satan was a defeated foe. They had cast their lot with the wrong side!

JESUS EMPTIED PARADISE

When Jesus rose from the grave He took to heaven with Him the souls of all those who were in Paradise. This seems to be what the Apostle Paul meant by Jesus "leading the captives captive" when He was resurrected, the captives referring to those waiting for God's promised redemption to be completed (Ephesians 4:8–10).

Since the resurrection of Jesus, whenever a believer dies, his soul and spirit go immediately to be face-to-face with Jesus in heaven (see 2 Corinthians 5:8 and Philippians 1:21–23). It doesn't make any difference where his body goes—whether it's buried, cremated, chewed up by man-eating sharks, or mummified! At the Rapture it will come back together again and be united with its soul and spirit, never again to know pain, weakness, or heartache.

But not so with the unbelievers. The soul of everyone of every era who dies without receiving God's provision for forgiveness of sin will go to "Torments" and stay there until his body is resurrected from the grave at the end of the Millennium and united with his suffering soul.

THE ORDER OF RESURRECTION

In this chapter of Revelation a first and a second resurrection are mentioned. The first one has several phases to it, and is made up of believers only. The second resurrection is at the end of the Millennium and is for unbelievers.

Let's briefly consider the four phases of the first resurrection. First Corinthians 15:20–25 tells us that Christ was the "first fruits of the resurrection." The word "first fruits" is taken from the feasts of the Nation of Israel, and means that since Christ was the first man to be permanently raised from the dead, with a body that could never see death, destruction, or decay, we can be assured that others will follow and be resurrected in the same way. Jesus' resurrection was the *first phase* of the "first resurrection" mentioned in Revelation 20.

The *second phase* of this first resurrection takes place when the Church is caught up at the Rapture. In this stage all the deceased and living believers who have trusted in Christ from the day of Pentecost until the Rapture will be *bodily* taken into heaven.

Old Testament believers, however, will not be bodily resurrected until the *third phase* of the resurrection. This will take place *after* the Tribulation, when Christ returns to the earth. At this point all the Old Testament saints and all the martyred Tribulation believers will have their bodies brought out of the grave and united with their souls and spirits. They will receive immortal, eternal bodies and go right into the Kingdom (see Daniel 12:1–3).

The mortal believers who live through the thousand-year millenial Kingdom will be the final ones to receive eternal bodies. These make up the *fourth phase* of the first resurrection. Apparently there will be no death for believers during the Kingdom, though there will be the immediate judgment of death for *unbelievers* if they persist in serious sins.

WHO'S ON THE THRONES?

In Revelation 20:4 John said he saw thrones with an unidentified group of people sitting on them, people with the authority to mete out judgment of some kind. We're not told here specifically who these rulers could be, but several other places in the Bible say that believers will rule over cities and even angels during the Millennium (1 Corinthians 6:2, 3). I think this group John saw is probably a representative group of Church-age believers and perhaps Christ Himself.

John also saw the souls of the martyred Tribulation saints united with their bodies and elevated to a ruling role with Christ for the next thousand years.

A question that many people ask is, "Whom will the believers rule over?"

We can't be absolutely certain, but in some way believers will help Christ govern the universe with all its diverse creation. It will be a rule of love, but there will be a tremendous number of people on the earth, and they will need some direction to their activities.

PHASE THREE — SATAN IS UNBOUND AND JUDGED

(7) And when the thousand years come to an end, Satan shall be loosed out of his prison, (8) and shall go out to deceive the nations which are in the four quarters of the earth, Gog and Magog, to gather them together to battle; the number of whom is as the sand of the sea. (9) And they went up on the breadth of earth, surrounded the camp of the saints, and the beloved city; and fire came down from God out of heaven, and devoured them. (10) And the Devil who deceived them was cast into the Lake of Fire and brimstone, where the Beast and the False Prophet are, and shall be tormented day and night forever and ever. REVELATION 20:7–10

Why is Satan released again after 1,000 years of imprisonment? Why does the history of man begin with perfect environment and end the same way?

I believe these two questions are inseparably related. We know from such Bible verses as Matthew 25:31–46 that the millennial Kingdom will begin with believers only. But apparently many of the children born during this period will not truly believe in Jesus as their Savior, and they will be deceived by Satan after he is loosed and will follow him.

Even though there'll be great security, equality, prosperity, and peace, as well as perfect ecology and government, there'll still be those who reject Christ and His forgiveness and secretly harbor rebellion in their hearts. What the Prophet Jeremiah said about man will be proven forever: "The heart is the most deceitful thing there is, and desperately wicked. No one can really know how bad it is" (Jeremiah 17:9, *TLB*).

PERFECT ENVIRONMENT IS NOT THE SOLUTION

I believe the great lesson God wants us to learn from this is that even though history begins with man in a perfect environment with all his needs met and ends the same way, the rebellion in a man's heart isn't caused by his environment. It may be aggravated by it, but the real root cause of rebellion against God is a bitter heart of sin that's never been healed by a new birth.

Almost everyone recognizes that man has a radical problem of some kind. Many diagnoses have been made in an effort to find solutions. The psychologist blames a "behavior disorder," and the sociologist calls it "cultural lag." Minority groups cite "racism" and the Communist calls it "class struggle."

But God stepped out of eternity into time nineteen centuries ago and called man's problem *sin!* You can't have an effective cure without an accurate diagnosis, and God alone has correctly diagnosed man's problem as sin and spiritual separation from Him!

THE DEVIL DOES IT AGAIN

The first thing Satan does when he is released from the abyss after the Millennium is to organize a war. War is one of his favorite enterprises. He gets together some of the descendents of the enemies of Israel (Gog and Magog) who were born during the Millennium, and surrounds Jerusalem. But the rebellion doesn't even get off the ground. God zaps them all with fire from heaven and they are annihilated.

This event ends the Devil's career of evil. God casts him into the Lake of Fire, and there with his evil companions, the Antichrist and the False Prophet, he is tormented forever. I'm sure this doesn't bring any joy to God's heart. This creature, Satan, was God's most beautiful creation and here he ends in terrible infamy. Yet in the light of the great misery and suffering he has caused, it's a time for great thanksgiving, and I'm sure the universe breathes a sigh of relief at his final banishment.

PHASE FOUR — THE LAST JUDGMENT OF GOD

(11) And I saw a Great White Throne, and Him who sat on it, from whose face the earth and the heaven fled away, and there was found no place for them. (12) And I saw the dead, small and great, stand before God, and the books were opened; and another book was opened, which is the Book of Life. And the dead were judged out of those things which were written in the books, according to their works. (13) And the sea gave up the dead that were in it, and death and hades delivered up the dead that were in them; and they were judged every man according to their works. (14) And those from death and hades were cast into the Lake of Fire. This is the second death. (15) And whoever was not found written in the Book of Life was cast into the Lake of Fire.   REVELATION 20:11–15

It's a great burden for me to write about this awesome and irreversible judgment of God. It gives me no pleasure to talk about my fellowmen being thrown alive into a lake that burns with an unquenchable fire for eternity.

The reason that eternal hell-fire is so hard for many people to believe is that it seems out of character with a God of love and peace. I hope by now you've seen how longsuffering and patient God is with men, and how reluctant He is to discharge these awful judgments.

It must also be fairly stated that God never made hell for men. It was made for Satan and his demons. The only men who will be sent there are those who genuinely did not want God's provision of pardon. For some reason known only to them, they would not repent of their sins after gracious warnings by God and knowledge of the alternative—hell.

THE SECOND RESURRECTION

Jesus predicted that there would be a resurrection of life and a resurrection of damnation (John 5:29). These correspond to the two resurrections of Revelation 20. The resurrection of damnation is that final gathering at the Great White Throne of God of all the bodies and souls of the unbelieving dead of all ages. This is the second resurrection.

WHY A FINAL JUDGMENT?

We've already seen that the souls of those who die without receiving God's pardon go directly into a place of punishment called Torments. Jesus emphasized the certainty of this when He said of Himself, "He who believes in Me is not condemned, but he who does not believe in Me is condemned already, because he has not believed in the name of the only begotten Son of God" (John 3:18).

If the unbeliever is *already* condemned, then the big question is, "What is the purpose of the last judgment at the Great White Throne of God?"

The purpose of this final confrontation between God and unbelieving man is to clearly demonstrate to the unbeliever *why* he is already condemned.

THE CELESTIAL BOOKS ARE OPENED

John tells us in verse 12 that the books were opened, including one called "the Book of Life," and that all the unbelievers standing before the throne were judged one by one from these books. The identity of all these books is not revealed. We can only speculate as to what they are.

I believe the first book opened will be the "Book of God's Law." In numerous verses in the Bible, God's written Word is referred to as the "Book of the Law." We're told that anyone who's had exposure to God's Word is responsible to live according to it, and if he doesn't he's condemned by God. Paul says this when he quotes from the Old Testament as he rebukes the Galatians for trying to get God to accept them by their good works: "Cursed is everyone who does not continue in *all* things which are written in the Book of the Law" (Galatians 3:10).

No doubt there will be many standing before God who can honestly plead that their ears had never heard one word from God's Law in their lifetime. To them God will affirm what He inspired the Apostle Paul to write to the early Church, namely, that those who've never heard the Law have had it written instinctively in their consciences by God Himself, but that they haven't always followed the good which their consciences have dictated, and this itself has condemned them (Romans 2:11–16).

THE BOOK OF WORKS

The second book which will be opened is the "Book of Works." Evidently each person has a recording angel who is writing down all of his works. Every time he has an opportunity to receive Christ as Savior and turns it down, it's recorded in the book. Every bad deed as well as every good deed that's done with the wrong motive is also written down and will be held against the doer.

It doesn't make any difference whether the wrong deed was done in secret. Solomon wrote in the book of Ecclesiastes, "For God will judge us for everything we do, including every hidden thing, good or bad" (Ecclesiastes 12:14, *TLB*).

If you've received the forgiveness that God offers in His Son's death for you, then God has *already* judged all the wrong things you've done or will do; Jesus has already taken God's wrath against those sins in your behalf. Now God accepts you perfectly, and you don't have to worry that God will keep a list of all your evil deeds. He nailed your list to the Cross, and Jesus buried it in the grave!

THE BOOK OF LIFE

The last book to witness against those awaiting their sentences at God's throne is the "Book of Life." The New Testament refers to the "Book of Life" eight times, and although the Old Testament doesn't call it by that name, it refers three times to a book in which names are written.

This book contains the name of every person born into the world. If by the time he dies, a person has not received God's provision of sacrifice to remove sin, then his name is blotted out of this "Book of Life." Some persons standing there will have so hardened their hearts that they accepted the mark of the Beast during the Tribulation, and their names were *immediately* blotted out of the "Book of Life."

So when God opens this book at the Great White Throne Judgment, the only names left in it will be the names of those who have believed in Christ as Savior and Lord. That's why the name of the book is changed from the "Book of Life" to the "Lamb's Book of Life."

SUMMING IT ALL UP

Here is the heart-rending scene that's going to take place at this Judgment Seat of God. As each man steps before the throne, God will first open the "Book of the Law." He'll show the man what was required of him if he was to come to God by the merit of his own good deeds. He'll patiently go over each point of the Law, showing afresh that the standards are so high that no man could keep them. Then God will remind the offender that this is why He sent His Son—to perfectly fulfill the demands of the Law for us and in us.

After this God will open the "Book of Works," with this man's name on it. God will painstakingly compare it point-by-point with the "Book of the Law," showing the man how he failed to measure up to what the Law of God demanded in the way of righteousness. He'll show the many times that he failed to heed the prompting of God's still, small voice in his conscience which told him to get right with God while there was still time.

Then God will quietly lay down these two books and pick up the "Book of Life." It's quite evident by now that the first two books have confirmed the condemnation that has brought the man to this bar of judgment, but just to prove beyond doubt there has been no mistake, God checks His final record.

He solemnly opens the "Book of Life" and begins to scan the pages for the man's name. Those nail-scarred hands turn first one page, and then another, all the time wishing the man's name could be found there. Tragically, it can't be found on any page, and God slowly closes this final book of judgment and says with great reluctance: "Depart from me, accursed one, into the eternal fire which has been prepared for the Devil and his angels" (Matthew 25:41).

The man begins to tremble, and frantic words rush to his defense—"Lord, Lord, didn't I prophesy in Your name, and in

Your name cast out demons, and in Your name perform many miracles?" (Matthew 7:22, 23).

The Father slowly shakes His head and says, "I *never* knew you."

Those words will ring in the condemned man's ears for all eternity—"I *never* knew you, I *never* knew you, I *never* knew you. . . ."

Perhaps the reason God will not allow any believers to attend this awful moment of truth is that we wouldn't be able to bear having a friend or loved one turn to us and say with bewildering accusation, "Why didn't *you* warn me of this judgment and tell me about Jesus' forgiveness for these sins which have now condemned me to hell?"

TWENTY-ONE

The Coming New World

We sometimes deride a man who's all caught up with learning the Bible and serving God and has become a little irresponsible about his daily responsibilities. We say of him, "He's so heavenly-minded that he's no earthly good!"

Personally, I don't think that's the problem today. Nowadays most people are so earthly-minded they're no *heavenly* good! I believe that the more a Christian understands about his future destiny and the wonders which God has in store for him, the better and more enthusiastically he will be able to live in this world.

MISPLACED EMPHASIS

In an effort to win converts to Christ, some Christians have overemphasized the *immediate* benefits of salvation. I agree that it's important to know that Christ can give a person peace, purpose, and pardon in this life, but I also believe that it's time for us to reemphasize the fact that there's an eternal punishment in everlasting torment for everyone who rejects God's offer of forgiveness, and that there's a fantastic place prepared for each of God's children in a new world that's coming.

Most people refer to this eternal home with God as *heaven*, but this is a misnomer. Someone who dies before the Rapture will indeed go to be with Christ in a place called heaven, but that's not where believers are going to spend *eternity* with God. Between the heaven that exists now and the eternal home with God is the thousand-year millenial Kingdom on earth.

The final dwelling-place of the believers of all ages will be a re-created earth and virtually indescribable city called the New Jerusalem. I like to call it the "New J." In this chapter the Prophet John draws back the curtain of eternity future and gives us a dazzling glimpse of this City of God and the mansions which Jesus has been preparing for us, His bride.

GOD'S PLAN WAS PERFECT

Now that we're standing at the closing hours of John's revelation in this chapter, we can look back over God's ingenious plan for climaxing human history while at the same time administering justice to friend and foe alike.

The era of grace in which we live will end with all believers being taken off the earth and into heaven. This is known as the Rapture, or the "Great Snatch"! This event will be followed by seven years of horrible tribulation on the earth in which mankind will be punished for their rejection of God's Son. During this seven years the believers will be royally wedded to Jesus in heaven. They will also receive rewards for any and all Spirit-filled service done while on earth.

Then in the Battle of Armageddon at the end of the Tribulation God will vanquish His enemies, and the Antichrist and the False Prophet will be cast into the Lake of Fire. God will then restore the earth, though not to the extent of complete re-creation. The re-creation will take place *after* the Millennium and before the start of eternity itself.

Man will enjoy a peace-filled thousand years on this old earth. But at the end of this time, after the mortals have had perfect government by the perfect God-man in the most perfect surroundings imaginable, some will end up rebelling and blowing it again at their first opportunity!

This opportunity will come when Satan is loosed for a short time at the end of the Millennium to lead astray some of the mortals who were born during the Kingdom years. But God will promptly end the rebellion with a purge of fire and will exile Satan permanently to the Lake of Fire.

Then God will call all the unbelieving dead persons out of

their graves to stand before His Great White Throne for their final sentencing to the Lake of Fire.

This ends the Millennium, and eternity then begins with God destroying the old earth and re-creating a new heaven (universe) and earth. His crowning creation, however, is the New Jerusalem—that beautiful City of God.

Read all of Revelation 21:1 to 22:5 at one time for a big overview of this fabulous destiny of God's children. The first five verses of Chapter 22 are included because they also describe the New Jerusalem.

THE NEW HEAVEN, EARTH, AND JERUSALEM

(1) And I saw a new heaven and a new earth, for the first heaven and the first earth were passed away, and there was no more sea. (2) And I, John, actually saw the Holy City, New Jerusalem, coming down from God out of heaven, prepared as a bride adorned for her husband. (3) And I heard a great voice out of heaven saying, "Behold, the tabernacle of God is with men, and He will dwell with them, and they shall be His people, and God Himself shall be with them, and be their God. (4) And God shall wipe away all tears from their eyes, and there shall be no more death, or sorrow, or crying, neither shall there be any more pain, for the former things are passed away."

(5) And He who sat upon the throne said, "Behold, I am going to make all things new." And He said to me, "Write, for these words are true and faithful." (6) And He said to me, "It is done. I am Alpha and Omega, the beginning and the end. I will give to whoever is athirst of the fountain of the water of life freely. (7) He who overcomes shall inherit all things, and I will be his God, and he shall be My son. (8) But the fearful, and unbelieving, and the abominable, and murderers, and fornicators, and sorcerers, and idolators, and all liars, shall have their part in the lake which burns with fire and brimstone, which is the second death."

(9) And there came to me one of the seven angels who had the seven bowls full of the seven last plagues, and talked with me, saying, "Come here, I will show you the bride, the Lamb's wife." (10) And he carried me away in the Spirit to a great and high mountain, and showed me that great city, the Holy Jerusalem, descending out of heaven from God, (11) having the glory of God; and her light was like a stone most precious, even like a jasper stone, clear as crystal;

(12) it had a great, high wall, and had twelve gates, and at the gates were twelve angels, and names were written on the gates, which are the names of the twelve tribes of the children of Israel; (13) on the east three gates, on the north three gates, on the south three gates, and on the west three gates. (14) And the wall of the city had twelve foundations, and on them the names of the twelve apostles of the Lamb.

(15) And he who talked with me had a golden reed to measure the city and the gates of it, and its wall. (16) And the city lies foursquare, and the length is as large as the breadth; and he measured the city with the reed—fifteen hundred miles. The length and the breadth and the height of it are equal. (17) And he measured the wall of it—seventy-two yards, according to the measure of a man, which are also angelic measurements.

(18) And the building material of the wall was jasper; and the city was pure gold, like clear glass. (19) And the foundations of the wall of the city were garnished with all manner of precious stones. The first foundation was jasper; the second, sapphire; the third, chalcedony; the fourth, emerald; (20) the fifth, sardonyx; the sixth, sardius; the seventh, chrysolite; the eighth, beryl; the ninth, topaz; the tenth, chrysoprase; the eleventh, jacinth; the twelfth, amethyst. (21) And the twelve gates were twelve pearls; each one of the gates was of one pearl. And the street of the city was pure gold, as though it were transparent glass.

(22) And I saw no Temple in it, for the Lord God Almighty and the Lamb are the Temple of it. (23) And the city had no need of the sun, nor of the moon, to shine in it, for the glory of God lit it, and the Lamb is the lamp of it. (24) And the nations of those who are saved shall walk in the light of it, and the kings of the earth bring their glory and honor into it.

(25) And its gates shall not be shut at all by day, for there shall be no night there. (26) And they shall bring the glory and honor of the nations into it. (27) And there shall in no way enter into it anything that defiles or anyone who works abomination or makes a lie, but only those whose names are written in the "Lamb's Book of Life."

CHAPTER 22

(1) And he showed me a pure River of the Water of Life, clear as crystal, proceeding out of the throne of God and of the Lamb. (2) In the midst of its street, and on either side of the river, was the Tree of Life, which bore twelve kinds of fruits, yielding its fruit every month; and the leaves of the tree were for the healing of the nations.

(3) And there shall be no more curse, but the throne of God and of the Lamb shall be in it, and His servants shall serve Him; (4) And they shall see His face, and His name shall be upon their foreheads. (5) And there shall be no night there; and they need no lamp, neither light of the sun, for the Lord God gives them light, and they shall reign forever and ever.

REVELATION 21:2—22:5

THE QUADRILLION MEGATON EXPLOSION

The new heaven and earth is made possible by the complete disintegration of the old ones. Peter predicts how God will accomplish this incredible future judgment: "But the heavens and earth which are now, by the same word are stored *with fire*, reserved for the day of judgment and destruction of ungodly men" (2 Peter 3:7).

What Peter was unknowingly saying is that God has stored within the earth itself the mechanism that will turn it into a gigantic ball of fire!

Men could not understand this verse until the advent of nuclear science. But we know now that the building blocks of our universe are atoms. The force that holds the protons and neutrons together in the nucleus of the atom is so great that when neutrons are released in a chain reaction we have an almost-incomprehensible explosion.

Just think what will happen to this old ball of *terra firma* when God releases *all* the atoms in our earth and its surrounding universe! Peter describes this as follows: "But the day of the Lord will come as a thief in the night, in which the heavens shall pass away with a great noise, and the elements shall be disintegrated with intense heat; the earth also, and all its works, shall be burned up" (2 Peter 3:10).

OUR NEW ETERNAL HOME

There's really very little said about the nature of the new heaven and the new earth. The earth will definitely be populated, and it will be restored as it was in the Garden of Eden, so it will be quite a spot. It will be much different than what we're used to now, since there will be no oceans or seas, yet everything will be lush and green. There'll be no deserts or ice poles or snow. God Himself will supply all the natural resources that are needed to keep an earth running smoothly. He'll be the source of light and heat and water and much more that we'll see later.

The new earth as a whole will not be the principal residence of the believers, though they will have free access to it. The New Jerusalem is where Jesus has been preparing mansions for His own and is the capital from which He will rule. It will be the center of the new universe, with a beauty and a holiness that can hardly be fathomed. Revelation 21 and 22 describe the glories of this city.

WHERE WILL THE "NEW J" BE?

Let's briefly see where this city will be located, and then we'll look at its beauty.

In Revelation 21:2 John said he saw the Holy City coming down out of heaven from God. Some Bible interpreters believe that this city has existed from the time Jesus left the earth to go to prepare a place for His bride, the Church. If that's so, this city is in existence during our present age although it is invisible, and it will exist during both the Tribulation and the Millennium.

It may be that the Holy City will be suspended above the earth during the thousand-year Kingdom, and that the immortal believers will principally live there. This would help to explain the question of how mortal and immortal beings can live together in the Millennium, since the mortals (those believers who live through the Tribulation) will continue to marry, have children, and live ordinary lives. This, of course, won't be true of the immortal believers, since these saints will already have received their resurrection bodies.

If this view is correct, then the city would have to be temporarily withdrawn when the earth is destroyed at the end of the Millennium. After the re-creation of the earth, the city will apparently descend to the new earth and actually rest on it, since the New Jerusalem is said to have *foundations*, which implies a firm means of support. Also, the New J has twelve gates through which the peoples of the nations will go in and out of the city.

In any case, the New J will be the center of the universe. All light will emanate from it and all life in the universe will revolve around it.

WHO WILL INHABIT THE "NEW J"?

John pictures this magnificent city as a new bride adorned for her husband. Because of the term "bride," some interpreters feel that only the bride of Christ, the Church, will live in this city.

However, we know that Abraham was promised a city, for the writer of the Book of Hebrews tells us, "For he looked for a city which has foundations, whose builder and maker is

God. . . . But now they desire a better country, that is, a heavenly one; wherefore, God is not ashamed to be called their God; for He has prepared for them a city" (Hebrews 11:10, 16).

There can be no question that this promised city is the New Jerusalem. While it may be the bride's city, it also has other permanent inhabitants—the saved of the house of Israel.

You'll notice that the foundation stones of the city have the twelve apostles' names on them, while the twelve gates are named for the twelve tribes of Israel. These twenty-four spiritual leaders represent the two main groups who will inhabit this city: they symbolize the *foundation* and *access* to the New J.

A third group of people will also have access to the city, though their principal place of residence will be the new earth. This group is called the "nations," which means "peoples" or Gentiles. They will be comprised of believers who didn't happen to be among Israel in the Old Testament or the Church in the New Testament.

Noah would be one of these, since he was not an Israelite. Naaman the leper would also be in this group, since he wasn't a Jew either. Many other Old Testament people knew God and believed in Him and found salvation, but were never part of Israel. All the Gentiles who are saved during the Tribulation will also be in this company of believers.

WHAT WILL THE "NEW J" BE LIKE?

The most important thing about this new city and new earth is that God will be there in person, and we'll see Him face-to-face. There are a number of Bible verses which promise this. For instance, in First Corinthians 13:12 it says, "For now we see through a glass darkly, but then face-to-face." John tells us that we'll see Christ as He is and become like Him ourselves (1 John 3:2).

Jesus' glorified human body is the "tabernacle of God" which John says has now come among men (Revelation 21:3). He will have His glorified body for all eternity, and we will have ours, so face-to-face fellowship will be no problem.

In verse 4 we're told that we'll be free from all sorrow in the New Jerusalem. God will wipe every tear from our eyes. Death will be gone forever, and so will its painful shadow—mourning.

The greatest enemy of mankind, totally unconquered by science, is death. We have cancer societies and heart funds, but have you ever heard of an anti-death research organization? In eternity the cemeteries will be gone forever!

All sickness and pain will be forgotten in the wonder of our new surroundings. Even our old sin natures will be removed at last, so that we'll never lose patience with one another again! No more bitter words or repressed hostilities—only love and peace!

God Himself tells John that only *overcomers* will be in the new world. They will be in an absolutely unique relationship with God. Though we call God our Father now, we can't yet fully appreciate that relationship because He's an absentee Father. But there in the new world we'll experience the unfathomable dimensions of the love of a perfect Father toward His much-beloved children. Best of all, we'll be able to love Him back with the kind of love He deserves, the kind we've never been able to give Him before!

THE VIEW FROM THE TOP WILL BE GREAT!

We're not sure whether the city is in the shape of a cube or a pyramid, but we know that at the bottom it's square. It's 1,500 miles in each direction, from side to side as well as straight up. This covers a lot of territory, and it implies that millions upon millions of redeemed saints will be there!

Sometimes Christians feel that very few have responded to the gospel and that they're only a tiny minority. Not so! I think we'll be very pleasantly surprised by some of the people who will come up and say "Hi" in the New J!

One of my greatest bonuses in eternity will be to have someone walk up and say, "Hal, remember when you talked to me about Jesus that time? Well, it finally sank in, and I just want to thank you from the bottom of my heart for making it possible for me to be with Christ in this fantastic place forever!"

That's when the Lord will have to come with his heavenly hanky and wipe some joyful tears out of my eyes!

The city itself is made of clear gold of some kind. Not only are the streets paved with it, but it's the actual material used to construct the buildings. You can see through it.

The walls surrounding the city are made of jasper (very

similar to diamonds) and are also transparent. I think the reason you can see through everything is that no one has anything to hide! Also, no one wants to be out of sight of Jesus for very long, and this way you can see Him twenty-four hours a day!

Somewhere along the line the story got started that Saint Peter was the doorkeeper of heaven, and that he stood at the pearly gates deciding who got in and who didn't. Only half of that is right. Saint Peter doesn't stand at the door of heaven or the New Jerusalem, but there *are* pearly gates.

As a matter of fact, the New J has *twelve* gates, and they're all made of pearl. Someone has said that the pearl is the perfect jewel to represent the entrance into God's presence, since it so beautifully symbolizes what Jesus did to make man fit for heaven. Just as a pearl begins from a small, irritating piece of sand in an oyster and is wrapped in layer after layer of pearl to make it beautiful, so the believer is an unfit vessel until he's been wrapped in the righteous cloak of Jesus, which makes him beautiful in God's sight!

The foundation stones of the city wall of the New J are studded with precious jewels of every kind. We learned in Chapter 19 that our heavenly bride clothes will also be covered with gold, silver, and precious stones.

The whole city has been designed by God to give his loved ones the greatest pleasure and joy. All our desires for comfort, ease, and aesthetic beauty have been anticipated and planned for.

Jesus Replaces the Temple

As John gazes at this New Jerusalem, he notices that the Temple is conspicuously missing. Though it once had an extremely prominent place in the history of God's dealings with man both on earth and in heaven, the Temple is now no longer needed. Everything it portrayed has come to pass, and the focal point of all its symbolism, Jesus, is now the Temple, along with God the Father.

The glory and brilliance of Christ and the Father are all that's needed to illumine the entire universe. Think what power must have been required to condense this glory into the humanity of Jesus and to keep it veiled for the thirty-three years He lived on earth! That's the marvel of the Incarnation!

One of the great questions that believers have about eternity is whether we will see all three members of the divine Godhead or whether we'll see only one—and if so, which one.

I personally believe that all three members of the trinity—God the Father, God the Son, and God the Holy Spirit—will be present in Person. John mentions two of the Godhead when he says in this chapter that there won't be any material Temple in the New J because the Lord God Almighty *and* the Lamb will be the Temple. He also speaks of a "River of the Water of Life" coming from the throne of God *and* the Lamb.

I can't understand what God the Father will look like, or how He and the Son will share the role of leadership in this City of God. The closest I can come to understanding my relationship to both of them is as a *brother* to Jesus (joint-heir to the Father's riches), and as a *child* of God my heavenly Father.

Personally, I'd like to relate to each of them in these ways through eternity. Though I've never had a physical brother, I've had some fantastic relationships with brothers in Christ. We've sat by the hour rapping about everything under the sun, and we could hardly tear ourselves away because we enjoyed the fellowship so much! I'm really looking forward to doing this for eons and eons of time with these brothers and our "elder brother," Jesus!

My dad has been a great example of a father here on earth. He did everything that was humanly possible to provide all my needs as I was growing up. If I had a problem, I knew Dad would have the answer. If I needed the car or money for a date, I knew I could count on Dad to slip in an extra buck or two. He gave me my share of lickings, too, and I know now that it really was for my good, though at the time I didn't think so!

I'd like to feel that my heavenly Father will take up where my dad left off—that for all the years of eternity I can go to Him with anything that's on my heart and find in Him the comfort that only the Creator can give!

RIVERS OF LIVING WATER

The angel showed John a river which came down the middle of the street of the heavenly city and was lined on both sides with trees that bore a different kind of fruit every month of the year. The source of this river was the throne of God and the

Lamb who sat on the throne, and it was called a *River of the Water of Life.*

Water meant a great deal in the ancient world; some cities rose and fell on the flow of their water supply. But I don't think this river is in the Holy City just to remind man of the refreshing aspects of the old rivers back on earth. Everything is new in this celestial city, and there's every reason to believe this river is something quite new and beyond our present experience to appreciate.

I personally believe that this River of the Water of Life will somehow be a tangible manifestation of the Holy Spirit. As we partake of the fruit of this river's nourishment, the Holy Spirit will continue the active relationship with believers that He has now.

The outpouring of the Holy Spirit has often been likened to rivers of refreshing and renewing life. Isaiah the prophet spoke of this when he said, "For I will pour water upon the one who is thirsty, and floods upon the dry ground; I will pour out My Spirit upon your children, and My blessing upon your offspring" (Isaiah 44:3).

The same Apostle John who penned this revelation wrote about the "rivers of living water" a few years later in the Gospel which bears his name. He quoted Jesus as saying, "If any man thirst, let him come to Me and drink. He who believes in Me, as the Scripture has said, out of his heart shall flow rivers of living water. (But this He spoke concerning the Spirit, whom those who believed in Him were to receive)" (John 7:37b–39a).

THE OUTPOURING OF THE SPIRIT

I don't think it's farfetched to regard this crystal-clear river from the throne of God the Father and God the Son as the continual outpouring of God the Holy Spirit. The Tree of Life drawing upon its waters produces fruit, even as the believer who draws deeply from the indwelling Holy Spirit today will produce the fruit of the Spirit. In this way the Holy Spirit takes from the Father and nourishes the believer.

As the River of Water of Life courses forth from the throne in the New Jerusalem, the Tree of Life draws from the Father and Son; then, as the believers enjoy its fruit, they are nourished in a growing relationship with the triune God.

Even the leaves of this Tree of Life draw strength from the river, and they provide a growing health and vigor among the people who dwell on the new earth. The word "healing" which is used in verse 2 really means "health."

There's obviously something unique about this tree in the New City, and it's not the first time we've run across it in God's dealing with men. The Tree of Life first appeared in the Garden of Eden at the beginning of man's history on *earth*, and here it is again at the beginning of his *eternity*.

After Adam and Eve had eaten of another tree in the Garden, the Tree of Knowledge of Good and Evil, they died spiritually. They were still alive physically, but their relationship with God was dead! God immediately barred them from access to the Tree of Life, since its fruit would enable them to live forever. God didn't want spiritually-dead people to live forever on the earth in bodies that have fallen natures.

Someone has said that the most important history of the earth has revolved around three trees. The first is the Tree of the Knowledge of Good and Evil, the second is the Tree of Life found in the Garden of Eden and again in the New J, and the third is the tree on Golgotha's hill.

The first tree took away man's spiritual life; the tree on the lonely hill of Calvary made it possible for believing man to have his spiritual life restored again; and the Tree of Life in the New Jerusalem assures man of everlasting life in fellowship with the Father, Son, and Holy Spirit.

A NEW OCCUPATION FOR MAN

We're not going to sit around apathetically in the New J. Revelation 22:3 says that we will *serve* the Lord, adding in verse 5 that we'll also *reign* forever and ever with Him.

The service we'll give to the Lord will be just about as laborious as a bride waiting on her new groom during their honeymoon! It will be pure delight, with none of our burdensome implications of "service."

It's exciting to think about kneeling at God's feet one minute and sitting beside His throne the next! There's no chance of eternity being boring with that kind of challenge alternating with adoring service!

There's no clear indication in Scripture whom we will reign

over or whom we will intercede for in our role as priests. But I'm convinced that these aren't just idle words dropped into the narrative. If John was told that the believers would rule with Christ, then someone or something needs governing.

The Apostle Paul suggests who it may possibly be when he says that we'll rule over angels (1 Corinthians 6:3). Jesus also hinted at our future role as rulers when He said that the servant who had been faithful in ten things in this life would rule over ten cities in the next (Luke 19:15–19).

Since the role of angels in the new earth and the City of God is not described (except as guardians of the twelve gates), it's possible that they will inhabit some of the galaxies and believers will reign over them. It's also possible that there is intelligent life on other planets which God will reveal to us in eternity.

WHAT'S THE BIG DEAL?

To some readers of this book, almost everything mentioned so far may sound like a wild fairytale, with the most fanciful part being the New Jerusalem. To others, the realization of what's in store for them in eternity is so thrilling that they can hardly wait to get there!

Why is it so important to know and meditate on what God has planned for us in the future?

It's important because this life has many disappointments and heartaches, but knowing there *is* a new world coming for God's people gives us patience and strength to joyfully bear the burdens of this life.

That's what Paul was talking about when he testified, "That is why we never give up. Though our bodies are dying, our inner strength in the Lord is growing every day. These troubles and sufferings of ours are, after all, quite small and won't last very long. Yet, this short time of distress will result in God's richest blessing upon us forever and ever! So we don't look at what we can see right now, the troubles all around us, but we look forward to the joys in heaven which we have not yet seen. The troubles will soon be over, but the joys to come will last forever" (2 Corinthians 4:16–18, *TLB*).

TWENTY-TWO

"An Offer You Can't Refuse" —GOD

This chapter brings us to the final scenes of John's divine revelation and deposits our feet firmly on the shores of eternity. Nothing of God's great plan to redeem man and the earth has been left unfulfilled. All His lofty purposes have been attained.

God has dealt with the rebellion of angels and men and has established Himself as King of Kings and Lord of Lords. He has His saints in glory with Him and His handiwork of creation has been renewed.

Before God deposits John back on his lonely island of exile, Patmos, and while the heavenly revelations are still consuming his mind, the revealing angel and Jesus impress upon John the shortness of time and the urgency of getting the prophetic message out. They give him final instructions of what to write about this incredible apocalyptic journey he's been on.

Read these verses carefully, keeping in mind that they are the last will and testament of God to men, His final prophetic message to stress the critical hour on God's great time-clock of eternity.

"I AM COMING SOON"

> *(6) And he said to me, "These words are faithful and true." And the Lord God of the holy prophets sent His angel to show to His servants the*

things which must shortly be done. (7) "Behold, I am coming quickly. Blessed is he who takes to heart the words of the prophecy of this Book."

(8) And I, John, saw these things, and heard them. And when I had heard and seen, I fell down to worship before the feet of the angel who showed me these things. (9) Then he said to me, "Don't do that, for I am your fellow servant, and of your brothers, the prophets, and of those who keep the words of this Book. Worship God."

(10) And he said to me, "Don't seal the words of the prophecy of this Book, for the time is at hand. (11) He who is unjust, let him be unjust still: and he who is filthy, let him be filthy still; and he who is righteous, let him be righteous still; and he who is holy, let him be holy still.

(12) "Behold, I am coming quickly, and My reward is with Me, to give to every man according to his work. (13) I am Alpha and Omega, the beginning and the end, the first and the last. (14) Blessed are those who wash their robes, that they may have the right to the Tree of Life, and may enter in through the gates into the city. (15) For outside are dogs, and sorcerers, and fornicators, and murderers, and idolators, and whoever loves and makes a lie. (16) I, Jesus, have sent My angel to testify to you these things in the churches. I am the root and the offspring of David, and the Bright and Morning Star."

(17) And the Spirit and the bride say, "Come." And let the one who hears say, "Come." And let the one who is thirsty come; let everyone who wills take the water of life freely. (18) For I testify to every man who hears the words of the prophecy of this book: If any man shall add to these things, God will add to him the plagues which are written in this book: (19) and if any man shall take away from the words of the book of this prophecy, God shall take away his part from the Tree of Life, and out of the Holy City, and from the things which are written in this book. (20) He who testifies these things says, "Surely, I am coming quickly. Amen." Even so, come, Lord Jesus.

(21) The grace of our Lord Jesus Christ be with you all. Amen.
REVELATION 22:6–21

THE REVELATION IS TRUSTWORTHY

It hardly seems necessary for the angel to affirm to John that the words of this divine revelation are true. Surely, John didn't need any further convincing after all he'd seen!

God knows the blindness of unbelief, and he realized that men down through the ages would read this book of prophecy and turn away convinced that John had had a nightmare. Thus, no other book in the Bible has so many affirmations of its truthfulness and divine source.

It's true that men must approach this book with trust in its divine Author—or at least with an openness to be convinced of its truthfulness by the Spirit of God. If a person will read this book of Revelation with an honest heart, he or she doesn't need to be afraid of the consequences. If we who are already believers have erred in our full acceptance of its message, then we're in very good company with the saints and the martyrs, the wise and the good of many ages and nations!

PROMISED BLESSING

Unfortunately, many Christians of all ages have avoided reading or studying the book of Revelation because they've felt it was too difficult to understand. Comparatively few preachers teach from it, and it really has been, as Daniel the prophet said so long ago, a "sealed" book.

This reluctance to plumb the depths of God's great prophetic plan is the work of the enemy of believers, Satan himself. He has more to lose than anyone else by people learning about the details of his demise. He doesn't want anyone to know more about the heaven to be gained and the hell to be shunned.

Twice this revelation of Jesus promises its readers and "heeders" a special blessing. No other book in the Bible does this. The fact that you've read this book means that God is promise-bound to bless you in a special way. And this blessing is compounded in the proportion that you *heed* and *respond* to the message of the book of Revelation.

EFFECT OF THE VISION ON JOHN

The revealing angel spoke to John with the words of Christ so often that John, in a moment of impulse and honest confusion, falls down at his feet and begins to worship him. But the angel, recognizing the true motivation behind John's gesture, admonishes him not to do it and then does a very gracious thing. He puts himself on the same level with John, calling himself a fellow servant of John and his prophetic brothers, and then he magnanimously includes in that prestigious company everyone of every era who reads the record of this vision and heeds it.

GET THE MESSAGE OUT!

When you stop and think about it, you realize what an awesome responsibility was placed in John's hands by this revelation that had been given to him. He didn't seek it. God picked him out and laid on him the weighty burden of faithfully recording what he saw and heard. From his island exile, there would be little he could do to disseminate personally this momentous revelation.

You'll remember that about midway through the apocalyptic vision, just as John was about to write down the ominous message of the seven peals of thunder, a voice from heaven told him to stop and to seal up this phase of the vision. He wasn't even to write it down! All he could do was bury the burdensome message in his heart and keep it there until divinely commissioned to release it. Nowhere in the revelation is he later told to reveal what those thunderous voices said.

But here in this final moment of future unveilings John is commanded *not* to seal up or keep to himself the words of this prophecy. He's to use every means available to get this message out to the churches. He still can't reveal the part that was sealed in his heart, but there's enough power in what *is* revealed to bring lost men to their knees in repentance and redeemed men to their knees in praise.

For some reason, God put a great love for the prophetic message in my heart as a new believer. The urgency of history's hour as set forth in Bible prophecy was the impetus for me to attend seminary and to go into the teaching and writing of Biblical truths.

From my very first faltering message on the second coming of Christ until this very day, I've been utterly amazed at the phenomenal interest and response on the part of believers and nonbelievers alike to the prophetic message. There is no comparable message for this hour in history!

God told the Prophet Daniel that no one would understand his prophecies until the end times, so the fact that men are now beginning to unravel the intricacies of these prophecies in the light of current events shows us the lateness of the hour.

THERE'S NO CHANCE AFTER DEATH!

The angel made an obscure statement to John that carries an ominous message. He said, "He who is unjust, let him be unjust still; and he who is filthy, let him be filthy still; and he who is righteous, let him be righteous still; and he who is holy, let him be holy still" (verse 11).

The point here is that a person who reads this prophetic revelation and rejects its warnings confirms his alienation from God. If he's unjust now, and dies that way, he will remain so throughout eternity. If he's morally filthy when he checks out of this life, he'll be filthy for eons and eons to come.

Contrary to the teachings of some groups, there is *no* second chance to repent or reform after death. If the love and grace of God doesn't produce a changed heart in this life, even a sampling of the horrors of eternal damnation won't cause men to repent. Even if someone could come back from the dead to warn men of hell, it would not produce a change of heart. Jesus made this very clear in the true story He told about a beggar named Lazarus and a rich man.

LAZARUS AND THE "RICH BEGGAR"

"There was a certain rich man," Jesus said, "who was splendidly clothed and lived each day in mirth and luxury. One day Lazarus, a diseased beggar, was laid at his door. As he lay there longing for scraps from the rich man's table, the dogs would come and lick his open sores. Finally the beggar died and was carried by the angels to be with Abraham in the place of the righteous dead. The rich man also died and was buried, and his soul went into hell. There, in torment, he saw Lazarus in the far distance with Abraham.

" 'Father Abraham,' he shouted, 'have some pity! Send Lazarus over here if only to dip the tip of his finger in water and cool my tongue, for I am in anguish in these flames.'

"But Abraham said to him, 'Son, remember that during your lifetime you had everything you wanted, and Lazarus had nothing. So now he is here being comforted and you are in anguish. And besides, there is a great chasm separating us, and anyone wanting to come to you from here is stopped at its edge; and no one over there can cross to us.'

"Then the rich man said, 'O Father Abraham, then please send him to my father's home—for I have five brothers—to warn them about this place of torment lest they come here when they die.'

"But Abraham said, 'The Scriptures have warned them again and again. Your brothers can read them any time they want to.'

"The rich man replied, 'No, Father Abraham, they won't bother to read them. But if someone is sent to them from the dead, then they will turn from their sins.'

"But Abraham said, 'If they won't listen to Moses and the prophets, they won't listen even though someone rises from the dead' " (Luke 16:19–31, *TLB*).

Some religious leaders teach that we can come back to this life in another person or form and give the world the benefit of the knowledge we've gained in our various lifetimes. This idea is very strong in the book, *Jonathan Livingston Seagull*. However, nowhere in the *Bible* is this philosophy alluded to, and it's diametrically opposed to the specific teachings of both the Old and New Testaments.

The writer of the book of Hebrews says, "It's appointed to all men to die once, and then comes their judgment" (Hebrews 9:27). This makes it clear that there is no "second time around." This sobering thought deserves careful consideration before one turns down the message of salvation.

IS JESUS COMING SOON?

When Jesus tells John that He's coming "quickly," I think He means that each of His appearances will occur suddenly in relation to the timetable marking the Rapture, the end of the Tribulation, and the Great White Throne Judgment. It won't be gradual or prolonged when the right time has arrived for His coming.

At each appearance of Christ, His judgment deals with men according to their works (verse 12). At the Rapture the *believers'* works are evaluated. At the Battle of Armageddon the evil works of the *nations* are judged. At the throne of God the *unbelievers* are judged for failing to live completely according to the Law of God and for spurning the Savior which their failure necessitated.

Because people haven't understood what Jesus meant when He said He would come quickly, skeptics have used His long-delayed return as an argument that He isn't coming at all, or at least not soon enough to get stirred up about it.

Yet the return of Jesus to take away His followers has been an any-moment possibility since the day He left. Believers have been urged to always keep looking for His coming. In fact, a crown of righteousness is promised to all who have loved His appearing (2 Timothy 4:8). This "hope" has been a strong motivation for holy living and for keeping priorities straight.

I've often been asked by people who've heard me preach that Jesus' return is near whether they should quit school or their jobs and start Christian training or join some evangelistic organization. Some want to know if they should save money for their kids' education or continue to make investments for the future.

My answer is that God has a perfect plan for each person, and *He* is the One to consult for these decisions. I do feel, however, that the expectation of Jesus' return places an extra responsibility on a believer. We need to realize that we're His *only* ambassadors on earth to get out the message of His coming, and we need to be sure we're in the center of His plan. Can you think of anything as important as this message?

To the skeptic who says that Christ is not coming soon, I would ask him to put the book of Revelation in one hand and the daily newspaper in the other, and then sincerely ask God to show him where we are on His prophetic time-clock.

ALPHA AND OMEGA

One of the most descriptive titles of Jesus is *Alpha and Omega*—the first and the last, the beginning and the end. In the first book of the Bible, Genesis, the seed of the woman is introduced as the coming Champion of man. That seed is none other than Jesus Christ Himself. He is the *Alpha*, the first ray of hope given to fallen man in the Garden of Eden.

Here in the last book of the Bible we see Him as the *Omega*, the final Champion who has defeated the enemy in combat, and now stands astride the universe as Victor. The hope kindled in Genesis blazes in Revelation as Jesus nullifies the folly of Adam and the malice of Satan.

Jesus tells John that the angel who has been revealing God's secrets was *specially sent* by Him to reveal this prophetic message to the churches. With this kind of mandate from the lips of Jesus Himself, I don't see how a single church today can fail to emphasize a study of the book of Revelation. Not to do so is a direct violation of an express command of Jesus!

DON'T TAMPER WITH THE BOOK!

This book is admittedly difficult to understand in places and there are devout scholars who disagree on some points. But what is meant by "adding to" or "taking away" is a warning not to change the message of Christ's work as Savior, Lord, and Judge. To do so is to risk incurring all the plagues in the revelation and a loss of citizenship in the New Jerusalem. Believe me, that's a terrible risk!

I personally feel that an individual who deliberately avoids studying or teaching this book is getting *very close* to the same thing as "taking away" from it. It's so foolish to neglect this jewel of truth when such promised blessings result from knowing its storehouse of treasures!

EVEN SO COME, LORD JESUS, COME!

The word "Come" is a favorite word of the Lord. W. A. Criswell put it beautifully in his book, *Expository Sermons on Revelation*.[1]

> In the face of the terrible judgment of the flood, the Lord commanded Noah to build an ark, and when it was built He said to Noah, "*Come*, Noah, *come*, you and your family, into the ark of safety—*come*."
>
> The great lawgiver, Moses, standing in the midst of the camp among his people in idolatry and in an orgy of sin, said, "Let him who is on the Lord's side, let him *come* and stand by me."
>
> "*Come* now, and let us reason together," saith the Lord; "though your sins be as scarlet, they shall be as white as snow; though they be red like crimson, they shall be as wool."
>
> "Ho, every one that thirsts, *come* to the waters . . . *come*, buy . . . without money and without price."

In this final prophetic message between God and men, there are two invitations to "Come." One is *to* the Lord to hasten His return, and the other is *from* Him toward all mankind.

"The Spirit and the bride say, '*Come*.'" The Holy Spirit was sent by God to draw men to Jesus for salvation. The Spirit has prepared the world for the coming of Jesus as King of Kings.

[1]W. A. Criswell, *Expository Sermons on Revelation*, Zondervan, 1969.

Here we see that His purposes have been accomplished; so now, instead of staying the judgment of God any longer in order to extend the opportunity for salvation, He says to Jesus, "Come on down. We're ready for You!"

The eager bride, the Church, sends forth her "Come" as she awaits her Groom. Those who've welcomed the message of the Church and have had it confirmed to them by the Spirit add their "Come" to the upward chorus. Finally, John himself joins in and urges the appearance of the beloved Lamb, whose unfolded revelation of justice, righteousness, and love he has just witnessed in his apocalyptic journey.

AN OFFER YOU CAN'T REFUSE—"COME"

The final "Come" is an invitation from Jesus for the person who is still thirsting in his soul for fulfillment. Jesus offers Himself as the thirst-quenching Water of Life. When a man drinks of this fountain, he never again thirsts in the depths of his soul.

If you look very closely at the outstretched hands of the One who asks you to come, you'll notice nailprints there. They were suffered for you, so that every awful judgment you have read about in this book might not come upon you. All you need to do is *"Come."*

My sincerest prayer is that I'll see you in the NEW WORLD THAT'S COMING.

HAL LINDSEY